Introduction to the

DANCE

Introduction to the

DANCE

By John Martin

A DANCE HORIZONS REPUBLICATION

This is an unabridged republication of the
original edition, first published in 1939,
by W. W. Norton & Co., Inc., New York

Copyright 1965 by John Martin

Second Printing 1968, Third Printing 1969
Standard Book No. 87127-002-1
Library of Congress Catalog Card No. 65-24216

Dance Horizons, Incorporated
1801 East 26th Street, Brooklyn, N.Y. 11229

Printed in the United States of America

FOREWORD

❧❧❧

Since *Introduction to the Dance* was first published in 1939 the dance in America, as elsewhere, has undergone many changes —in direction, quality, quantity and public reception.

To be sure, any art that managed to remain static for more than a quarter of a century would scarcely justify chronicling at all. Nevertheless, the march of events has inevitably made the latter half of the present text more or less passé as a historical record of achievement in our time.

On the other hand, much of the basic material here set forth has not been treated elsewhere, and there has been a persistent demand for its re-issuance. Immediately the question is raised of how much up-dating is desirable. After long and serious consideration, the answer seems to be that there should be none at all.

Any genuine up-dating would result of necessity in an altogether new and different book, for not only does an art change and develop with the passing of time, but so also does one's critical attitude toward it. It has seemed, then, to be more useful and more honest to keep the text within the framework of the period that produced it, as itself a manifestation of the times. On that basis, accordingly, it is here re-offered for what it is worth.

JOHN MARTIN

April 15, 1965

Contents

Illustrations

(THE PICTURES BEGIN AT PAGE 315)

9

Chapter One

APPROACH TO THE DANCE

❧❧❧❧❧

O N first thought, it seems strange that any book should
be needed to clarify the spectator's response to the dance,
for all art is itself a basic means of communication between men. Instead of having to be explained in words, it actually comes into the scheme of human experience in order to
explain those things for which words are not adequate. Common
usage acknowledges in a number of popular phrases the existence of such a verbal inadequacy, as when we say that something "beggars description" or "must be seen to be appreciated"
or is "too beautiful for words." It is in this category of things
and experiences too beautiful for words—or too ugly or too in-
tensive in some direction—that the artist finds his material and
justifies his art as a medium of use to society.

By words, of course, one does not mean in this connection the
stuff of poetry, for poetry is a manipulation of words and their
juxtapositions to achieve meanings and colors apart from the
literal and the matter-of-fact. But even the best words in the language, whether colloquially spoken or developed into the most
refined of scientific terminologies, cannot convey melody, gesture, color, form. These and all the other elements of the arts
awaken a direct response without any intermediary devices to

help them along, and in general talking or writing about them serves merely to make them less vivid.

If there should be some one who had never seen the color red, it might explain its existence to him to tell him about the spectrum and the range of red wave lengths in millimicrons, but it would give him no experience of the color and no means of recognizing it if perchance he should see it at some future time. Similarly, how vivid does it make the identity of, say, C$\sharp$ to cite the number of its vibrations per second? The only way to make it clear is to sound it. All the materials of art are equally outside the realm of description or translation into factual terms.

Good art speaks directly from its creator's emotions to our own, provided that our native response mechanisms are in working condition, and this kind of contact constitutes the only real experience of art. The proviso, however, is a fairly large one, for the response mechanisms of a great many of us have become pretty well clogged up with extraneous theories and the rust of disuse. Since theories are largely matters of words, words are perhaps the best possible means for exploding them. Thus a verbal attempt to clarify the spectator's approach to the dance becomes largely a clearing away of the underbrush of erroneous theory so that the free channels may function. To be sure, no amount of reading about the dance is of any avail in itself; it needs to be accompanied by attendance at performances of all forms of the living art, and if possible some practice of its nonprofessional aspects. There is perhaps nothing so potent for a full grasp of the subject as getting the "feel" of movement in one's own body, however remote the idea may be of becoming a performer or even an amateur virtuoso.

The dance antedates all other forms of art because it employs no instrument but the body itself which everyone has always with him and which, in the final analysis, is the most eloquent and responsive of all instruments. In spite of this fundamental character and simple basis, however, the dance, in common with the more derivative and complex arts, has grown away from the comprehension of the average man and consequently requires reinterpretation.

The division between artist and spectator is easy to understand. It has become proverbial that the creative artist is "ahead of his time," and all the great figures in the history of the arts tend to give credence to the idea. Recognition and acceptance of the work of a great creator seldom come in his own generation and generally only after the passage of considerable time. This is natural when it is considered that the artist does not deal with the obvious and already accepted facts of daily living; he enunciates new truths which perhaps he alone senses, and new truths in whatever department of life are almost inevitably rejected upon their first presentation. Such a statement as this involves nothing of cynicism, but states a perfectly reasonable fact. Every new truth involves the abandonment of certain old truths which have constituted the basis of satisfactory practice, and human beings are interested enough in self-preservation to be extremely wary about casting aside theories that have proved workable for others that have not been tested. If there is something of inertia involved, there is also more than a little native common sense. Thus the very intuitive talent that makes a man an artist also patently separates him in a degree from his fellows.

In simpler cultures than our own we find a mass of art actually created and practiced by the people as a whole. As soon as an individual in such societies advances any strikingly personal concepts of art, he is set apart by his fellows either as an offender against tradition, in which case he is punished perhaps with death, or as a recipient of divine revelation, in which case he is made prophet, priest, shaman, medicine man. In these societies a special gift of this kind is recognized as having meaning for the whole group, for in a closely integrated culture, art (and especially the dance) is the very voice of religion and magic which govern all the affairs of daily life. Through them benevolent spirits are pleased and hostile ones appeased; the rain is danced out of the sky and the corn out of the ground, the youth is danced into manhood, the sick into health, the dead into quiescence, the enemy into defeat, the quarry into capture.

For us art no longer has these important connotations, but along with religion and magic has been separated from daily living and deprived of practical function. Instead of playing an integral part in the activities of providing food, shelter and safety for us, it is relegated to those hours and those energies which we can spare from such activities. Thus, though the artist has always been set apart even in simple societies, he has become ever more widely separated from the rest of his group in our highly departmentalized scheme of things. Since he does not deal with tangible stuffs, measured by the yard, the pound, the acre, he is considered by men of affairs to live in a different, impractical and frankly incomprehensible world; while he in turn is inclined to despise the world of affairs (perhaps partly to compensate for its neglect of him), and to turn his own type of activity toward fantasy and abstraction. The unfortunate consequence is a great chasm between the artist and the group from which he springs and whose ideals and impulses he must interpret. It is a chasm, furthermore, that is continually widened by erosion on both sides.

The artist, left to himself, tends to deal less and less with the life around him and finally to see art as an end in itself. Out of this point of view grow cults of aestheticism, producing works so involved in formalism and so attenuated in content that the layman could scarcely be expected to respond to them. The layman, on his part, is not only legitimately discouraged by contacts with overspecialization and preciousness, but is also unreasonably addicted tᵣ grubbing in literalism, and finally admits into his categories of art only the old, the banal, the familiar, if he does not turn completely away from all art. The twofold result is that when he is faced with a living and unaffected work of some kind, his deadened response mechanisms make him unable to recognize it. Thus develops the ironic necessity of having to explain the artist to the very people from whom he springs, whose voice and intuition he is, in order to bridge the chasm and restore art to its natural social and cultural function.

This explaining can be done in two ways. One has to do altogether with analyzing the systems, the forms, the specialized technics and the devices which artists and schools have built up. This is designed to show the layman how the machinery operates, but there is no guarantee that it will give him any experience of art, any more than the analysis of red and of C♯ will give him any experience of color and tone. The second way devotes itself rather to piercing through these formalistic surfaces, attempting to awaken the dormant capacity for response, and laying bare the basic stuff of art itself. As a matter of fact, both methods must be employed if practical results are to be obtained. The former alone implies an acceptance of art as nothing more than an agglomeration of technical orthodoxies to be learned by rote; the latter alone turns its back on reality, for where elaborate systems have become entrenched it is virtually impossible to penetrate to the core of the matter without first dissolving the accumulation of formalistic mysteries which hide it from all save the initiate.

Obviously there cannot be any art without form, any more than there can be a building without structure or a body without a skeleton. Similarly there must be technical methods to make possible the achievement of the desired results in the most efficient manner, just as there must be adequate tools and skill in using them to build a house or row a boat. These things, however, do not constitute the finished product and are of no interest whatever to the man who merely wants to live in the house or be carried to the other side of the lake in the boat.

Sometimes, unfortunately, they are made to seem the principal concern in the arts. This theory is inherent in the tenets of two oddly assorted schools of thought which find here their only common ground. One school consists of the ultra-conservative who will not accept anything that has not been hallowed by a certain amount of antiquity, and the other consists of the violent nonconformists who reject all but the very latest manifestations of technical ingenuity.

Radical innovations of the past, quite shocking and frequently unaccepted in their own day, have found themselves eventually transformed by militant disciples into orthodoxies which must not be violated on pain of excommunication from the fellowship of artists. This kind of arbitrary practice serves only to hamper growth and foster sterility, for as long as man progresses and civilization advances there must be a continuous development of new tools and new forms to meet the new needs of life. In the technics of building we have seen the picturesque method of wooden-pegged beams give way to the use of nails, of steel girders and rivets, of welding. Today, however much we may admire the homes of our colonial ancestors when seen in the frame of their own time, it would be sheer affectation to build a house with pegged beams, and many types of structure for commercial or industrial use could not even be put together by such means. As more suitable materials and better methods are found in the practical world, they are generally adopted; not so in the world of art, where frequently tradition is placed before function.

At the other extreme are those artists who make novelty and invention their first demands. Their experiments with materials and technics undoubtedly confer a benefit upon the arts in that through developing new skills and discovering new devices they extend the range of technics in general. It is rarely, however, that they achieve substantial art themselves, for their attention is focused on means rather than matter. It is as if the builder were to put together beams and bolts for the sheer pleasure of craftsmanship with no consideration for what he was making, counting on the connoisseur to appreciate his workmanship without looking at the total structure. But it is the total structure, the accomplished purpose, that concerns the ultimate consumer. The average man, when he rides in an automobile, usually does so in order to get somewhere or to enjoy the scenery en route or even for the thrill of speed; it is an exceptionally fanatical devotee of mechanics indeed who rides merely to listen to the performance of the motor. Art has inherently and historically a social function; it is not made for a select caste of connoisseurs but for all the members of the group from which it issues, whether they all choose to enjoy it or not.

Means and materials, though they are of great importance to the artist, do not concern the spectator and should not be allowed to obscure the real purpose of art. The experience of art should enrich the intangible, emotional life and should not consist of mathematical puzzles or exercises in discovering violations of rules. This is not to infer that all art must be emotionally overwhelming and contain only profound implications. The fine arts are wide enough to include everything from *Oedipus Rex* to Mickey Mouse, but fine art without content on some emotional level is inconceivable. Those whose concern is with craftsmanship, forms, stuffs, have a rich field to work in in the decorative arts where content does not enter into the picture at all. Each of the major fields of art contains departments which classify as "decorative" rather than "fine." Not only are there such things as textile designs, wallpaper, and other products of the painter and the draftsman, which come most readily to mind when the term is mentioned, but in music there is jazz, in the theater the revue, in literature the limerick and the mystery story, in the dance tap, "step" and various other forms of theater dancing—all of which can be excellently, even exquisitely, conceived and executed.

In general, then, to establish a rapprochement between the layman and the artist two things are necessary. In the first place, since orthodoxies have grown up and been accepted as tradition, obliterating to a considerable extent the original and still the cardinal function of art, it is necessary to cut through these arbitrary codes to discover what the real experience of art is. In the second place, since a great quantity of highly respected art has been created within these orthodoxies, it becomes essential to know the bases of the systems upon which they have been built unless we are to discard altogether a large portion of the art heritage of the past.

When we come to consider the dance in particular, there are other obstacles, also, to be overcome, for of all the arts the dance has had the most difficult problem to face in making its identity felt in our day. It remained in an almost unparalleled period of neglect and abuse until virtually yesterday when Isadora Duncan restored its expressional principles and Michel Fokine delivered the ballet from servitude. To be sure, there had been folk dancing of real vitality and function through the ages, but with the advance of the machine in industry, the life of the folk was steadily changed until by the end of the nineteenth century the arts of the countryside had all but ceased to function.

The fine art of the dance had similarly declined until it was nothing more than a second-rate decorative art in which the dancers, now almost altogether women, made no attempt to say anything in their performances, but concentrated on exploiting themselves as charming personalities. One of the great teachers of the early nineteenth century, Auguste Vestris, a man who in his youth had been the first dancer of his day in the ballet of the Paris Opéra, actually instructed his pupils that their chief and only purpose should be to make every one in the audience fall in love with them.

This was in a sense only an advanced stage of a disease that had always threatened the art of the ballet, born as it was out of the social festivities of the medieval and Renaissance nobles of France and Italy. Both before and after it had become a professional art in the public theaters, all its inspired leaders in every period had struggled to lift it from this heritage and give it unity, meaning and relation to life. The great Noverre voiced an exalted creed in the middle of the eighteenth century, but during the momentous era that followed—an era that included the French Revolution and major world changes—no new Noverre arose to carry on the fight, and a hundred and fifty years later the ballet, the only art dance of its time, was all acrobatics and sugar-coating.

In spite of the fact that since then Fokine, the greatest reformer in the entire history of the ballet, has carried out brilliantly all the ideals of Noverre and more besides in what we have come to know as the Russian ballet; in spite of the rise of Isadora Duncan, who extended the free creative capacity of the dance art as it had not been extended since the Golden Age of the Greeks, there still endures among us that spurious orthodoxy of approach that prevailed in the last century and that brands dancing as an exclusively frivolous art, devoted to time-pleasing, prettiness and eroticism, and incapable of substantial utterance such as is credited to the other arts.

It is not unnatural that a theory of this kind should have taken hold in the Victorian era when intellectualism was almost a fetish and prudery was at its height. All the arts live in the realm of the irrational which the intellectualist abhors, and none of them has its being so wholeheartedly in this world of intuition and emotional activation as the dance. Similarly, since it deals entirely in terms of the body, it could reasonably be expected to draw the chief fire of prudery. Today with our broader, franker and eminently saner attitude toward the body, the stuff of the dance becomes not only more approachable but also far more potent to awaken an emotional response.

This latter point brings us to the last and most important of the special obstacles standing in the way of a full appreciation of the dance. In the light of these attitudes which have formed, consciously or unconsciously, the background of our cultural training and tradition, it is easy to see that we have grown insensible to the medium in which the dance operates, namely, the movement of the body. We have lost all awareness of the fact that movement can be and is a means of communication, of the objectification of inner feeling—in short, of art expression. We have forgotten how to look at movement and how to respond to it.

It is much as if we had lost our ability to respond to sound as a conveyor of meaning, and consequently employed the essential stuff of music for nothing more important than to procure a pleasing combination of tones for a set of clock chimes or a not too raucous ring for the telephone bell. Under such conditions it can readily be seen what would happen to the musical arts. Before the normal response which belongs inherently to everybody could be restored, it would be necessary to cultivate the experience of sound as a means of communication; but first, perhaps, it might even be necessary to make ourselves aware of the fact that sound can be such a medium and to learn how it functions as such. In other words, we should have to be taught how to listen intelligently, instead of merely allowing sound waves to vibrate against our eardrums and bounce off, leaving no impression behind.

This seems a fantastic theory because music has been so long and so steadily a recognized part of our cultural life that it is inconceivable for any one not actually tone deaf to fail to react to it in some degree. With movement, however, the case is altogether different. Until the past decade or so, the dance had not been a part of the educational system since the days of antiquity, nor was it a respected or even a respectable part of the program of polished and gentle living. Furthermore, it was quick to accept the position of triviality imposed upon it by the nineteenth century and made little effort to maintain its integrity. Throughout the great period of musical romanticism, when the conveying of emotional concepts from artist to listener became once more a conscious purpose of the composer, the dance was content to devote itself to two general types of movement. One consisted of naturalistic gesture, pantomime, dumb show, which really belong to acting rather than to dancing; the other was made up of combinations of lines and balances designed to display the body to its best decorative advantage or in its most skillful acrobatic aspects. To revert again to the analogy of sound, it is as if music consisted exclusively of two types of sound: one which we call speech and which is not really music at all, and one which attracts the ear by reason of either its resonance or its novel timbre. On such a basis as this, there could not imaginably have grown up a great musical art, and it is equally impossible on the same basis to build up a great dance art.

Music, moreover, is in a more favorable position than the

dance because of the fact that it has a standard method of notation which the dance lacks. If music were faced with a period of barrenness such as fell upon the dance in the nineteenth century, it could still maintain what it had achieved in the past even though progress might be temporarily halted. The existence of a wealth of literature would serve not only to supply current demands but also to provide a source of influence for a possible renascence.

Not so the dance. A barren period in its life can only feed on itself and become increasingly barren, waiting for some new creative force to rise and assert itself. No recourse to the repertory of the past is possible for the maintenance of a level even of competence. With no written recordings of repertory, no revival of any work is possible except by means of the memory of some one who has participated either in the original production or some previous revival. That such a memory is likely to be faulty in the first place is obvious, and that material thus transmitted rapidly loses its validity as it is handed down from memory to memory is equally evident. Lacking some persistently forward-looking creative spirit, then, any dance period is inevitably one of deterioration, for the dance is unhappily an illiterate art.

Efforts have been made, to be sure, throughout the centuries to establish a satisfactory method of notation and to make it universally intelligible, but none has attained more than transitory success. It is quite possible for the student to go back to the opening of the eighteenth century and find a system of notation by Feuillet in which are recorded many dances of the day; later in the century others made modifications and simplifications of Feuillet's method, and in the early years of the next century fresh beginnings were made on a different basis by Saint-Léon and Zorn, and the results of their labors are still available and serve adequately to fulfill their purpose. With the advent of the new dance of Isadora Duncan, however, all these methods became immediately obsolete, for whereas they dealt with vocabularies of movement which were standardized, the new dance discarded set vocabularies and worked in a freer and wider field.

This complicated the problem of satisfactory notation considerably but not insuperably. A number of contemporary systems have been devised which are suitable not only for the ballet and other dance styles which employ specific vocabularies of movement, but also for the freer styles of dance and even for gymnastics and other forms of nonartistic movement. Of these methods the one which has gained the most ground, largely because of its adaptability and general simplicity, is that devised by Rudolf von Laban. The entire repertoire of the Jooss Ballet has been recorded in this system of script and its use has been started auspiciously in America. On the basis of what has already been accomplished in this young medium, there is reason for hope that dance illiteracy will be wiped out within a generation or two. This, however, will have no effect, unfortunately, upon the great wealth of material of the past that has been irretrievably lost.

Certainly, whatever the causes of the decline of the art of the dance in the nineteenth century, the lack of a script and a basic literature to fall back on hastened and intensified it. By the turn of the century the scene was desolate, indeed. The concept of movement as a medium of communication was in a state of total eclipse and the very theory of it lost and forgotten. That sterile tradition, in spite of the heroic work of Duncan, Fokine and those who have come after them, is still largely our heritage.

To sum up then: the misconceptions and omissions which constitute the stumbling blocks to a full reaction to the dance, and which must be removed practically and specifically before an intelligent approach to the subject is possible, come under four principal headings. First, it is necessary to establish an appreciation of the stuff of which the dance is made, namely, the movement of the human body. Perhaps because it is the commonest of all experiences, it has been taken for granted to the point where we have become unaware of its multifold offices and must be reminded of them. Chief among these offices for our immediate purpose is the capacity of movement for conveying meaning. Such a topic necessarily takes us away from the immediate discussion of the dance as such and into the field of general aesthetics.

The second topic for consideration is that of form, or the arrangement of this essential material of movement into such sequences and relationships that it assumes significance for the onlooker.

The third topic has to do with the effect that time, place and background have upon both movement and the forms into which it is cast, an effect that is generally classified as style. Through its influence there have developed specific vocabularies of movement, that is, sets of standardized gestures and figures, which have been set up as the language, so to speak, of certain kinds of dance. A nodding acquaintance with some of these vocabularies is needed if the language is to be understood.

The fourth and largest topic is the classification of the dance according to the particular functions and purposes of its various types, and the discussion of them in some detail. Obviously, if one's only experience of the dance consists of the waltz and the rhumba, there will be little understanding of the performance of a Pavlova; or if nothing has been seen except the Russian Ballet, there will be no basis for passing judgment upon a Wigman. Though all dance is essentially one in so far as it is the externalization of inner, emotional force of some kind in terms of bodily movement, there are different motives for such an externalization and as many different objects for it to accomplish. This discussion, to which Part Two is entirely devoted, comprises the main body of our concern. If we are really to understand the basis and functions of the dance, however, we cannot jump at once to considerations of its highly developed forms, but must first go fairly far afield to establish the foundations upon which they rest.

To treat each of these matters separately is not to produce a sense of division but rather to show how by the neatest of dovetailing an art with many ramifications attains fullness and unity.

Part One

THE DANCE IN THEORY

Chapter Two

THE NATURE OF MOVEMENT

❦❦❦❦❦

IN spite of the fact that the dance is perhaps the least generally understood of all the arts, it employs as its medium a material that is closer to life experience than that employed by any of the other arts, namely, the movement of the body in its reactions to its environment. This, indeed, is the very stuff of life. Instead of contributing to the easy understanding of the dance, however, this fact has actually worked in the opposite direction. The movement of the body is so habitual, so continuous, and so largely automatic that we are in the main quite unconscious of its range and potentialities. Familiarity breeds not contempt, perhaps, but certainly neglect. We are most likely to forget altogether that, besides its more obvious functions of locomotion and the like, movement is a vigorous medium for both expression and perception. If we are to have any practical concept of the dance, however, we must become keenly aware of it in both these capacities, for not only does the dancer employ movement to express his ideas, but, strange as it may seem, the spectator must also employ movement in order to respond to the dancer's intention and understand what he is trying to convey.

It is imperative here, accordingly, that we postpone all concentration on the dance itself until we shall have familiarized ourselves with the processes that underlie it. This will take us necessarily into a consideration of the psychological factors that make movement a means of perception, of its functions in the practical and the imaginative life, and of the part it plays in all art experience. It is not until we have isolated the substance of which dance is made, as we shall do in this chapter, and have seen the process of composition by which it is put into intelligible form, as we shall do in the next chapter, that the dance can begin to emerge whole.

In everyday life our first reaction to every object and circumstance is in terms of movement, for, as we shall see presently, that is the way living creatures are constituted for their protection and survival. It is natural, therefore, that the earliest art impulses to make their appearance in human history use this most elementary of all mediums as their material. As a matter of fact, even most of the lower animals, including birds and fish, are known to dance.

When primitive man wants to experience something that his immediate environment does not provide for him, he creates an imaginary environment in which he can realize these needs, at least temporarily. Since his capacity for life experience at the moment exceeds his opportunity for living, he must provide himself with a synthetic outlet as much like life experience as possible. To this imaginary environment that he creates for the purpose, he responds just as if it were actual; that is, he reacts first in terms of movement, or in other words, he dances. His activity is perhaps play rather than art at this level, since it may lack altogether the element of communication, but of that more later. For the present, let it suffice that the medium in which the art impulse first expresses itself is that of movement. No matter how many later developments it may undergo which may refine the element of overt movement to the vanishing point, no matter how sophisticated, how abstract, how involved it may become, movement is still its root.

The spectator's approach brings another angle to bear on the essential facts of movement. All too frequently the spectator is believed to have nothing to do except to bring himself into the general vicinity of a symphony, a painting, a dance, and let something mysterious called beauty or art pour itself over him as sunlight pours itself over a table that chances to be in its path. But if a man made no more active response to art than the table to sunlight he would experience no more reaction. On the other hand, there are many conscientious followers of the arts who go to the opposite extreme. Realizing that they must play some more active part than this in their contact with art, they accordingly concentrate all their intellectual powers on analyzing its make-up, figuring out its technical details, and trying to deduce its probable meaning from these data. It would be hard to say which approach is the more futile and unrewarding.

It is virtually a truism that nothing is ever understood until it is translated into terms of experience. We may accept something in theory if it comes to us on reliable authority, but it is not actually ours until we have put it into action, whether it happens to be a cooking receipt, an engineering formula, a route of travel, a landscape, or a work of art. The question, then, is how do we put a work of art into action so that it becomes ours? Let us resort to a crude analogy.

When a Christmas pudding is set before us, we go at it with delight, knowing from previous association with Christmas puddings what an agreeable experience it is. But the pudding means nothing at all to us until we taste it, and even then there is only a momentary gustatory pleasure which contains no satisfaction. On the contrary, it merely whets the appetite, and the adventure is not complete until we have actually eaten the pudding. We have really enjoyed the experience and profited by it only when the pudding has gone through the processes of deglutition and digestion and its nutritious elements have been absorbed into the system to build up blood, bone, muscle. In other words, the total experience of pudding involves the breaking down of the whole into its essential components and the distribution of these where they will be efficacious. We cannot simply subject ourselves to a Christmas pudding, nor is there any known means by which it can automatically inject itself into the system in toto as an entity; it must first be changed into a more assimilable form. The greater part of this transformation is, of course, automatic; once we have chewed and swallowed the delightful morsel, our volitional part of the activity is over.

The enjoyment of a work of art is in the main a parallel process. It is possible to stop at the stage of merely "tasting" it—that is, admiring its color, shape, rhythm—but that is an unsatisfying and profitless method of procedure, in spite of its prevalence. The actual digestion of a work of art demands no more deliberate activity than that of a pudding, but it must be "chewed" and "swallowed" so that it can be brought into contact with the necessary mechanism. The rest is done without effort of will, but it is done, nevertheless, by dynamic processes. We have no experience of art until it has been transmuted into assimilable stuff, and this assimilable stuff is the stuff of life experience, which in its basic terms is movement.

In our reception of a work of art, it is those elements in it which awaken experiences out of our own background that give it value for us, for nothing outside experience can possibly have meaning. Art is not, however, merely a means for reliving the past; its only relation to the past is to give it focus, drawing out of the haphazard miscellany which constitutes one's background a clearly defined body of experiences, seen now for the first time

under the artist's stimulus, as belonging not to an isolated period gone by but as giving meaning to the present. Thus in the
instant of revelation, past and present illumine each other, and
the process itself adds a still further immediate experience, a
quickening synthesis which actual life environment at the moment could not provide alone.

The artist, who in all likelihood does not even know of our
personal existence, much less of our particular backgrounds, has
built in terms of universal experience as he has touched it in his
own life, and in proportion to the breadth of contacts with universal experience which each of us has stored up, his work is
capable of awakening us to a moment of richer and fuller living.
There is a widespread sentimental attitude toward art which assumes that its sole function is the bringing up of images of roses,
babies' smiles, and other fortuitous fantasies, but actually its evocations are not of promiscuous and random images of any sort.
The artist's efforts are directed toward touching into life specific
experiences definitely related to the material he has selected, and
his arrangement of it is all to this end. Though the entire activity
takes place below the intellectual level, it is not for this reason
vague or indeterminate, nor are its results extraneous to its substance and content.

For some of us certain components of any work of art will
probably produce keener reactions than others, so that not all of
us will react alike. In the eating of the pudding, one man may
merely have endured the raisins, another have wished that the
citron had been omitted, a third may have had a cold in the head
and tasted the whole pudding less sharply, and a fourth may
have found it too rich and too heavy and passed it by altogether.
Our total reactions, whether to pudding or work of art, depend
upon the equipment we bring to bear upon it, our past experience and present expectation.

We may like or dislike a work of art as we may a pudding, and this decision is not necessarily either arbitrary or whimsical but functional. When we are left unmoved it is either because our background does not contain associations of the nature demanded, or what is far more likely, because our apparatus for aesthetic digestion is unable to cope with the situation. Obviously all cases of aesthetic indigestion come from inability to break down works of art into assimilable material, that is, into terms of life experience, which is only another way of saying movement.

Work, Play and Art

It may be a totally unfamiliar idea to many people to have life experience made synonymous with movement in this way, for movement is taken pretty thoroughly for granted. It is easy to overlook the fact that it constitutes the chief substance of daily living and thinking. The common habit is to divide experience into two departments, action and thought, and to consider the latter somehow on a higher plane. When the subject is examined a little more closely, however, thinking itself is seen to be dynamic; no matter how deeply introspective it may be, it must go back ultimately to some concrete experience with the outside world, which is to say, some experience of movement. Otherwise it would have to exist virtually in a vacuum, and having nothing to deal with, could not actually exist at all.

Like thinking, art cannot exist in a vacuum, but must have constant reference to life, and this, obviously, through the ordinary functions of movement. It is well, then, to consider in a brief and general way what the ordinary functions of movement are in daily life, and their possibilities for translation into art.

In the illustration of the pudding, its essential value was found to consist in its contribution to the "inner man," and this provides a fitting point of attack upon the problem. It has become a kind of standard joke to refer to eating as appeasing the "inner man," and like many other jokes, it comes nearer to the truth than we are likely to realize. No doubt the reference is habitually turned into playfulness because of our inheritance from the Victorian age of the notion that the body and all its organic functionings are gross and inferior while the higher nature consists entirely of cerebration and fantasy. It would consequently be a trifle grotesque with such an upbringing to admit that the "inner man," the nucleus of the personality, is primarily concerned with eating and drinking and other equally low and vulgar matters. Nevertheless, if we are willing to put aside pretty poetic concepts, in the interest of something nearer to biological truth, we shall see that cerebration and fantasy and all the many ramifications of the so-called higher mental life have been evolved and exist solely for the service of the somewhat crude "inner man" about which we jest so lightly.

The actual inner man, which dominates the personality with its demands, consists of those elements of the organism which serve to maintain life and keep it functioning at a harmonious level. They are made up in general of what are sometimes called the vital organs, along with a virtually independent nervous system of their own. Here, with due apologies to our Victorian forebears for the indelicacy of the idea, is where our emotional life is born, rather than in any ethereal departments of the mind, for our emotions are nothing more than stirred-up states resulting from the action of these prosaic organs when they are confronted with objects or situations which have bearing upon their well-being, either to menace or to augment it. Manifestly a stirred-up state is not a state in which life can function at a harmonious level, and must be alleviated before the inner man can proceed at his normal pace. In the alleviation of these states most of our life experience and all of our art is brought into being. In an uninterrupted and self-perpetuating vegetative state there would be no demands, no upheavals, no art, and no growth.

Nature, however, has apparently decreed that there shall be no such static condition. The inner man must get food from his environment and must be protected from anything in that environment that might tend to injure or destroy him. The very fact that obviously he must exist in an environment of some sort, provides the necessity for all sorts of contacts—with objects that are desirable to acquire, with those that must be fled from, and with those that must be destroyed. Indeed, not maintenance of life alone constitutes nature's minimum requirement, but growth as well, for the one cannot exist without the other.

But not being able to live in his own self-contained universe puts the inner man into something of a predicament. Consisting as he does of a few organs with definitely limited functions, he would be doomed to practically immediate annihilation if he did not have some outside assistance. He has no means whatever for providing himself with food, and if something should come along and threaten to trample him underfoot he is without any way of removing himself from the zone of danger. Tucked neatly away somewhere in the middle of the body, he has no powers of locomotion and no direct contact with the outside world. He can only make his wants known—and this he can do with some vigor—and leave it to some other agency to fulfill them.

This outward body that he is tucked inside of comprises the agency that nature has evolved for him for this purpose, and a remarkably delicate and dexterous agency it is in its entirety. It contains a number of bony levers and an intricate structure of active muscles to operate them so as to make it possible to move toward objects or away from them, to acquire them or destroy them; countless sense organs placed strategically so as to serve as channels for becoming aware of these objects in the outside world and for reporting their character; and a complex system of nerves and brain cells to co-ordinate the senses' reports on such objects with the inner man's estimate of them, and to make the necessary connections for appropriate action of muscles, arms and legs, etc., toward them. The inner man alone determines what he needs and desires and must have; it is up to the outer man to locate these necessities, figure out how to secure them, and bring them into the sphere of the inner man's activity.

This problem involves a number of different kinds of action, since the necessities of the inner man are many and varied. Action, of course, means movement; and movement in general, therefore, divides itself automatically into several major classifications according to the exigencies of the situation.

There are, first of all, those movements which supply the bare essentials of life, with the emotional nature left as much out of consideration as it is possible to leave it in theory. These are grouped together in the category of work, and include the getting of food, the chopping of wood and drawing of water, the maintaining of cleanliness, protection from the elements—in short, all the routine of sustaining life on the most harmonious level with the smallest expenditure of energy. A great many of these movements are instinctive, while a great many others are the result of learning and are actually highly specialized skills.

It is possible theoretically to conceive of an environment in which the needs of the inner man are so nicely balanced with the ability of the outer man to supply them that no other forms of activity are necessary to maintain the organism in perfect trim. This is an environment, however, that is entirely nonexistent, for in any actual life situation there occur conditions which tend to overtax the ability of the outer man, and which consequently increase the demands of the inner man beyond the point where an even balance of harmonious functioning is possible. In a complex world where there are conflicts and repressions on every hand, the demands of the emotional life become far greater than can be easily satisfied in the actual life situation. It is necessary, then, for the ingenious outer man from time to time to create a fictitious, a synthetic, an ideal life situation in which satisfaction is possible.

Play and art are the chief divisions of this creative life. They are closely related to each other, and obviously cannot depart entirely from the character of work movements, since these are the only movements that come naturally into experience. They are, however, an extension and adaptation of work movements beyond their normal limitations, or else they would serve no end that work itself might not serve.

Play, whether it takes the form of daydreaming or of strenuous physical exercise, is essentially an ingoing activity, so to speak. In it the child (or the man, for that matter) employs skills which his life situation tends to stultify, or extends them beyond the point where they have been proved safe in practical life. If a second person is involved, it is only to intensify the player's reaction. For example, it gives a keener pleasure to dance in unison with others than to dance alone, in that each dancer is thus able to participate in a total movement experience greater in strength and scope than any of them could create alone. There is, however, no exchange of emotional concepts, nothing created. The relationship between them is one of mutual awareness rather than of communication.

Art, on the other hand, is an outgoing activity. It demands response or the expectation of response. The poet, the musician, the painter, the actor, or the dancer, does not create his work for the mere pleasure of the process but always with the vision that the work itself, once created, will give back to those who see or hear it something of what he has put into it. From this vision he derives his satisfaction. He makes art only because he conceives of truths which cannot be realized in his current daily experience but which must nevertheless be realized and recognized as truths if only in a synthetic world. Since he has conceived them he must externalize them. These truths inevitably involve not the artist alone but a sense of the potentialities that exist in the relationship between men or between man and his environment, and hence cannot be objectified in solitude. He is perhaps asking for co-operation in the attainment of a fuller and richer life which he has glimpsed and cannot attain without the aid of his fellows. At the least he is recording a revelation which he himself may return to and re-enjoy in the capacity of spectator.

The ultimate distinction, then, between play and art is this matter of communication, which the former lacks and the latter demands. Whatever the specific forms of either may be, however, they must be referred back ultimately to the inner man for approval, no matter how successful they may seem to the reason and ingenuity of the outer man who has made them. He does not feel, he only thinks and devises.

By our sterner ancestors both play and art were frowned upon as impractical, wasteful, a flight into unreality, and hence immoral, and the same viewpoint prevails among ascetics of various types today. That it is an untenable position to take, however, needs hardly to be argued. In play, aside from its immediate satisfactions, the child learns skills and adaptations, both physical and emotional, which develop enormously his capacity for meeting the problems of practical life. Its values have become so widely recognized that it now finds a place in the formal educational program in all enlightened communities. Similarly, art provides an extension of the emotional potentialities, leading to easier adjustments, larger tolerances, broader visions. When vague and half-felt needs are brought to light and synthetically satisfied for a moment in the imaginative world of art, the first step has been taken on the road to their more realistic satisfaction in life. Thus, though the senses, nerves and muscles have no traffic whatever with morality, their ultimate action in both play and art is to increase the powers and extend the range of all men's lives.

Movement Sense

SINCE the efforts of the outer man to carry out his orders from within constitute the sum total of what we are aware of as the business of living, whether in work, play or art, it is well to consider briefly not only the motivations of such efforts, but also what they consist of fundamentally and how they operate.

As has already been pointed out, our only possible contact with the outside world is through the senses. When a sense impression is made upon any of the countless receptors provided for the purpose in the eyes, ears, skin, etc., it is borne at once through the nerves to the spinal cord and brain, where, as in an elaborate telephone exchange, it is instantly transformed into an outgoing impulse over other nerves to certain appropriate muscles and glands to prepare them for movement. When it is recalled that the entire sense mechanism has evolved purely to establish contact with outside objects so that they can be adapted to the use of the organism, it will be readily seen that the only function of sense impressions is to prepare the body for appropriate movement with relation to the objects reported upon. It follows, then, that we are made aware of any object only in terms of the appropriate movement we are prepared to make with relation to it.

It is not necessary, to be sure, for the body to make all the movements for which it is prepared by the reports of the senses; past experience has shown, for example, that many noises that strike the ear are not indicative of dangers that must be fled from, and the actual carrying out of the movement for which the muscles are prepared is inhibited by this knowledge. The impulse is, so to speak, short-circuited. Also, many circuits of sense impression and movement have become so familiar with repetition that they have made well-worn paths for themselves in the neuromuscular system and now operate without our even being aware of them. A circuit that is often traversed becomes, as in any other travel route, increasingly familiar with each repetition until it is virtually automatic.

Manifestly the number of sense impressions and their corresponding motor preparations in a day is tremendous, for we are constantly seeing, hearing, touching, smelling, and tasting things. But the sum total of all these sensorimotor experiences is still less than those which come from another source, a source which is commonly ignored altogether. However little we are aware of it, we are fortunately equipped with a sixth sense which concerns not so much the outside world directly as that elaborate and intricate world which is comprised in the body itself. This is a movement sense. Sense organs are to be found in the tissue of the muscles and in the joints, which respond to movements of the body in much the same way that the eye responds to light or the ear to sound. They register change of posture however small throughout the body, and thus tend to keep it always in alignment, so to speak.

When a traveler picks up his suitcase its weight would probably pull him off his feet if it were not that he has sense receptors which report the movement he has made and give a signal, as it were, to set up an equal pull elsewhere in the body to offset the strain. A moment later he is stepping with one foot upon a high coach step and would again be in a precarious condition if his body were not given sufficient information to establish the proper compensations. Consider, also, the predicament of the pianist if, literally as well as figuratively speaking, his left hand did not know what his right hand were doing. Or what might happen to the baseball pitcher when he winds up if his body were not kept constantly informed of his movements so as to make the necessary adjustments? Or what of the dancer poised *en arabesque* on the tip of one toe? Or the oarsman if he could not pull equally on both sides? Or the surgeon if he had no way of sensing the gradations of movement involved in a delicate operation?

These movement-sense receptors comprise certainly the busiest system in the entire body, for we are in a continual state of postural change, far greater than we realize, from the movement of the eyeballs in following an object, to the periodic contractions of the stomach. Besides the receptors in the muscle tissue, there are also semicircular canals in the ears which collaborate in recording data concerning our balance and tendencies to shift from it. If we did not have this testimony, we should be perpetually falling down, or even unaware of whether we were right side up or upside down. Through the agency of movement sense we are able to regulate the force of our movements, to co-ordinate them so that objects can be picked up or put down, and to make hundreds more otherwise impossible motor adjustments without which we could not begin to carry on a single day's normal activity.

Just as we found some paths well worn in that part of the sensorimotor system which deals with reports of the outside world, so we find similar beaten tracks in this inner system. These well-established patterns provide us with a great deal of background information and save us incalculable effort and experimentation. To take a simple example: when we consider the weight of a log that we chance to see lying across the path, there is awakened in us a pattern of movement responses based on memory of previous experiences with the weight of objects, which prepares us through our movement sense for the muscular forces that will be brought into play and the energy involved in lifting this particular log. We need not actually lift it, therefore, to know that it is heavy, and approximately how heavy. The report made by the eye is sufficient to open one of many beaten tracks in our neuromuscular experience and associate this object with previous objects with which we have had contact. When we pronounce the log heavy, then, we are actually describing not so much the log itself which we have not even touched, as the motor reactions which occur in our own bodies at sight of it. Perhaps we have never lifted any large log, so that there is no such exact experience for us to be reminded of; but we have certainly had many experiences with bulk and with density, whether we are actually aware of them at the moment or not, and the sight of this particular combination of bulk and density arouses in our musculature an approximate estimate of the weight of this particular log. Such an estimate, to be sure, has nothing to do with pounds and ounces for these are arbitrary, intellectually determined units adopted for convenience, and the muscles know nothing of them. Only the man who works habitually with scale divisions and has learned to associate the degree of muscular energy they stand for with various masses and densities will be able to make a fair guess of the weight of the log in pounds, but the rest of us will know at least how its weight compares with that of a stovepipe or a solid steel cylinder of equal dimensions.

All our perceptions are similarly matters of motor reaction. Otherwise they would not be perceptions at all, but mere sensations. Obviously, however, nobody who has lived in the world can have a simple sensation, for it must inevitably arouse associations with other sensations and the actions resulting from them. Thus when we find qualities in objects, such as hard and soft, rough and smooth, loud and faint, near and far, bright and dim, hot and cold, sweet and sour, square and round, high and low, we are actually describing the motor patterns which are set up in us by contact with such objects. If any object is broken down into its constituent elements, it will reveal the presence of no such ingredient as squareness or highness or hardness for these are qualities that do not constitute any part of the object itself but exist only in our experience of it. It would be nearer the truth to say that the squareness, the highness, the hardness, are in us, for they are essentially the names we give to neuromuscular experiences. If it were not for the presence of these movement-sense receptors throughout the body, constantly registering our postural changes and general movement activity, there would be no such thing as a smooth or a soft or a heavy object in the world, for nobody would be capable of distinguishing qualitative differences and everything would consequently appear to be exactly alike. Far more serious consequences than this would follow as well, to be sure, but in so far as aesthetics is concerned this would be serious enough.

Mere perception, however, is not the whole story of our relation to objects by any means, for there are also involved, besides the action we take or are prepared to take toward them, our feelings about such action which we call broadly emotion. Logically enough, the sense organs which report movement and postural change are closely connected with that part of the nervous system which belongs primarily to the inner man where emotions are generated. It follows naturally, then, that every emotional experience tends to make what we might call records of itself in motor patterns, setting up more of those well-worn paths in the neuromuscular system and adding new phases to those already set up. Thus in the rich storehouse of associations which life is always replenishing for us, the pathways from incoming sense impressions to the outgoing movements made in response to them lead through the territory of the inner man, and accordingly acquire for themselves inseparable emotional connotations. Our contact with an object, therefore, does not consist merely of recognizing it for what it is, but includes also an awakening of our feelings toward it. We live in a constant stream of emotional reactions, greeting every object, every situation, with favor or disfavor in varying degrees, reviving memories of previous experiences over the same neuromuscular paths, and making movements or preparations for movement according to the resultant of all these sources of testimony.

"Inner Mimicry"

PERCEPTIONS of objects affect us even more intimately than this, however, for it is virtually impossible for us to resist translating what we see or hear into our own present and active experience. To take a common example, when we see some one sucking a lemon we are more than likely to feel a distinct activity in the mouth and throat just as if it were we who were tasting the acid. When we look at bloodshot eyes, our own eyes are likely to water; if somebody yawns, we yawn; if somebody laughs, we laugh; if somebody cries, we frequently feel a lump rising in our own throats. If it were not for this propensity for experiencing synthetically whatever is presented to us, we should very often fail to understand the situation in which we chanced to find ourselves. When, for instance, we see signs of anger or rage in another, we are able to recognize them as such only because we have experienced them ourselves. Translating them automatically into a memory of these personal experiences, we understand at once the state of mind they represent and have warning to protect ourselves against a possible outburst of temper directed against us. Signs of fatigue in another are translated into a sympathetic awareness in our own bodies, and all types of gesture and facial expression convey meaning to us automatically because we have felt similar muscular experiences ourselves and recognize the postural attitudes and their emotional connotations as having happened to us.

Nor is this true only of our relations to other persons; it applies to impersonal objects as well. If we look at a building with columns supporting a mass above, we shall form a definite opinion as to whether the proportion is good or bad according to whether the mass that is supported seems easily supportable by the columns in question or too heavy for them. This reaction has nothing to do with any knowledge of architecture; it is a motor response. The building becomes for the moment a kind of replica of ourselves and we feel any undue strains as if they were in our own bodies. The reaction is exactly the same as the familiar sympathetic muscular strain we feel when we watch some one lift a tremendous weight or carry a staggering burden. "It makes me ache to watch him!" is the customary phrase for it, and the ache is present whether the "him" happens to be a person or an inanimate object. A sense of this sympathetic motor response to the function of the architectural column must have played some part, conscious or unconscious, in the mind of the designer of the Erechtheum when he caused one of its

porches to be supported by the figures of maidens, thus presenting the supporting force as actually occurring in the human
body. What an agonizing building it would have been if he
had made the maidens too small or the mass they had to bear
too heavy! A column not so suggestively personalized is only
slightly less productive of motor response in the onlooker, and
the same principle is at work in all our relations to architecture.

This faculty for transferring to our own consciousness those
motor experiences which an inanimate object before us would
undergo if it were capable of undergoing conscious experiences,
has been aptly termed "inner mimicry." It rarely results in very
clear outward or visible action, though it is true that we tend
to elongate the body when we look at a tall building or tower
and to spread ourselves broadly and comfortably before a low,
wide structure. Inwardly, however, we respond with vigor.
Psychologists have discovered changes in the postural condition
of the muscles in response even to shapes, though there is no
outward movement of any kind visible.

When reduced to theoretical statement, all this sounds a little
strange and perhaps even esoteric, yet it is simple and eminently
familiar in practice. We indulge in it every time we resort to
gesture to fill in verbal lapses, when we use our hands to
describe objects, or almost literally re-enact an incident we are
trying to tell. When we were children most of us have at one
time or another assumed a careful look of innocence and asked
an unsuspecting victim to tell us what a spiral staircase is, only
to burst into laughter when he has immediately resorted to
making descriptive circles in the air with his hand, as we had
known all along that he would do.

Again, if a large rock is seen on the ground with its longest
dimension parallel to the earth, it will almost inevitably be
described as lying on the ground, but if the same rock happens

to have its longest dimension extending into the air, it will be described as standing. This is a natural translation of the rock's position into that of our own bodies under similar circumstances. When a child bumps himself against a chair, it is a favorite device of parents to persuade him that the chair was hurt, also, and to induce him to rub its bruises. All this immediately suggests the animism of our primitive ancestors, and makes it clear that animism was no chance development but grew out of functional premises. It also provides a clearer understanding than any number of scholarly tomes could do of the close relationship that can exist between man and his environment, as well as between his religion, his art and his daily life.

We are continually attributing our own actions and reactions to the objects about us, and as a result the idiom of daily speech is so full of verbs of action used with inanimate subjects that the dictionaries record the usage as accepted. Hills roll and mountains rise, though they are perfectly stationary; the rolling and the rising are activities in us when we look at them. The wind howls and whistles shriek, because those are what we would call our actions if we were producing similar sounds. Examples are innumerable on every hand of the ease with which we personify the things about us.

There is an old joke about a farmer who found his lost horse by putting himself in the horse's place and just letting himself go naturally where the horse would go under the circumstances. This is an excellent formula for finding things even more elusive than a lost horse. If we want to "find" the Washington Monument or the Taj Mahal, Niagara Falls or the Grand Canyon, in terms of experience, we must do exactly as the farmer did, and have a similar imaginary transference of personality, so to speak. If we want really to "find" a Beethoven symphony we must hear it as our own voice with its emotional

cadences and timbres, its breath phrase, pulse beat and body
rhythms, arranged in the orderly utterance of a great experience
and extended to a range far beyond that of ordinary life. To
listen to it for its formal structure or its instrumentation is to
have perhaps an intellectual pleasure in it but to miss its compulsive import and its essential vitality. We must *become* reflex-
ively the Discobolus, the Mona Lisa, Hedda Gabler, Siegfried.
It is because we are built with a central spine that we require
of a painting that its masses balance about a central axis. Strict
bilateral symmetry is perhaps too literal to be interesting, but
too great a departure from it gives rise to an uncomfortable
feeling of lopsidedness.

It is useless to approach any work of art with the notion that
it must be understood before it can be responded to. Understanding is a process of rationalization after the experience; first
there must be the experience or there is nothing to rationalize
about. This all-important experience is to be gained in no better
way than by following the old farmer's example.

From what has been said about the perception of objects as
a motor function, it will be seen that there is a duality of
approach involved. We were dealing a few pages back with a
log across the path whose weight was sensed by looking at it,
and a bit later with a stone whose implied action of standing
or lying was judged by a translation of its "experience" into
ourselves. The perception of any object has both these aspects
inseparably; on the one hand we are concerned with what it is
and on the other with what it is doing. This must inevitably
follow since every object that has being has also an implication
of action; if it is doing nothing more vigorous, it is at least
standing or lying or sitting or spreading or rising or waving
or flowing—or something of the sort.

Qualitative and quantitative attributes we know through contacts made by those senses which report on the outside world and through the motor patterns set up by these contacts. Action, on the other hand, we recognize only through having experienced it in ourselves. In the first instance, that of the log, we regard the object as a thing totally apart from ourselves with which we may have to deal in some indicated way. In the second instance, that of the stone, we identify ourselves with the object in a degree, in that we are aware of its state of action only in terms of our own experience of it; we look out from it, in a sense, instead of looking merely at it.

In daily life, where perception is an automatic function, the interoperation of these two processes takes care of itself naturally and easily. In art, however, where perception is in a certain degree a conscious process, we are more than likely to concentrate our attention upon the qualitative, the static element, leaving the vital factor of action virtually unperceived. That this does untoward things to the response to any work of art is evident, but what it does in the case of the dance is injurious beyond measure.

Response to the Dance

THUS far, little or nothing has been said directly about the response to the dance, for that, as must be clear by now, is potentially the simplest of all art responses. When the dancer appears on the stage, he presents to us movement of the human body, the very element in which we live. It is manifestly impossible, as we have seen, for him to make any movement which has not been either submitted to the inner man for his approval or dictated by him in the first place. In other words, the dancer's movements must inevitably have emotional connotations; he cannot make any other kind of movements unless his nervous system is pathological. (Even when movement is pathological, a tic or some other form of motor uncontrol is likely to appear grotesque because of its apparent implications of meaning quite inappropriate to the situation.) No movement of the human body is possible without definite relation to life experience, even if it is random or inadvertent.

Since we respond muscularly to the strains in architectural masses and the attitudes of rocks, it is plain to be seen that we will respond even more vigorously to the action of a body exactly like our own. We shall cease to be mere spectators and become participants in the movement that is presented to us, and though to all outward appearances we shall be sitting quietly in our chairs, we shall nevertheless be dancing synthetically with all our musculature. Naturally these motor responses are registered by our movement-sense receptors, and awaken appropriate emotional associations akin to those which have animated the dancer in the first place. It is the dancer's whole function to lead us into imitating his actions with our faculty for inner mimicry in order that we may experience his feelings. Facts he could tell us, but feelings he cannot convey in any other way than by arousing them in us through sympathetic action.

Obviously it is not the dancer's, or any other artist's, purpose simply to arouse us to feel emotion in a general sense, to stir us up to no end. It is his purpose, rather, to arouse us to feel a certain emotion about a particular object or situation. He wants to change our feeling about something, to increase our experience, to lead us from some habitual reaction which he has discovered to be perhaps merely inertia or otherwise limited and restrictive, to a new reaction which has an awareness of life in it and is liberating and beneficent. It becomes necessary for him, therefore, to do considerably more than just to work himself up into an excited emotional state and hop about in response to the whim of the moment. He must organize his material so that it will induce those specific reactions in us that will communicate his purpose. Only thus can he reveal to our experience the new reaction he has had and wishes us to have toward some particular object or situation.

An important part of his task is to make sure that he presents to us a clear grasp of this object or situation itself as well as of the state of feeling it arouses in him. The latter without the former tells us nothing, however much it may benefit the dancer by releasing his pent-up emotional energy. With the desire for communication, then, there comes the necessity for form and the beginning of art. This is a subject that requires discussion by itself.

Meantime, there remains an apparent contradiction to be reconciled. At the beginning of this chapter it was stated that the dance was perhaps the least generally grasped of all the arts, and now it is maintained that response to the dance is the simplest of all art responses. The two statements are both true and are brought into relation to each other by a third statement, previously made, to the effect that our total reaction to a work of art depends upon the equipment we bring to bear upon it, our past experience and present expectation. There is no disposition here to claim that the average spectator approaches the dance with anything but a perfectly functioning neuromuscular system and an equally healthy general physical organism, nor can there be any doubt that he has a wealth of associational material to serve as background. Where the difficulty is usually to be found is in the matter of his present expectation. He goes to a dance performance looking perhaps for storytelling, or musical rhythms, or sex appeal, or with almost any expectation except that of motor response. Obviously, under these conditions it is all but impossible for the dancer to make an impression on him.

Music would function no better if we did not listen to it. If we were to go to a symphony concert to concentrate on making a diagram of the conductor's arm movements, or to keep count of the total number of musical beats in each composition, or perhaps to study the walls and furnishings of the hall with an eye to redecoration, the best music in the world would become nothing but meaningless noise.

Painting would be similarly ineffectual if we looked at it merely to count the number of different colors, estimating the area of each and computing its proportion to the total area of the canvas. Here we should be using the correct and indeed the only visual instruments, but receiving no impression at all of the work of art. A great many people go through life totally insensitive to architecture because they see only a door here, a window there, and enough wall space between to place the grand piano against. They, too, are looking with the proper organs but they are seeing nothing at all of architecture.

It is essential when approaching the dance to carry along the expectation of response to movement and a reliance on the faculty of "inner mimicry." Because this is likely to be a new idea, it sometimes proves difficult at first; there is so much curiosity in the functioning of the "inner mimicry" itself that it often becomes the object of complete concentration. In that case it ceases to function, of course, and the dance goes by all but unnoticed. A bit of practice and persistence, however, will inevitably rectify this overenthusiasm for watching the wheels go round, and the dance will begin to function as an art of movement.

Chapter Three

FORM AND COMPOSITION

❦❦❦

FOR all the tremendous importance of form, the spectator needs to know remarkably little about it in order to enjoy a full and rewarding experience of art. Only when formulas are encountered is there need for any special knowledge, and then, it is true, the spectator must be something of a connoisseur. Normally, however, it is the business of the artist alone to bother about the laws of form and the solution of problems of composition; the spectator is concerned with nothing but the result. It is up to him to approve or disapprove, to accept or reject the finished work that is presented to him, on the basis of the reactions that are set up in him, and it is not his province to worry about how the reactions were achieved.

There is no other aspect of the arts about which so much nonsense has been talked, and none that has been transformed into such a hobgoblin to frighten away the layman. Form, to be sure, demands of the artist a knowledge of his materials and a skill in their manipulation, but it does not become thereby a matter of academic pedantry. Similarly, it requires intuition and sensibility of the highest order, but this does not place it in the realm of mysticism. Yet cults of form of both the academic and the mystical varieties flourish in all the arts, and increase incalculably the chasm between the artist and his rightful audience. Actually every normal adult is supplied by nature with all he needs in the way of equipment to react to form. This consists simply of the mechanisms of inner mimicry, motor response and association.

Form is not a separate entity, and cannot exist apart from materials. Like size or weight it is only an aspect of an object. Except as a useful term for philosophical speculation, "pure" form is as fantastic a concept as "pure" size or "pure" weight, and can exist no more in art than in nature. In so far as the definition of form is concerned, there is no difference at all between the form of a work of art and that of a chair or a door or an ocean liner, or for that matter, of a man or a tree or a horse. In any case, the purpose of form is the shaping of material so that it fulfills a specific function, and the resultant form itself is the particular disposition of elements thus arrived at by which the whole becomes something more than merely the sum of its parts.

A chair is not merely so many pieces of wood, it is something to sit upon; a door makes possible the closing and opening of an entry at will, and is therefore something quite different from a mere assemblage of boards. To be sure, some chairs and some doors are better formed than others, though all may perform adequately the function that makes them respectively chairs and doors. Workmanship that considers the most comfortable height and pitch of a chair seat, or the easy hang of a door on its hinges, undoubtedly produces better-formed objects. A heightening of form, and subtly of function as well, is obtained merely by the employment of pleasing proportion, by the arrangement of lines and masses so that a comfortable sense of balance and generally harmonious adjustments are aroused. As consumers we do not have to be instructed as to which object is the better; if we are insensitive and do not mind physical discomfort, the less well-formed objects will perhaps serve us satisfactorily, but mere contact with the better-formed will in all likelihood increase our immediate demands and raise our ultimate standards. Only if the door has a secret mechanism, however, or the chair must be sat in at a certain angle, shall we have to have any instruction regarding their functions and consequent desirability.

With art the situation is identical. The separate elements of which a work is composed must be held together in such a way that a unified experience, a total meaning, will result which would not otherwise exist. Three major considerations control the procedure of the composer. He must obviously have in mind the function for which his work is designed, he must know what materials to choose and how to handle them, and he must be aware of the mechanism of response in his audience in order not to overtax or understimulate it. Again, it is precisely the same procedure as that which directs the chairmaker. He does not take a casual armful of boards and sticks and play with them until he has put them together in some accidental fashion; he determines in advance what the end result is to be and is therefore not faced with the necessity of figuring out some purpose for the object once he has made it. Secondly, he knows better than to employ materials with such unsuitable modes of behavior as, say, tissue paper or wax for this purpose, and understands how to manipulate in the most efficient way the pieces of whatever material he does select. Thirdly, he does not make the legs of his chair four feet high, or its seat six inches wide; he is guided by his knowledge of the anatomical structure of the man who is to sit on the finished object.

The artist is likely to employ improvisation to some extent in the development of his composition, but he starts out with as clear a sense of the goal as the chairmaker does. Though he is generally not aware in advance of the details of the process, he knows the specific function for which his work is designed. This may vary over a wide range, from the conveying of a deeply stirring emotional truth to nothing more than the presentation of colors, lines and masses in arrangements calculated only to arouse a feeling of pleasant and orderly being, but its minimum function is the transference of an emotional experience of some kind and degree to the spectator. If it does less than this, it is not a work of art no matter how many facts it may state, events it may report or rules of procedure it may obey.

There is an element of compulsion about artistic creation that takes care in advance of the aim and purpose of any particular work, so that this does not become a matter for debate and selection. But the remaining factors, which involve the materialization of this compulsive inspiration—namely, the knowledge of materials and their behavior, and the judgment of the capacity for response that the spectator can be counted upon to possess—are less definitely indicated in advance. By the reconciliation of these three elements, however, the ultimate form of any work of art is determined. This reconciliation is effected largely by the method of trial and error, for composition is not a science in spite of the fact that there are pedagogues who try to teach it as if it were. Academic formulas have been devised from time to time only to be proved barren, since every work of art makes its own requirements as to form and there are no ready-made containers into which the substance of the artist's vision may be poured and still retain its individual force and character.

It is necessary at the outset to distinguish clearly between organic form and arbitrary forms. Organic form is that relationship of elements by which a self-determined identity is created with an inherent function emanating from the interoperation of its constituents, each of which is indispensably related to the whole. Arbitrary forms are arrangements of materials according to patterns agreed upon for reasons outside the inherent functions of the materials themselves.

In primitive art, for example, we sometimes find motifs repeated four, or eight, or nine times, according to whichever number happens to be sacred to the tribe. This is an entirely extraneous basis for form, but one that gives satisfaction to those who know and accept it. In more intellectual societies arrangements such as the rondel, rondeau, ballade and sonnet were invented and developed by rhetoricians equally without organic basis, and these, too, give pleasure to those with sufficient special knowledge to be able to accept them as basic forms. Pleasure in arbitrary forms is always less a matter of natural response than of specific training, and because of this, the subject of form in art often resolves itself in the popular mind into the learning and observance of formulas. Certain patterns are evolved in every period which become fashionable for a while and pass out of use, but the principle of organic form is the same now as it was in the earliest days of prehistory.

The application of this principle in the actual process of composition involves intuition and that faculty for self-criticism without which an artist can never hope to compose. Even in the midst of the most inspired moments of creativeness, the real artist is aware that a certain portion of himself is standing apart, passing judgment in the capacity of spectator. The artist who lacks this percentage of objectivity, who "loses himself in his art," is reasonably sure to leave his audience equally lost in it, though not in the same rapturous and intoxicated way. On the other hand, the composer who intellectualizes and analyzes his methods too closely is likely to find his productions stillborn.

The Character of Materials

AT the moment, however,·the purpose is not to look at the subject of composition through the eyes of the composer in the throes of giving form to his inspirations, but rather to peer over his shoulder at the array of problems confronting him. If he were ever to see them spread out thus coldly before him in all their range and complexity, he would probably flee in terror from the prospect of having to master them. He works, however, from within his medium and allows it to carry him along to a large extent; he does not stand coldly outside it and manipulate it intellectually. For those of us, however, who wish to have some quite impersonal conception of the elements involved in dance composition, a fairly detailed analysis of the behavior of materials and the appeal to spectator response-capacity can do no harm. Happily, as spectators we need have no practical dealings with them, and once our curiosity has been satisfied, can put the whole matter out of mind.

As in any other art or craft, the nature and behavior of materials in the dance amount to inherent laws. Though the dancer makes some use of music, costume, architecture, acting, the painter's sense of color in décor and lighting, and in a small way even poetry where his titles are concerned, the actual stuff in which he works is movement.

All motion exists in the three dimensions of space, time and dynamics, and these must be considered not alone in their separate characters but also in the fusions and overlappings which give rise to such secondary phenomena as rhythm and phrasing, sequence and counterpoint. First, however, it is necessary to realize that dance employs a particular type of motion which affects all calculations. An inanimate object may be in motion if it is dropped or hurled or pushed, but the dance deals with the animate human body, not merely tossed about through the application of outside force, but in motion through its own volition. In other words, the body *moves,* whereas inanimate objects *are moved.* This obviously puts a definite color of motivation upon every phase of activity in any of the three dimensions of motion—upon direction, for example, and speed, and gradations of energy. Ultimately, it is true, all the other arts have similar demands to meet, and none of them can permit unmotivated and arbitrary lines, sounds, colors, masses. The dance, however, works in the most personal of all mediums, and the body that is seen making arbitrary and unmotivated movements is more than likely either to be unintelligible or to present a picture of insanity, since the normally co-ordinated human being does not make functionless movements in life. "Pure" form and "pure" line become therefore manifestly impossible in the dance, for in any movement or posture, however based merely on laws of design, there is bound to be an implication either of motivation or else of the inco-ordinations of mental unbalance.

This is perhaps the cardinal consideration in the approach to dance composition, namely, that movement of whatever kind carries within itself the implications of mood, purpose, function, emotion. The dancer does not work with an objective instrument like a piano or a palette of colors; he is himself the instrument. This makes it impossible for him to escape from connotations of the realism of human behavior, even though as a dancer he necessarily departs entirely from representationalism and all possible suggestion of pantomime. Thus, if he extends his leg so that his foot is higher than his head and sustains the position long enough (certainly an attitude without representational implications) he will most probably evoke applause from an audience; not because he has awakened any sense of abstract beauty by the obtuse angle he has formed, but because the muscular strain (a recognizable part of human behavior) which he has been able to withstand has surpassed normal endurance and his feat has been admired. The same thing will happen if he makes a great many turns at a great rate of speed, or performs any other series of extraordinarily rapid or manifestly difficult movements which in themselves are not expressive and might be counted on to function simply as elements of pure decoration or geometrics of motion. A succession of movements of this sort can become extremely exciting to an audience, by the evocation of sympathetic muscular experience, and it will sooner or later have to find a vent for its synthetically stirred-up state by shouting and beating its hands together. The niceties of pure aesthetic design, however, will have counted for little or nothing if, indeed, they have chanced to be present; the link exists in the connotations, however remote, of human behavior. The body is totally incapable of becoming an abstraction itself or of producing movement that is abstract in the sense of divorced from behavior.

It is easy to see how this situation affects the dance composer's dimensions of space, time and dynamics. His use of them is dictated first of all by the character of what he has to say and not by any extraneous principles of design. That there is another factor that tends to exert pressure upon him in the opposite direction we shall see in a moment, but it can safely be stated that the content of a work of art is the primary determinant of its form, just as water, sand, coal, milk and the uses to which they are to be put, determine the shape and texture of vessels suitable to contain them.

The dance is the only art that makes equal use of space, time and dynamics, but it is, of course, impossible to consider it as consisting of elements of space plus elements of time plus elements of dynamics, for they are not separable. It is possible, however, for the sake of analysis to consider the whole from the point of view of one of these aspects at a time.

Spatial problems have been treated most cavalierly by composers in general; it has frequently been thought quite enough to keep the face toward the audience and to balance a sortie to the right with a sortie to the left. Instinctively the better composers have discovered other and more respectable devices from time to time, but not until the advent of Rudolf von Laban with his theory, and more particularly Mary Wigman with her incomparable practice, was the subject of space given the attention it deserves.

By the dancer's prevailing awareness of the space in which and through which he moves, he relates himself consciously and visibly to his environment, and not only to the physical aspects of that environment but also to its emotional overtones. He places himself, as it were, in his universe, recognizing the existence of outside forces, benign and hostile. The dancer, on the other hand, who lacks this consciousness of the immediate world that surrounds him must necessarily concentrate on the exploitation of his person and his skills.

On this basis a wholly spectacular department of the dance has been built up, ranging from the bald exhibition of an ego in a vacuum to the development in the academic ballet of an exquisitely classic art. Following the line of classic practice in general, this departs by intention from the main stream of the dance as a biological phenomenon, so to speak, and sets up a self-contained existence upon the premise of an invented code of laws, quite unrelated to natural impulse and subjective experience and in no wise concerned with the illumination of man's relation to man or to his universe. Being thus cut off from the parent body of the dance, it is affected only in part by the operation of its laws. There is perhaps no more crucial point of division than that arising out of the spatial issue.

The pervasive presence of space, nevertheless, is the dancer's native realm, in much the same sense that air is the bird's or water the fish's, and it makes imperious demands upon both the performer and the composer. For the latter there is first of all the question of the amount of space to be employed and its character. Some compositions involve the extensive traversing of ground up to the utilization of the whole area available, while others unfold without change of base, that is, with the dancer remaining virtually in one spot. Because of the spatial values in the dance, stage setting and lighting assume a closer integrality with the composition itself than in other types of theatrical production. Here they do not serve merely as decoration or as descriptive place backgrounds, but take on the functional responsibilities of defining and delimiting the dancer's working area. Platforms, steps, ramps, pedestals and other structural forms are made to serve variously to break up a perhaps too monotonous expanse of merely empty stage with points of orientation, to afford areas where sheer height is available, to provide levels of contrasting elevation and different modes of access to them. Light can be used to restrict area and to increase it at will, to establish localized areas of different quality and accent, to cut off or to accentuate height, to blot out all tangible background and suggest limitless range.

These synthetic controls of space must, of course, be completely under the direction of the composer, who knows when he needs artificial elevation, points of orientation and constriction or expansion of working area. In the hands of stage designers working independently, they can become ruinous examples of mere visual ingenuity, impeding movement and throwing their own formal intentions athwart the dancer's design. The first important developments in this auxiliary branch of dance production were made in the years just before the World War by Appia, Salzman and Dalcroze in Hellerau, but little was done afterwards until Arch Lauterer turned his attention to the subject at the Bennington Festivals and produced for Hanya Holm's "Trend" in 1937 the first truly collaborative and functional stage setting for the dance to be seen in America.

But to return to the specific concern of the composer. Once the working area has been determined, there arise considerations of the possible disposition of the figure in the space available. It will achieve varying degrees of emphasis by being placed in the center of the area or at one side, forward or back; by clinging to the perimeter or by using the free body of the stage. In the matter of direction of movement, the forward and backward, the sideward, the diagonal, the curvilinear path, the broken line of progress, the turn in place, the shift of direction, all have definite values of their own.

Then there are the manifest differences of implication in the vertical aspects of the body—when it is seated or kneeling or lying on the ground, when it is crouching or stooped, when it is upright, when it is elevated upon the toes, when it is leaping into the air, and when it is falling. None of these things is a matter of free choice or pure invention for the creative choreographer, but will evolve for him in the main out of inner impulsion.

Also touching in a measure upon the category of space problems is the consideration of whether the movement of the individual is simple, as when the entire body unites in the performance of a single action, or complex, as when parts of the body move in opposition to each other. When this essential problem is increased in dimensions, with different dancers, instead of different parts of the same body, working in opposition to each other, there can be no question that space problems are involved, for here we have a definite instance of spatial counterpoint. With a composition involving more than one dancer, all space relations are intensified. Aside from the subtleties and the selective aspects of composition, it becomes necessary at once to guard against such major dangers as simple confusion in which some figures interfere with the activity of others and nothing emerges with clarity. It is manifestly impossible to move a stageful of dancers always in uniform mass, and the evolving of simultaneous patterns in space necessitates the careful maintenance of relationships so that emphasis falls only where it should for the adequate development of the central plan. The cardinal issue here is how much the spectator can be counted upon to perceive; and of that, more later.

All these problems of space involve elements of time as well, for manifestly it is impossible to move through space without occupying time. Thus the number and variety of impressions made by spatial conduct are increased in geometrical progression by the added consideration of their time aspects.

With such elementary matters as speed and slowness, gradual accelerations and retardations, or sudden shifts in the rate of movement there are no bewilderments. It is when we approach more complicated involvements in which time and dynamics are concerned together that difficulties appear. This is the category in which the vexed subject of rhythm exists, with its corollaries, phrasing and sequential development. Indeed, as soon as rhythm is mentioned, we are likely to find ourselves enveloped in as dense a fog of mysticism and vagueness as that which beclouds the subject of form itself.

It is wise when considering rhythm in the dance to put aside all preconceptions deriving from musical rhythm. The latter, it is true, originates at the same source, namely, the natural movement of the body, but as music has been developed as an absolute art, its relation to bodily experience has become increasingly attenuated until in many instances it approaches the point of disappearance.

All rhythms are products of dynamics, concerned only incidentally with time. They consist basically of the alternations of accent and unaccent; the time element enters only with the periodicity of the alternations.

Bodily rhythms are made up of the successive contractions and relaxations of muscles. The most persuasive of them, because they are continuous, organic, generally regular, and above all, because we are aware of them, are the pulse of the blood and the process of breathing. Against these as a background, we are inclined subconsciously to measure all other rhythms, phrasings and tempos.

Walking, hammering and similar repetitive activities are readily seen to be rhythmic successions of contractions and relaxations, fairly simple in character. Any movement is rhythmic, however, even though there is not such a marked contrast between its strong and weak elements, if it maintains a comfortable alternation of contractions and relaxations. It is not necessary for the two elements to be of equal duration, for this is frequently not the case even in movements that appear to be regular, like breathing.

Rhythm in the dance, being merely a concentrated adaptation of the rhythms of the body, is similarly based on alternation and recurrence, but it need not therefore be the monotonous succession of single units like the action of hammering. Once the presence of a periodic dynamic alternation has been established, almost limitless variations may be played upon it. The pattern of each variation may then be set up as a larger rhythmic unit in itself, namely, the phrase, to be subjected in turn to alternation and recurrence. Variations, to be sure, cannot be arbitrary, for it is perhaps necessary to repeat that the dancer cannot dodge the responsibility for setting up implications of function and intention by whatever he does. The larger rhythmic unit, the motor phrase, must therefore have some organic logic about its development. If the motor phrase were subjected to definition it would probably be described as a succession of movements from a common impulse, not necessarily sufficient to constitute a complete statement of action but containing either the introduction of a theme or a response to such a theme already introduced.

To illustrate, it might consist, let us say, of some such elements as a sequence of steps to the front ending with one foot raised, while the arms complete a wide circle upwards. Or perhaps in a more clearly functional manifestation, it might be made up of an initial movement which tends to throw the body out of equilibrium and those succeeding movements in the course of which equilibrium is restored. In any case, the series of movements would necessarily have a characteristic pulse, though they need not inevitably be evenly spaced or timed, and would possess a unity that set them apart from what had been done previously or what was to follow. This unity would be the natural outcome of the fact that the phrase was the result of a single impulse, a single motor idea, so to speak.

There is no prescribed length for a motor phrase nor any fixed regulation as to how much material it must contain. A complete statement of action comparable to a sentence in rhetoric or a period in music may demand several phrases, consisting not only of a subject and a response but perhaps also of the introduction of new subjects before the first has been resolved. The content of the projected work is the sole arbiter. Thus we are led at once into the matter of sequential development, and a composition is seen to be built up by the juxtaposition of motor phrases.

In dance rhythms and phrases, time will play the smallest conscious part, and the spectator will be aware of them chiefly in terms of recurrent spatial patterns with dynamic variations. Dynamism, indeed, is the heart and soul of rhythm and the vital-izer of the whole art. All movements exist between the extremes of complete tension and complete relaxation, and dance compo-sition concerns itself accordingly not only with the distribution of movement through space and time, but also with the amount of movement to be utilized. As music consists of a continuous stream of sound—punctuated by brief pauses and modified in pitch, speed and intensity, but still a continuous stream—so dance consists of a continuous stream of movement, similarly modified. Spasmodic bursts of movement scattered through space no more constitute a dance than separate bits of marble scattered through space constitute a sculpture. A unity of substance, a continuum, so to speak, is required, which in the dance consists of a sustained muscular tone, a heightened dynamic state, which is never allowed to lapse, though it is constantly varied, until the dance is over.

This dynamic continuum is primarily a matter of quantity determining whether dance movement exists at all and in what degree, but its variations constitute that aspect of movement which we call quality. In the field of comparative intensities lie all increases and diminutions of force, all degrees of sharp-ness of attack, rigidity and fluidity, gradations of accent and unaccent, flexions, extensions, and rotations, leaps and falls, de-vitalization and rest.

Demands of the Spectator

So much for the subject of the materials of dance and their behavior; now to consider the manipulation of them in such a fashion that a finality is achieved and the spectator is left with a sense of satisfaction.

Experience of spectator response through many generations has made certain methods of procedure virtually mandatory, not by academy decree, but for functional reasons discovered by the painful trial-and-error system. Many of them, though perhaps not all, are commonplaces, for though we have not all been composers, we have all been on the receiving side of the process innumerable times, and our demands, whether we have made them overtly or not, have been along well-defined lines.

It is the composer's responsibility to capture the attention, hold it on the basis of climactic building of interest, and release it only with the culmination of his project, making sure that the release will have in it sufficient compensation for the expenditure of energy demanded up to this point. A beginning must be made simply and relationships between various thematic elements established gradually. To be thrust at once into a complicated situation is rather like opening one's eyes in a maze with nothing to suggest the way out.

It is of the utmost importance to indicate the path of progress step by step in advance. Unfamiliar material is far more difficult to follow than familiar, and must therefore be carefully prepared for and anticipated. If it is completely strange and unexpected, it is likely to produce no effect whatever, like words spoken in an unknown language. On the other hand, if it is too familiar, the response is likely to be almost mechanical and require so little effort of the attention that the mind will be allowed to

wander off to more exciting fields. The problem then is to provide enough novelty to keep the interest, but to build on a
groundwork of reasonable familiarity and with due preparation.
The unknown, as in any type of activity, must be couched in
terms of the known. Continuity—which is only another way of
saying a cleared path for the attention—is attained simply by
preparing for each successive step within the preceding one, so
that when it arrives it has a comfortable enough feeling of
familiarity about it to support that element which is new. Even
those elements which are planned for surprise must be prepared
for, at least to the extent of a warning to expect the unexpected.

The first preparation is made by the title, which in effect sets
the stage before the work begins. It may indicate the subject
matter of what is to follow, or the mood in which it is to be
cast, or something of its pattern, any of which is helpful in
establishing a point of contact. A poor title or a vague one often
seriously hampers a dance composition by leading the expectation into the wrong channels. The title is, of course, no part of
the work itself, but an extraneous device to facilitate its reception
by setting up certain associations that can be built upon when
the composition gets under way. Thus the basis for continuity
is established even before the opening phrase.

Continuity in itself is obviously not enough to insure attention,
any more than the sight of a cleared road is an irresistible lure
to travel it irrespective of its destination and the scenery by the
wayside. Along with continuity, a state of expectancy must be
maintained and its fulfillment ever promised but ever postponed.
This quality of suspense may rely merely on the natural urge
for the completion of an act begun, or it may be heightened by
the introduction of a counterelement which tends always to
turn the act away from its logical completion and is not conquered until the last moment. Devices to prolong the state of

unfulfillment serve to increase the pleasure of the final resolution by increasing the vigor and insistence of the demand. The process is not unlike that of hunger, in that the longer food is delayed or the more the appetite is increased by such synthetic devices as cocktails, the greater the pleasure in the eating and the larger the amount that can be consumed. The experience of hunger is not in itself a pleasant one, to be sure, and if there is no guarantee of food ahead it can become an exceedingly painful one, but the natural unpleasantness of the experience can be completely transformed by the anticipation of pleasurable fulfillment.

In art it is possible for us to extend the range of our experience into unpleasantnesses which in life we must avoid, because we have always ahead of us the assurance of a pleasurable resolution, and hence a much sharper experience of pleasure than the mere level routine of safe living can provide. In its use of suspense, art provides us with an extension of experience into the enthralling realm of danger, with the certainty of complete safety. To be harrowed and wracked—within limits, of course—becomes not painful but pleasant with the anticipation of a proportionate recompense. To be sure, not all art is as dramatic and emotionally stirring as this, but even if the issue is no greater than the threatened incompletion of an aesthetic design, the fringe of adventure has been touched.

Aside from the consideration of familiarity and unfamiliarity, some material is easier of reception than other. Because it is the nature of the organism to defend itself against inharmonious adjustments and to invite harmonious ones, that material is most easily effective which awakens pleasurable associations. The clear, bright color, the soft tone, the gentle modulation, the curved line, the smooth and even-flowing movement, invite no resistance, whereas the discordant tone combination, the angular line, the irregular rhythm, the abrupt attack, arouse defensive and even avertive reactions and conflicting adjustments. The work of art, therefore, which wins the most widespread popularity is the one which deals in materials of the easiest reception.

Those works, however, which have the most momentous consequences in art and in the redefining of human values are always those which require the receptive consciousness to extend itself beyond these rather lazy boundaries. By demanding unfacile adjustments and the resolution of irregular and antagonistic combinations, they compel an extension of the grasp and practice of universal order. This has been true of every important work (though not every popular work) in the history of art, and a means of extending the range of art both in the depth of human values and in technical mastery from generation to generation. This is not to be attributed to any deliberate intention of the artist to be moralistic or educational, but simply to the fact that as an artist he is more sensitive to his environment than the majority of those about him and is faced first with the necessity for making new adjustments.

In the handling of thematic material, repetition, up to the point where it becomes monotonous, is increasingly pleasurable, providing an opportunity for recognition both of what has been previously presented and of its manner of presentation. When a phrase or a complete statement is brought into play a second or a third time, it travels over a path already cleared but not traversed so often as to have become virtually automatic. On the basis of repetition, variations may be introduced, relying on the familiarity of the material to sustain them, and even to make them doubly pleasurable because of a comfortable margin of novelty and an element of contrast. The pleasure of repetition is also increased if in the meantime material of another character has been introduced, for, again, contrast heightens the intensity of the recognition.

Responses, however, like muscles, are subject to fatigue. Persistence on a single theme produces ennui just as readily as the overtaxing of a single muscle. Endurance of interest is lengthened if there is a wider distribution of attack, always with the proviso that the spread is not so great as to produce a sense of disunity.

This spread may involve not only alternation and variation of theme in sequence, but may also consist of presenting simultaneous themes or basic movement materials too large to be performed by a single dancer. As a rule it is easier to sustain attention with the unified activity of a group of dancers than it is with a single figure, for there is a wider field of interest and less necessity for close concentration; but it is above all essential that such activity shall be unified. Attention is lost if it is required to focus on more than one thing at a time. If two things occur simultaneously in a composition they must either be so related as to become virtually one or else so arranged that one is comparatively negligible—perhaps a mere marking of time or else the continuous repetition of a simple theme of moderate accentuation which can be easily registered as a background for more striking action. Because of differences in the processes of seeing and hearing, musical harmony and counterpoint are considerably freer in range and can indulge in greater elaborations than their spatial equivalents, for visual objects do not blend as sounds do. Whether this is due in part to lack of experience in looking at spatial counterpoint or altogether to essential differences in the respective powers of the eye and the ear to focus is for the psychologists to say.

Even with a broader attack, however, it is necessary, in order to sustain vigor of response, that greater and greater stimulation be provided as the work progresses. A simple beginning is indicated, therefore, not only because it is difficult for the spectator to grasp an involved one, but also because it is difficult to build upward from a starting point that is already high.

Musical Forms

THUS far what has been discussed has obviously more relation to the elements of organic form and the compositional approach to its realization than to any particular dance forms. As a matter of fact, the dance is virtually free from predetermined forms. This was not always the case, and in primitive societies where rituals prevail, it is still not so. Nevertheless, in the art dance of the present time, the routine approach that so grieved Noverre in the eighteenth century and the reformers who came after him, no longer exists. The overturning which took place in the wake of Isadora Duncan destroyed the old stereotypes pretty effectively.

The dance today is singularly unfettered. There is nothing even approximately equivalent to the sonnet or the sonata, where a definite procedure is prescribed. Perhaps the nearest approach to it is the pas de deux which is still seen in the formal manner in revivals of nineteenth century ballets—and approximations of their style—that is, first, an adagio section in which the ballerina is exhibited by her partner; then a solo, called a variation, by each of them; and finally a coda in which they are together again, this time in allegro movements. Nowadays, however, even this term has lost its set meaning, and pas de deux signifies any dance for two, without formal restrictions.

Sometimes antique dances such as the sarabande, the courante, the galliard, the minuet, are referred to as dance forms, but this is a loose manner of speaking. Even in the days of their practice in the ballrooms of the nobles of the Renaissance and later, few if any of them were rightly to be considered as forms. Today, their choreographic aspects have been generally forgotten, and in the line of direct survival they have come down to us only through their musical influences. Music written according to the patterns of certain of them was employed in contrasting combination to make up the musical suite, but since this popular musical device long outlasted the dances on which it was patterned, it is only natural that it should have become thoroughly musicalized and progressively isolated from its source material. Actually it does little more than retain the characteristic rhythm phrases and the general spirit of the original dances.

The antique dances, particularly in the sketchy state in which we know them, are not to be considered in any sense as forms, therefore, but rather as rhythmic schemes, and step patterns, in much the same way that the waltz, the fox-trot, the tango, are rhythmic schemes, and step patterns. They are comparable not to such a self-contained form as the sonnet, but rather to the type of verse that characterizes it, that is, the iambic foot in a five-foot line. A form is necessarily a definitive structure with beginning and end, and is not to be confused with the details of design which it may employ. A room, for example, has form in that it demands a minimum number of surfaces in order to be a room; but the wallpaper which decorates it consists merely of a series of repeated units of design which may continue indefinitely. Any of these rhythmic schemes may be put into form by a composer if he chooses to employ them, but they do not constitute forms in themselves.

What accent there is on predetermined forms in the dance today is largely the effect of that dependence upon music which grew, as an inadvertent by-product, out of Isadora Duncan's practice, and which has not yet been totally overcome. Though

Isadora overthrew all the old choreographic formulas, she subjected the new and free substance of her dance to the influence of highly organized musical forms which completely dominated it structurally. In her published writings she has stated that her use of such music was no part of her theory but only an immediate personal necessity, since from no other source could she obtain the inspiration she required. By many of those who followed her, however, the superimposing of musical forms upon dance material was seized upon as a definite method and has continued in force to some extent ever since. This is true not only of those types of dance which obviously owe their beginnings to Isadora, but of the ballet as well. If the musical composer has already put his ideas into form, the dance composer apparently feels that he need not bother to do likewise but can lean instead upon the musician's work.

Logically enough, when the more progressive choreographer first sees the need for breaking away from this hampering dependence upon music, he is more than likely to take with him as his basis for independent composition those practices which he has automatically acquired from the musician. By reason of this inertia, it is the frequent procedure of dancers, even when composing entirely without the aid of music, to follow musical formulas, in spite of the fact that forms devised specifically to solve musical problems are generally unsuitable to dance.

The basic principles of organic musical form, to be sure, are at one with those of organic dance form and stem from the same root. Dance and music are extremely close and in their origins virtually inseparable. Dance without song or song without dance is a relatively late development, and then only in the Western world. An independent musical art exists nowhere else and an independent dance art is equally unthinkable. Manifestly, the man who is totally possessed by the impulse to externalize his emotional state will not omit any instrumentality at his command, and complete dance must involve voice as well as movement. If the dancer has insufficient breath for both, the song can be delegated to others. No matter who does the singing, however, it is always essentially the dancer's voice that is being represented, and this becomes no less pressing a necessity even after the song has evolved into wordless and orchestral music.

When the combination of dance and song is dissolved into its separate halves and each half goes its own way without regard for the original relationship, their higher individualistic developments become remote and irreconcilable. When they are put together again into a joint function, it is necessary to turn them back to that point near their common origin at which they began to part. Since music has been developed to a far higher degree in its own sphere, its realliance with dance entails a considerable sacrifice of purely formal musical progress. For this reason many musicians will not consent to write for dance because of the retrogression involved, and even more are unable to do so because of a widespread inability to grasp, in anything but theory, the original dance aspects of music with which they have had no personal contact.

Nevertheless, if the chief musical forms are examined, it will be seen that those few which are actually forms in the organic sense are as much dance forms as they are musical. Some of them are not even definitive entities but merely combinations and devices, and hence fall outside the classification of forms in spite of accepted usage.

The one-section type of composition, typified by some of the simpler folk songs and an occasional prelude by a more sophisticated composer, is, of course, equally applicable to short types of dance, and is an entirely organic manifestation of form, being merely a single complete statement of rhythmic action.

The two-section form is certainly as much a dance form as a musical. It is only a further extension of the essential base of rhythm; the next larger step after the balancing of phrases to make a section is the balancing of sections according to the same plan. In spite of its increased dimensions, it is still in effect a contraction followed by a relaxation—a statement and a response, a question and an answer. This is obviously founded on an organic principle, though the mere use of the letter of the device without regard for the inner relation of the material in the two sections is no guarantee that organic form will be realized.

The three-section form, commonly referred to as A-B-A, states a theme, follows with another of contrasting character, and repeats the first. There is, again, an inherent possibility of formal completeness in such a program of action, which belongs to the dance as well as to music and is frequently employed by it. There are innumerable implications possible in its use. For example, it is as if in the emphatic statement of a point the composer wishes to say: "This first statement is true; this second statement may also be true; but the important thing is that this first statement is true." Or perhaps, more dramatically, the first section makes a compelling statement, the second attempts to deny it, and the repetition of the first refutes the denial. Or again, it may be an enlargement of the two-section form for clarity and emphasis. To take an example from the nursery jingle: "What are little girls made of?" (First section.) "Sugar and spice and everything nice." (Second section.) "That's what little girls are made of." (Repetition, not only on a more positive basis, but also to point out that the recipe in the second section was not a mere digression but was strictly on the original subject.)

This form bears a close relation to the rondo, which is often said to have grown out of it but which may just as logically have given birth to it. The rondo consists of a single basic theme followed by any number of other themes with a return to the basic theme after each, as A-B-A-C-A-D-A, etc. Since there is no limit to the numbers of themes that may be introduced, this is manifestly not a definitive form. One of its early usages is in the choral dance-song in celebration of the exploits of a hero, in which the legend is told by a leader with periodic interruptions by a group in a refrain. The form is completed when the story is completed. Here it is actually the material that supplies the definitive element. Another and perhaps slightly less extraneous manner of drawing the form to a conclusion is to be seen in a type of ancient round in which the dancers circle in a characteristic figure, and each dancer in turn takes the center to perform a figure of his own. The whole is given shape of sorts by the fact that the dance is not complete until every participant has made his contribution. It is possible to consider the A-B-A form as perhaps one man's share in such a dance as this—a group figure, the emergence of a soloist, his return to the group. Certain "longways" country dances employ something of the same plan, each couple executing a figure in turn and rejoining the entire company for a repetition of a general figure between. Again, the end is determined in advance by the number of participants. It was in such a form as this that the early French ballet and opera couched the inevitable grand chaconne of its final act.

For the rest, there are no clean-cut organic claims to be made. Sonata form is an elaboration of the two-section form, with nothing at all inevitable about the manner in which it has been elaborated. Changes in tonality play an important part that the dance cannot possibly hope to parallel, and it is, indeed, a purely musical development, with an arbitrary logic of its own, and no organic structural basis. The sonata as a whole, consisting of several movements of which "sonata form" usually shapes only the first, is an outgrowth of the old dance suite, but nothing remains of the original except the contrasting character of the various movements, and frequently one movement in the pattern of the minuet.

The fugue, as Sir Donald Tovey has said of it, is "a texture rather than a form." Its end is in no wise implicit in its beginning; it may, indeed, run on forever, and in the hands of a composer only moderately skilled never acquire any aesthetic contours at all. It is not a form but a manner of procedure, its chief feature being the presentation of a leading theme or subject in each of a number of voices in turn, while the other voices continue with secondary material. Something in the nature of fugue or canon is frequently employed in the dance, as in certain longways dances in which each couple in turn performs a series of patterns introduced by the leading couple; but in dances designed to be seen by spectators, it is a device that can be used only incidentally and at some risk. Highly contrapuntal arrangements in any medium demand great mental concentration from an audience, and so much so in the dance that they are generally conducive of little besides visual confusion.

The theme with variations is not a specific form but rather a type of compound composition consisting of a number of individual forms. Each variation is a complete entity, and may be of virtually any type, while the whole is united by a common subject rather than by any structural unity. The varying of a theme is a widely used composing practice, whether in music or dance, but it does not constitute a definitive form, since it sets no limits for itself in either extent or procedure. Bach has employed as many as thirty variations in the Goldberg set, and Beethoven thirty-three in the Diabelli.

Music and dance are seen, thus, to have much in common along formal lines, but to be far from identical in their individualistic developments. Materials play so vital a part in the shaping of form that the application of any of these common principles to music and to dance produces quite different results, and there is actually no formal unity between them. The dancer, therefore, who takes any old rag-tag and bobtail of movement and depends upon its meticulous arrangement according to musical formulas to give it validity is doomed to failure from the start.

Doris Humphrey, a master of dance form, once gave a lecture in which she demonstrated all the standard procedures and formulas and concluded by remarking that though these were the accepted methods of composition, she herself never composed according to them. Her method, she said, was rather to let the central idea of a composition grow in her mind and eventually work itself out in a form of its own. Most mature artists, it is safe to say, work in some such manner, with the result that no handy compendium can be relied upon as a key to their creation, and to look always for musical form in them is virtually to insure missing the point.

Drama and Dance

IN many respects, the dance is more closely related to drama than to music, though especially since the days of Isadora Duncan, emphasis has been otherwise directed. The dancer and the actor are actually the same person in slightly different guises, but the dancer and the musician very early become two persons, supplementary to each other and engaged in separate divisions of the same art.

The musician takes the experience of the dance and attenuates it into a disembodied emotion, so to speak, leaving the personal performance behind. The actor, on the other hand, retains the element of personal performance, but instead of attempting any rarefaction, makes it more inclusive and more specific. The dancer in his performance represents only himself as a type of the race reacting in the present moment to the world about him; the actor becomes a particular individual in a particular plot situation. Both employ movement as their medium, and each adds a characteristic sound equivalent. Where the sound equivalent for the dancer has the same broadly symbolic quality as his movement, that for the actor falls into the more specific forms of speech, varying in its literalness from highly exalted verse to colloquial prose.

The division between dance and drama becomes at times exceedingly fine; indeed, the greater part of the existing dance repertory leans well over the line. The moment the dancer ceases to appear as himself experiencing a present emotion, and assumes a character, he steps into the actor's field, though not necessarily into the range of dramatic form. When in addition he retails some exploit, real or imaginary, he invokes automatically that particular sequential arrangement which belongs to dramatic form. A vast majority of the larger dance works designed for the stage are equipped with both characterization of sorts and plot; and the latter, even though it may be little more than a thread upon which to string incidental dances, frequently provides the only structure by which any semblance of formal unity is attained.

Dramatic form as such can be said to exist when the dance, instead of presenting the essence of an emotional experience, deals with a specific sequence of events out of which such an experience grows. The more literal its treatment, the less it has of dance about it. The essential basis of dramatic form is reducible to the following simple formula: the presentation of a

leading theme, the introduction of a countertheme in direct opposition to it, a clash between the two, and the emergence of one
of them as victor. This is eminently applicable to certain types
of dance composition, and can obviously be employed without
resort to the kind of highly detailed plot and closely identified
characterization that are required in storytelling. Dances of high
emotional content but of less inclusive form normally deal with
only the last of these sections, that is, with the summation of an
emotional experience. Dances of more lyric character naturally
eschew the dramatic form altogether.

Drama and dance are seen even more strikingly as merely different levels of the same art when they are viewed at a point before the element of form properly enters into consideration at
all. Composition, as the process of putting materials into form,
concerns itself first necessarily with materials, and the basic stuff
of drama and the basic stuff of dance are identical. The difference is altogether in the approach to it, for drama thinks of it as
action and dance thinks of it as movement.

Frequently the young dancer, along with the uninspired
among his elders, feels that he can rely upon musical principles
for his forms, but has no notion where to turn for his choreographic materials, that is, for the movement which is the substance of his dance. Music, his habitual guide and support, can
offer him no help here, having long since been developed away
from any direct concern with bodily action. In his plight, he generally follows one of three courses: either he allows music to
"inspire" him to improvise; or if perhaps he rightly mistrusts
this reliance on suggestibility, he invents arbitrary movements
that look "original" and uses them to fill in an objective pattern;
or he simply arranges and rearranges old familiar movements
without any thought whatever of creativeness of material.

The solution of his problem (unless, of course, he is dealing with a traditional type of dance with a rigidly determined vocabulary) lies in turning directly to the fact that the body reacts to all stimuli first in terms of movement, and that communicative movement suitable for dance can be drawn only from what might be termed his motor memory of emotion. He must learn how to call upon his emotional associations and translate them into action directly from life experience.

This is exactly the same fundamental problem that belongs to the actor's art, though the actor with his broader medium need not concentrate on sheer movement. This was the basis of Stanislavsky's discovery at the turn of the century by which, as director of the Moscow Art Theatre, he revolutionized theater practice. During those same years Isadora Duncan was discovering it to be the fundamental problem of the dancer's art, unrecognized since the days of antiquity, but more vital by far than any matters of form. Indeed, such matters were seen to be largely dependent upon the development of movement out of life experience.

Isadora has described in her autobiography her discovery of the origin of movement in the solar plexus, "the temporal home of the soul," and in this discovery, unscientific as it possibly is, she touched on the theory of movement evolved directly out of emotion which is the crux of the whole creative problem of the dance. Further, she tells of her efforts to discover a "first movement" based on a primary emotion from which a whole series of movements would flow as a kind of natural reaction without any mechanics of deliberate invention. Here is, indeed, the ideal pattern of the motor phrase. Such ideas were unheard of in the early nineteen hundreds, and are still far from being understood by the great majority of dance composers.

No movement sequence with the logic of emotion in it, however, is created by any other means, even though oftener than not it is only pure accident that produces an eloquent phrase. The fear of killing "inspiration" frequently prevents the tapping of the wellspring from which it flows, namely, experience seen in perspective. Certainly Stanislavsky's actors, with whom nothing was "inspirational" in the erroneous sense of improvisational, were never led into mechanical or routine performance by the application of the actor's approach to the same technic; it was that very thing, in fact, and nothing else, that saved them from mechanics and routine. Nothing else can perform a similar service for the contemporary dance, and put an end to the theory of excellence by accident as the only alternative to the three barren courses of action which prevail so widely in the dancer's approach to the discovery of his materials.

To be sure, highly personal emotional experiences cannot be taken in toto and put upon the stage as dances; they would be not only extremely embarrassing, as personal confessions always are, but also largely unintelligible because of their close relationship to the private and involved affairs of one individual's life. These experiences are only the ore from which the pure metal must be extracted, and the process of extraction is the most important element of dance composition and the one that makes the greatest demands on genius.

Here the actor and the dancer definitely part company, each to provide in his own way the necessary perspective by which personal experience is transformed into the stuff of art. The actor (or rather the dramatist who provides him with the composition he is to perform) turns to characterization. The emotional experience which is at the heart of the work is transferred to a fictitious personality, created synthetically from both inward and outward observation and endowed with such qualities that this experience can logically happen to him under a given set of fictitious circumstances. The element of personal confession is thus removed, since the surface that is presented is quite objective; the intricacy of personal detail is likewise eliminated by supplying only enough of such detail concerning the invented character to clarify the immediate situation, omitting the many extraneous complications which would attach to him if he were completely and naturalistically transcribed from life. Though he may give the impression of a fully rounded personality, he is, of course, nothing of the sort, for only that part of his life which has to do with one particular dramatic episode has been created. He has been greatly altered from the pattern of actuality in order to provide those emphases which the artist needs to make his point. Clearly Hecuba, Clytemnestra, Medea; Hamlet, Lear, Othello; Pantalone, Pierre Patelin, Tartuffe; Hedda Gabler, Paula Tanqueray, Salvation Nell; Rip Van Winkle, Simon Legree, Jeeter Lester—are all merely dramatic abstractions from life and not life itself.

To the extent that the dancer from time to time steps into this field of characterization, he employs the same method of abstraction. His characterization, however, is never as detailed as the actor's and usually is the characterization of a type rather than of an individual. When he is a warrior, he is never General So-and-so at the Battle of Such-and-such, but is the typification of all warriors; when he is a butterfly (which happily he is not impelled to be very often these days), or a peasant, or a hobgoblin, he is the typification of all butterflies, peasants and hobgoblins.

This also gives an inkling of his approach on the far more significant occasions when he is not adopting the actor's medium of characterization in any degree but is functioning purely as a dancer. Then he dances in his own person as the type of all men in contact with some emotional force. If he dances about war or death, spring or love, he does not personify them, but rather externalizes some new emotional insight into them which he wants the spectator to recognize as belonging potentially to himself and to all men.

Naturalistic gesture is immediately ruled out, for it is commonplace, personal and particular. The impulse behind gesture, however, is the kernel of the matter, for the urge to move in generally the same tone in response to the same stimuli is common to all men. Here we are on the threshold of a universal medium of communication. It remains only for this common impulse behind gesture to be materialized in the dancer's movement with such breadth of dimension and clarity of outline that it will awaken the spectator to recognition of its personal significance for him. Literal mimetics cannot accomplish this experience of identification, for they contain too much that is purely objective. The dancer's movements are abstract; that is, they have abstracted the essentials from a particular life experience, omitting all that is merely personal and without universal significance. If, for example, a dancer were to compose a dance of farewell, he would not feel called upon to insert wavings of the hand or tears or embracings of an imaginary partner. These are the external commonplaces of the situation and would not warrant the making of a dance at all. Just what he would feel called upon to do cannot be prophesied, for it would grow from a personal and inward illumination. His material, however, would be distinctly less superficial and more intuitive than these outward tokens, based on a keen inner realization of the emotional forces involved, and utterly unpredictable in detail.

Almost the only thing that can be said of any dance composition in advance is that it will definitely not be an exact or even an approximate reproduction of nature; it will certainly take nature as its base, but will reshape nature's forms so that the attributes which the composer is anxious to make clearer than they

are in life will be magnified, and those with which he is not concerned will be minimized or eliminated. Sometimes this process
results in a heightening of sensuous beauty, in which case it is
likely to be considered as idealization; sometimes it results in
quite the opposite state, in which case it is more than likely to
be called distortion. The process, however, is exactly the same,
and is inseparable from the business of composition. It is the
process, indeed, which differentiates art from life, and makes possible the creation of that compensatory world in which art
dwells.

Not all types of dance, to be sure, employ movement creatively in the manner here discussed. In spite of the fact that this
is the root of the whole art, according to history as well as to
internal evidence, in all periods and in all arts crystallizations of
method and vocabulary occur which gradually grow so habitual
for one reason or another that they become laws in themselves
and tend to supersede creative experience as the point of departure for the artist. The controlling reasons for this are many,
having to do with religious prescription, social caste, fashion,
academism, and all the other monopolistic institutions of conservatism.

Such tendencies begin early in history in the notoriously conservative society of primitive peoples. When a dance with religious or social significance has become accepted as ritual, it is
death to the dancer who changes the smallest detail of it. Thus
dances are kept superficially alive from generation to generation even after their original purposes have been forgotten and
the accompanying songs have degenerated into mere gibberish
through constant but uncomprehending repetition.

In many parts of the world, especially in the East, religious
traditionalism still maintains inviolable vocabularies of movement, in some cases so far removed from nature and spontaneous

creativeness that dancers must begin training as young children when their bodies are capable of being molded along lines of abnormal movement.

In the Western world, the Renaissance, which has been greatly overvalued for its service to art, applied its passion for standardization to the courtly dance, and paved the way for the setting up in the seventeenth century of an academy in France under charter from the king to make laws for the ballet from which it has never completely separated itself. To be sure, there have arisen reformers from time to time who have preached the rebellious doctrine of a return to nature, and through the generations there have been changes of many kinds in the body of the laws, but an academic ballet still exists which works from a premise quite apart from creative movement.

Even in the nominally free tradition of the dance which has grown out of the revolt of Isadora Duncan there are now to be seen many manifestations of the same tendency to establish systems and ready-made vocabularies. Methods of movement which an individual dancer may have discovered to be expressive and logical for his own body with its particular conformations and for his own temperament and mental attitude, are frequently transformed into standard technics and superimposed upon pupils with whose temperaments and bodily conformations they have nothing in common.

All such crystallizations, historical and personal, together with selective aesthetic approaches and those deeper racial and geographical influences which tend to shape the dancer's practices, go to make up that aspect of dance which is known as style. A consideration of its broader values, both positive and negative, can perhaps be calculated to illuminate certain phases of the subject which are otherwise likely to be obscure.

Chapter Four

THE BASIS OF STYLE

✥✥✥✥✥✥

THE object in considering style is a purely practical one,
namely, that works of art couched in unfamiliar idioms
may become intelligible. The idea of translating from language to language for the sake of intelligibility is a common one,
but it is not often recognized to what a large extent the same
process must be employed with the languages of music, painting,
architecture, dance. Time, place, race, religion, social customs, all
make so deep an impression on the arts that it is possible to say
that every group of people makes its art in a different language,
or at least a different patois, and that none of them is totally
familiar to any other group.

This point has not been stressed nearly as strongly as it deserves to be, with the result that where our art education is concerned we have been pretty thoroughly taken in by it, without
any apparent realization of the process involved. Our attention
has been directed almost exclusively to the translation of works
from other times and other parts of the world, to the marked
detriment of the artists who speak to us in our own tongue and
of our own time. We have been so busy learning other people's
languages, without even being aware that we were doing so, that
we have remained virtually illiterate in our own. This is pos-

sibly only a by-product of our general educational tradition, for to adjust to an alien art expression demands a certain definite intellectual process, and this is no doubt more "educational" than merely to respond without any major adjustment to a work that speaks directly to our emotional understanding and does not necessitate such formal intellectual preparation.

Nevertheless, though contemporary native art, the expression of our own mind, is sorely neglected in favor of the old and the alien, the world teems with great works stemming from all peoples and all periods which only the most abysmal provincialism would advocate ignoring. Moments of illumination, of insight into human living, captured by artists in environments remote from our own, more than repay the effort that is required of us to penetrate through the purely local surfaces with which they have of necessity clothed their visions, to the universal core within. Sometimes the effort is beyond our capabilities, as in the case of much of the art of the East, and we are unable to get past the exoticism of the surface. At other times the adjustment is simple and after a bit of experience becomes practically automatic, just as one who learns to speak a foreign language and speaks it habitually over a long period acquires the ability to think directly in its terms without having to formulate his thought first in his own language. As an example of a similar art experience, we have grown so familiar with the music of the nineteenth century Germans that we have come to take it as our own language and are inclined to resent it when any other musical language is spoken even by our own composers.

It should never be forgotten, however, that an adjustment is necessary for all art created outside one's particular environment. The impulses of art, its motivations and its necessities, are universal, but the forms in which it is materialized are inevitably localized. Our guides to art appreciation do not always make

this clear, and as a consequence leave us with a perhaps encyclo-
pedic analysis of particular masterpieces but no hint of a general
principle to work upon. Under no conditions can we expect to
receive from a work of art out of another culture or another
period a reaction identical with that which it produced in its
own group, for the background out of which it sprang is too
far removed from our experience. The more fully we can re-
create this background synthetically at the back of our minds,
the greater will be the reaction we enjoy, and the keener will be
our appreciation of the essential truth which the artist has attempted to voice.

The danger of the entire process of adjustment, however, lies
in the fact that studying alien art methods and remote backgrounds can become such an absorbing intellectual pursuit that
it completely obliterates the function of works of art as such.
Scholars are frequently to be found who know the most intimate
details about whole periods of art and yet give no evidence of
having ever really touched the aesthetic substance of any of it.
This kind of scholarship is generally the resort of those whose
natural response mechanism is not too vigorous, yet who are
nevertheless attracted to art and eager to have closer contact
with it. It is largely the result of developing the wrong instrument through unawareness of the right one. In any choice between the two instruments—intellectual knowledge and motor
responsiveness—the latter is by far the more rewarding. The incidental facts and theories surrounding the arts will come of
themselves bit by bit through continued association, though it is
undeniably true that against a background of strong motor responsiveness, a little outside preparation can be stimulating and
useful.

The basis of style goes back to the elementary fact that art is a
form of compensation. As was pointed out earlier, the artist

finds himself equipped with urgent potentialities which he cannot fulfill in his actual life environment, and creates a hypothetical environment in which these potentialities can be fulfilled. In the creation of this hypothetical environment he necessarily employs materials which are familiar to him. On these facts the structure of style is built: that every environment presents different limitations to be overcome, and offers different materials, including different patterns of behavior, as the agencies for overcoming them.

To take perhaps the most striking example, there is the contrast between those categories of art which belong to the south countries and those which belong to the north. Where nature is kind, food plentiful, shelter and clothing easily obtained, art is characterized by acquiescence. The artist does not struggle against nature, but seeks only to intensify the beneficence which he finds about him, to live ever more richly and fully. His music is melodious and voluptuous; his architecture is low and balanced, conforming to the line of the landscape and emphasizing it. In the northern countries all this is changed. Nature is not a willing ally but must be fought and tamed. Food is not easy to get, and must be stored for the future; shelter and clothing make large demands where bitter winds blow and half the year is burdened with snow and ice. Here art is characterized by a far greater intensification of the harmonious vision, for in it lies not pleasure alone but survival. In such art there are to be found purpose, determination, even defiance. The music stirs in emotional depths seeking to resolve doubts and unrests; the architecture rises at right angles to the line of the landscape, opposing it, and pointing upward into space with a gesture of freedom from the bondage of the earth.

A perfectly contented people might be expected to produce no art at all, since everything within their range of vision would already have been found to exist in life experience. In proportion as the vision of potential fulfillment exceeds the degree of present satisfaction, art takes on depth and substance and tends to transcend mere graciousness of surface. In the increasing complexity of contemporary Western civilization there is obviously a great incentive to creative art, in spite of the common opinion to the contrary. To an unprecedented extent man's vision of the possibilities of a fuller life and accomplishment has outrun his ability to realize in practical terms what he sees himself capable of, both individually and collectively, and the surplus must expend itself. That the art resulting from this expenditure is not more widely recognized as a great and characteristic expression is owing perhaps to the difference in its forms, its materials, its texture, from those of quieter, narrower and less idealistic times upon which we have been nurtured culturally.

In all times and in all places art has used the forms, materials, textures, with which it was familiar. To a great extent, these have been determined by geographical considerations, the rock, the soil, the weather, the type of raw stuff naturally available, and the social and economic systems that these have bred. Not only do such sources supply the actual stone for the architect and the sculptor, and the pigment for the painter, but they are responsible as well for the objects and the conditions of living which the artist pictures.

On the other hand, the nature of man himself unconsciously shapes his arts in his own image, for the determination of characteristic forms comes largely from within. By a kind of inversion of the process of "inner mimicry," we project ourselves into the forms of things we make just as we read our own impulses into the things we see. It is quite usual for the writer of dialogue to put his own phrases and habits of speech unconsciously into the mouths of his characters. Illustrators commonly put their own physical characteristics and postural habits upon the figures they draw. In a larger sense, it has been demonstrated that there is a marked unity of form between the physical qualities of the various racial types and their respective architectures. Irving K. Pond, following an earlier architect, Espérandieu, has dealt briefly but delightfully with the "ethnology of architectural forms" along these lines in *The Meaning of Architecture*.

Racial qualities of voice result in racial types of music, and even the instruments that are developed will tend to be those of similar timbres. Language itself grows similarly out of group thought and physical equipment. Certainly those peoples of the East whose legs are particularly supple and who sit on the floor instead of on chairs will evolve out of this single physical characteristic different forms of furniture, clothing, and social practice from those common to the Western world where legs are relatively stiff. There are infinite variations to be played on the theme, some of them built on readily apparent evidence, others so deeply rooted in unrationalized experience as to be virtually impossible of scientific verification. Art becomes thus clearly the product of the interplay between man and his environment, a fact that goes deeply to the roots of the whole subject.

Against the background of these fundamental distinctions, shaped and directed in the remotest periods of time, history marches through group cultures. Wars, the subjection of tribe by tribe, and nation by nation; empire; religious movements, philosophies, the establishment of ecclesiasticism; famines, plagues, pestilences; migrations, discoveries, inventions; revolutions, ideals of liberty, emancipations; industrialism, machinery, power—a tremendous succession of changing values, of sharpening cleavages, create new potentialities for man and along with them new limitations to their fulfillment. Manifestly the sympathetic response to any period's art lies far less in familiarity with how certain painters applied their color and certain musicians their harmony and counterpoint than with a grasp of the forces that controlled this eternal margin between the will of the time and its fruition.

Historical Periods

THE approach to the specific consideration of style in the dance differs rather widely from the approach in other arts, for the simple reason that the dance has no living past. It is possible to make firsthand contacts with works of art in virtually all other mediums at almost every stage of their historical development, but the dance of other periods is lost for lack of adequate recording. It is possible to make presumptive restorations from occasional fairly explanatory records, and there are traces of antiquity handed down, though with colossal changes, through folk practices, but generally speaking, there is no dance work that can be seen in its authentic state after it has once ceased to be performed regularly and passes into history.

For example, the oldest work now in the ballet repertory is Dauberval's "La Fille Mal Gardée," first produced in 1786 and still given from time to time chiefly by the Soviet State Ballets. That it is little more than a wraith of its original self, handed down from generation to generation by tradition, is safe to assume, and a solitary wraith at that, for none of its contemporaries remains to keep it company. From such a source as this there is obviously little to be learned of eighteenth century style, save by deduction.

Far younger works have been forgotten completely after brilliant successes in their own day. Of the great 1830-40 period, when romanticism captured the ballet, there remains not a single authentic work. "Giselle" has persisted continuously through the years, but it would be a dangerous business to guess how much of its original choreography survives. Popular ballets of the Petipa era are now chiefly disembodied reputations. Even so great a work as his "La Belle au Bois Dormant," first produced in 1890, had to be pieced together for revival in 1921 from notes and memories of dancers who had been associated with it in its previous incarnations, and then copiously filled in from other and more frankly imaginative sources. More recent works than this, however, have disappeared beyond hope of authentic revival. When Fokine was asked, shortly before the revival in 1935 of his "Thamar," originally created in 1912, if this was to be an accurate reproduction, he replied that he did not see how it could possibly be since even he himself did not remember it.

Of earlier days, nothing is to be looked for. Except for a bare handful of manuscripts in various methods of notation and not too readily decipherable, the entire court period, the time of Camargo and Sallé, the great reforms of Noverre, the works of Viganó, live only in historical reports about them and a few relevant technical data. On such external evidence as this, coupled with knowledge of the life of the times, must stylistic background be built.

No such condition exists in any other art, except perhaps that of the actor, which is really a subdivision of that of the dancer. In music, for example, scores are available from the early contrapuntalists, the troubadours, the madrigalists, and even before. There are the beginnings of opera, and ironically enough, the music for many of the early ballets. There are riches of all sorts from the seventeenth and eighteenth centuries, as well as the nineteenth and twentieth.

Perhaps something of the situation of the dance can be seen if a similar set of circumstances is imagined in music. Suppose in order to play a Tchaikovsky symphony, it were necessary to hunt up old musicians who had originally performed the work and piece together a score from their memories of what they had played! Or worse still, suppose that a Beethoven symphony had to be approximated from written accounts of its first perform-ance supplemented by whatever knowledge could be gleaned from outside sources of the prevailing musical practices of the day and to what extent Beethoven conformed to them. The re-sult would be at best an interesting thesis, but certainly not a symphonic score in any sense, and much less a particular score by Beethoven.

Revivals of old dance compositions are just as difficult as this and as unsatisfactory. Indeed, even the restoration of the general style of a period is altogether a matter of pastiche, and contains at least as much of the individual style and times of the artist making the restoration as it does of the period that is being re-stored.

The Greek dance provides an excellent illustration. There is nobody now living who has any definite knowledge of how the Greeks of the classic era danced, nor has any such knowledge existed in the world for many centuries. Nevertheless, for the past four hundred years at least there have been "revivals" of Greek dance. In the sixteenth century, under the influence of the Renaissance, musicians and poets were generally bent upon re-establishing the unities of the Greek choric drama. Ronsard, Baïf, and the group known as the Pléiade were active in Paris, and a few years later, Peri, Caccini, and the group known as the Came-rata were even more active in Florence. Naturally, the dance was not unaffected. Fabritio Caroso records efforts to compose dances for the ballrooms of Italy in spondees and dactyls to ally dance thus with poetry in what was meant to be the manner of the an-cient Greeks. In the court of Henry III of France, the "Ballet Comique de la Reine" told a story of Circe in a fashion which its creator, Beaujoyeux, and his contemporaries considered to be a well-realized restoration of the Greek choric drama, though its characters wore the còurt costumes of the time and the whole procedure differed from the customary court ballet of the day only in a somewhat greater unity of plot.

A century and a half later Greek gods and heroes peopled the ballet still clad in sumptuous elaborations of the contemporary court costume. In 1733 Marie Sallé created a scandal when she danced the role of Galatea without these trappings but in "a simple dress of muslin" which seemed to her to be more appropriate. A generation later Noverre was still somewhat radical when in his ballet, "La Toilette de Vénus," he left the conventional wide-skirted coat off his fauns, replaced the customary red-heeled shoe with a laced one suggesting the bark of a tree, and substituted for the customary white of gloves and stockings, a color to represent the flesh tint of "these forest inhabitants." A simple drapery of tiger skin covered part of the body, and the rest was allowed to give the appearance of nudity, but in order not to cause too violent a contrast with the costumes of the nymphs, a garland of flowers was thrown over the tiger skins.

In the days of Louis XVI and on into the next century, a new classical wave spread, stimulated by Winckelmann's researches into Greek art, and for the first time the ballet interested itself in a slightly more archeological style of dress for its continuing succession of Greek gods.

During none of these years had any thought whatever been given to the choreographic style that might have belonged to the ancients; instead there prevailed without question the fundamental vocabulary of movements established in the court ballet, crystallized in the academy of Lully, and revised and extended from within by the logical developments of time. Whether it even occurred to anybody that perhaps there was such a thing as a different idiom of movement seems altogether doubtful.

Indeed, at the end of the nineteenth century the idea seems to have been definitely established that there was not. Then in a dissertation on the antique Greek dance, Maurice Emmanuel examined sculpture and ceramic paintings and concluded that the Greek dance was much the same in vocabulary as the nineteenth century ballet. The bare feet depicted on dancing figures were often merely the result of an artist's convention, he contended, and he found reason to believe that the Greeks even danced on the points of their toes, though nobody else had ever done so, to be sure, until the Taglioni period. Significantly enough, Cecil Sharp, the eminent English folklorist, examining the same material a few years later, found it to contain many similarities to the contemporary folk dance of European peoples.

At the turn of our own century, Isadora Duncan, deeply impressed with Greek art but well aware that she was not in any sense reviving the antique dance, adopted the classic tunic as her costume, threw off corset, shoes and other time-honored impedimenta, including the technic of the ballet itself, and unwittingly started another Greek dance revival. In the Russian Ballet, Michel Fokine, a supreme stylist, created against a background of ballet training, though not in the traditional ballet manner, a number of Greek works, going for his source material to sculpture and ceramics, and achieving, at least in his "Daphnis and Chloe," a touch of the archaic manner of the ceramists. Nijinsky in his "L'Après-midi d'un Faune" employed a more exaggerated archaism of pose, working almost exclusively in the two-dimensional quality of a frieze. Virtually everywhere today there exists a type of simple, free and natural dance that calls itself Greek or "revived" Greek, though manifestly the "revival" is built on external information and intuition together with the

example of Isadora Duncan, rather than on any actual knowledge of the antique dance. In Greece itself, Eva Sikelianos and
Vassos Kanellos have separately re-created what their deep study
of the subject has made each of them believe to be the essential
spirit of the antique dance.

In the face of all these conflicting presentations, what is Greek
classic dance style? Apparently it is whatever you think it is. In
each of these instances, it is quite clear that the artist has looked
at ancient Greece and given his individual interpretation of it,
against the background of whatever his particular period has
known about it archeologically and felt about it emotionally. It
becomes necessary, then, to identify the period in which the
style is evolved equally with that period at which it aims. Thus,
if we would make ourselves clear, we must obviously refer to
Renaissance Greek, or Louis Seize Greek, or Isadora Duncan
Greek, or Russian Ballet Greek, for there is manifestly no such
thing as objective Greek dance.

The situation is substantially the same when the dancer attempts to reproduce the style of any other period, though of
course the Greek far outdistances all competitors in the race for
popular approximation. It is not, however, a very calamitous
situation. If there were dance works extant from other times, it
would be vitally necessary to know how to present them, but in
view of the fact that there are no such works pressing for performance, the occasion does not arise. Certainly there is as little
reason for any dancer to set out to create an authentic dance in a
remote style as there would be for a musician to compose an
authentic fifteenth century madrigal or a writer to adopt the
English of Chaucer. The creative artist may allow influences
from the past to enrich his style, or he may deliberately quote
from it, if to do so has point, or he may employ his special
knowledge or intuition to create an impression of it, but he

maintains his own approach and speaks inevitably to his own time. For the actor or the musician who is not an originator but a performer of an existing repertory extending back through the centuries, the case is somewhat different. It is imperative for him to have a knowledge of period and a sense of styles. Even here, however, the present colors his performance; he is interpreting and in a sense commenting upon another epoch, pointing out its characteristic flavors to his contemporaries. He lives in two worlds, as it were.

In the dance no such problem exists, for though many dancers perform what others compose for them, there is no repertory from the past to be concerned with. The nearest thing to such a problem is the approach to the traditional ballet, which in spite of a necessarily contemporary repertory retains certain fundamental principles established three hundred years ago and employs many traces of the past in its actual vocabulary of movement. It would be totally inaccurate, however, to consider the ballet style in itself as a period style, for it represents at bottom a particular approach to the dance which has nothing to do with time. The mere handful of specific works that have been handed down from earlier periods in word-of-mouth form are too few to constitute a problem. Illiteracy has taken care of that situation with devastating thoroughness.

The matter of period, then, presents little or no trouble to the spectator who has the average man's background of general history and social change, for the dance as we know it has no life outside the present. The limits of this present lie between the memory of the oldest dancer now active and the vision of the most forward-looking. It is within this range, then, that a practical consideration of style must function, rather than within some more orthodox range patterned after the necessities of the other arts.

Ethnic Influences

WITHIN the present there is only one category that presents serious obstacles, and these so serious, indeed, that they are in many cases insurmountable. This is the ethnic category. It is to all intents and purposes impossible for a Westerner to grasp the subtleties and symbolism of the dance arts of the East, intricately interwoven as they are with religion and social custom. For their decorative values, their unusual color, and their stimulation of interest through the sheer difference in their movement vocabularies they are frequently admired and applauded, but rarely, it is safe to say, for the proper reasons from the dancer's point of view.

In a certain degree this is also true of that ancient and highly involved composite that we call loosely the Spanish dance. Deeply rooted in the life and spirit of the people, it retains still the qualities of a folk expression even when it is taught with classic precision to the daughters of the élite or transplanted bodily to the stage. With the strong flavor of the East in its mobility of body, the constantly centripetal emphasis of its curving lines, its awareness of the earth beneath it, its passion and petulance, its bursts of song, the counterpoint of its castanets, snapping fingers and heel rhythms, its inviolable and inexplicable traditions make of it a magnificent, complex and utterly unique manifestation. La Argentina, by her genius for the theater and her impeccable taste, translated it into a universality which it generally does not have. Lacking such unique illumination, however, it is best approached as the exciting expression of a richly passionate people, and admired simply for what it seems to be. To grasp its many subtleties and traditionalisms can easily become a career in itself.

Possibly because in exotic types of dance it is only the surface that is seen and this seems striking and delightful, a quantity of pseudo-ethnic dancing has come into existence, reproducing sometimes most painstakingly all the superficial detail of the original, apparently with the firm belief on the dancer's part that he has penetrated to the heart of the matter. For the experienced spectator, even though he is without technical knowledge, the difference is readily recognizable, sensed rather than rationally understood. It is far easier to speak a foreign language without a trace of accent than it is to dance in a foreign idiom with complete purity of style. Indeed, if the former is difficult, the latter is practically impossible, for movement rises in the unintellectualized realm of experience and is likely to betray the pretender in spite of his most assiduous mental effort.

Ethnic influences, however, employed frankly as such, form a useful part of the dancer's resources, especially in the field of the ballet. It was part of Fokine's great reform in this medium that when its plots dealt with other races its movements should also conform to racial styles. Previously it had been the practice to make no differentiation whatever, but to present the peoples of all times and places in the conventional vocabulary of the academic ballet, and even to costume them in the standardized ballet costume of tights, fluffy tulle skirts, pink slippers, etc. The ladies dressed their hair in the latest fashion and wore any jewels they were lucky enough to possess, without regard for the racial or financial status of the characters they chanced to be portraying. The only nod in the direction of style consisted of a bit of characteristic decoration, such as a narrow border of Greek or Egyptian design on the edge of the skirt, an apron if the character happened to be a peasant maid, or a few beads and a quill in the hair for an Indian. Fokine put a definite end to all such practices. For him Greeks, Hindus, Egyptians, Persians, as well as the many native tribes of his own Russia, moved in a manner dictated by the most reliable research.

To say that such movement is authentic would be to misstate the case entirely, for authentic movement would simply get in the way of the artist's creative purpose in much the same way that the everyday naturalistic gesture would. The ballet itself is a convention of the Western theater, and though its choreographic action must be adapted to give the color of other styles it must remain always within the bounds of its own. Such a method is familiar in the musician's world. Remote ethnic melodic practices, rhythms and timbres are approximated by the conventional instruments of the Western orchestra and in the conventional Western musical forms. It is unheard of for any Western musician to compose authentic Eastern music, and the "Scheherazades" and the "Madame Butterflies" are frankly intended to be evocative rather than ethnically accurate.

Outside the ballet, there is the striking example of Ruth St. Denis and her many Oriental dances. The great majority of them were created before she had ever put foot in the Orient and were not meant to be museum pieces but a Western vision into an Eastern art. Their music, like Fokine's, was part of the approximation and made no pretense to authenticity.

Ethnic style, then, like period style, demands qualifications. Just as we must speak of Renaissance Greek and Louis Seize Greek, so we must speak of Fokine Chinese and St. Denis Hindu. The style of the artist who makes the adaptation is at least as important as that of the original dance being reproduced. The whole approach to both ethnic and period styles in the contemporary dance, therefore, resolves itself into a deliberate process of evocation by synthetic means. It consists in extracting a certain essence from authenticity and employing it to give flavor to the whole, with no notion of archeological or ethnological accuracy. It is dictated, in the same degree that considerations of form are dictated, by the dual necessity of the artist to say what he has to say and to say it with due regard for the capacity of response that he can count on from his audience.

Unfortunately, out of such a perfectly sound aesthetic practice abuses have grown, and countless stylistic clichés have come into existence and been accepted in certain quarters as standard. Instead of going to original sources, it has been easier to go to some artist's successful adaptations and take them as a routine vocabulary. It does not matter at all that the same artist has probably employed a totally different approach and even different materials in other dances deriving from the same ethnic or period background. Thus we see a kind of standard Egyptian dance which presupposes that the ancients were exclusively two-dimensional creatures and that their representation in the early paintings was realistic portraiture. In this same category of art, Chinese dancers always shuffle about either with hands in sleeves or with index fingers pointing upward; "Orientals" are a half-clad composite of India and the state-fair midway, and indulge almost entirely in undulations of the hips accompanied by ripples of the arms. There are similar stereotypes to be found under the labels of Greek, Japanese, Russian, American Indian, Negro, Spanish, Dutch, and even "peasant." These are perhaps best classified as dancing school styles, but, unhappily, so to classify them does not remove them from the scene where they do a great deal of damage in the shaping of popular taste.

If there are distinctive differences of style to be found between groups of people who are of various races, cultures and backgrounds, there are also countless deviations from the particular norm within each group. Indeed, it is necessary to consider style as without any very clearly determinable boundaries, and certainly not as a static and specific thing that can be neatly pigeonholed. It varies markedly from individual to individual, and in the arts this is an element of some importance. The outstanding artist is invariably endowed with a highly personal style, inescapably related, it is true, to the style of the group of which he is a member and an interpreter, but departing from the norm of the group in indefinable ways. To describe or account for the particularities of personal style is as impossible as to describe or account for the particularities of physiognomy or complexion. In its less attractive phases it manifests itself as mannerisms and eccentricities, but when it belongs to a poised and richly endowed artist, it transcends surface trivialities and becomes a kind of luminous epitome of individuality.

Such qualities are easily recognized even in mediums in which the vocabulary and methods of procedure are codified and fixed by tradition. In the realm of the academic ballet, for example, an intangible combination of forces sets Alicia Markova apart, as it set Anna Pavlova apart, though the vocabulary of movement is the same academic vocabulary that is used by hundreds of other dancers. If we go farther afield into the alien art of the Spanish dance, the great exponents of our day, La Argentina, Argentinita, and Escudero furnish even more notable examples, as different from each other as possible, yet all elevated far above the rank and file of Spanish dancers by subtleties of carriage, of insight into the use of materials, of intuitive flavor.

The freer type of dance which follows in the footsteps of Isadora Duncan has recognized the existence of individuality to such an extent that it has built its approach largely on this ground. Mere freedom from established routine, however, does not automatically produce greatness of personal style, and it is still some inexplicable balance of factors that results in a Mary Wigman or a Martha Graham.

Ironically enough, we find that in this field of dance that is based on personal vision and personal style and is meaningless without them, the very strength of the theory is in danger of becoming its weakness. The emergence of striking personalities with highly individual manners of moving has led to little coteries of disciples at the feet of each, modeling their movements, their styles, their approach to costuming, composition, content, as closely as possible upon those of their leaders, utterly unmindful of the fact that they are denying the very theory of the type of dance they have embraced. Thus personal style is seen to lead to crystallizations just as ethnic and period styles do, retaining in each case only the surface aspects of a fresh and creative art adventure, erecting out of them a standardized vocabulary and a traditional approach and setting up new classicisms beside the old.

Classicism and Romanticism

TREMENDOUS confusions exist with regard to the relationships between classicism, romanticism and modernism in the dance. No sooner do we get it all straightened out on what seems to be a perfectly satisfactory basis that the ballet is altogether classic, the dance of Isadora Duncan and the "interpretative" school romantic, and that of Wigman, Graham and Humphrey modern, than we begin to hear troublesome rumors. Some one will talk, for example, of the romantic ballet of Taglioni, and as if that were not enough in itself, will add bewilderingly that though this was romantic, it is really what we mean today by classic. Some one else will make disturbing references to Fokine both as a master of the ballet and as a romantic revolutionist, or Isadora will be declared to be a modern, or Kurt Jooss will be said to make ballets out of modern dance.

To resolve these difficulties in a categorical manner is not to bring any fundamental enlightenment to the subject as a whole. Indeed, before it is possible to discuss any of these artists or their characteristic styles, there must be some clarification of the main issue, for we are inclined to be rather cloudy about these three selective aesthetic approaches in themselves quite apart from the dance.

For example, when a work of art is said to be classical, it may prove to be any one of six things: it may have to do with ancient Greece or Rome; it may be a work from another period that has managed to survive, usually in the schoolroom; it may be composed according to specific and stereotyped rules of form; it may employ a standard, codified vocabulary; it may be couched in a style that is cool, unemotional and neatly balanced in design; or it may be simply something outside the range of what is immediately and cheaply popular. Thus we find the academic ballet and the dance of Isadora Duncan, the symphonies of Haydn and those of Tchaikovsky, the *Iliad* and *Uncle Tom's Cabin,* all subjected to the same epithet!

Romanticism is likely to suggest to us lovers meeting clandestinely by moonlight or wasting away with phthisis, for we have inherited from our fathers that flavor of the tag-end of the last century. If we were asked to define modernism, we should find it virtually impossible to do so without resort to such words as angularity, cacophony, intellectualism, and it would be an effort to keep away from neurosis, decadence and primitivism.

All three of these approaches, however, are historic influences closely related to the life of the times in which they have developed, and in their periodic alternations and recurrences they have in every case arisen out of the essential drives of a particular environmental situation. Only a recourse to history, therefore, can clarify their fundamental natures by revealing the living impetus behind them, and save them from being treated as nothing but opposing "schools."

Perhaps the definitive character of classicism consists in its guidance by objective criteria and its faith in the cumulative wisdom of traditional procedure.

In the direct line of the arts of the Western world, it has its beginning in the Hellenistic period, with Alexander the Great as its father and Aristotle certainly in no lesser capacity than that of godfather. Before this time, it is true, great works of the past were reverenced; Homer and the glowing figures of the fifth century had long been part of a prized and consciously permanent background. Even before the rise of Greek culture there had been libraries of some magnificence in Egypt and Babylonia. When Alexander swept across the scene, however, the attitude toward the past's accumulation of artistic and intellectual treasures was vastly changed, and with it the future of Western culture. With a passion for Hellenizing that far exceeded mere avariciousness or political ambition, he embraced the whole barbarian world in the name of the Greek way of life. The culture of Greece had been spreading outside its own borders slowly and genuinely for many years by reason of its inherent persuasiveness; now the process was intensified manyfold, and the authority of Greek pre-eminence was established by official action. Local rulers and subrulers hastened to assume and advocate the utmost of Greekishness irrespective of conviction, and everything Hellenic became the fashion.

Obviously, this could be nothing but a forced culture over a large area of the civilized world. The native creativeness of the conquered peoples was stifled under this onrush of official superiority. Libraries were established, the great works of Greek writers were collected, studied, and diligently copied. That there was an enormous increase in specific cultural activity cannot be questioned, but whether its tendencies toward pedanticism and self-consciousness represented any advance in ultimate values over the natural and living manifestations that it displaced and destroyed is another matter.

In Alexandria in the third century B.C. we find the organized study of the foremost writers, orators, and philosophers of the past under way, critical editions of Homer being issued, and, what interests us most at the moment, lists drawn up of those writers who were officially decreed by the scholars to be best. It was still a long time before such selected works were actually called classics, but that is what they were in fact. The term itself did not arise until five centuries later in the Roman period, when the grammarian, Aulus Gellius, made a parallel between various grades of writers and the classes of Roman society. His comparison took as its model the social division set up in the ancient constitution attributed to Servius Tullius, in which all men were divided into six classes on a basis of property, the highest being the classici, and the lowest or propertyless, the proletarii. To this scheme Gellius made the writer conform, the highest type being denominated a scriptor classicus and the lowest a scriptor proletarius. Thus the classics were specifically named and defined, and endowed with a kind of snobbism that has extended far beyond the day of Gellius.

So great was the effect of Alexander's conquest upon a posterity more remote than he could even have envisioned in his day, that we still find the barbarian world being supplied with its lists of officially correct art out of the past and its correlative rules of officially acceptable procedure for the creation of art in the present. The artist who makes bold to violate these laws pronounces himself, today as in ages past, a barbarian and an aesthetically propertyless, ungrounded proletarian. It is interesting to note that the concern in the first place is exclusively with literature, and that it is literary men who make up the approved lists. Apparently none of the other arts seemed to them important enough to bother with.

At any rate, if the select works of literature and the canonized methods of guaranteeing this same selectness for the future were maintained in all their purity, history was conforming to no such carefully regulated pattern. Dynasty followed dynasty, power succeeded power, until in the early years of the Middle Ages life is seen to be rather remote from Hellenism, for all the careful nurture of the classics. The very language of the classics of the Alexandrians has by now become unintelligible to all save a handful of scholars, and even the literary Latin of more recent centuries is known only to the clergy and the courtiers.

The common speech does not derive from the highly inflected literary language but is a purely colloquial tongue. Being a part of the daily life of the ordinary man, free, colorful, utilitarian, it evolves its rules out of the necessities of communication, and not from academic code and culture. Such a system makes, of course, for diversity rather than standardization, each group slowly developing its own variations to fill its own requirements. In those days, that part of the world that had constituted the old Roman Empire was known as Romania, and its various dialects, developed from the popular spoken Latin that had been the basic tongue, came, naturally enough, to be referred to as Romanic or Romance languages. The tales sung or written in these languages were dubbed, accordingly, romances.

They were ebullient tales, indeed, unrestrained by convention, dealing with the adventures of common men, rogues, and fighters, with the exploits of kings and heroes out of classic myth and tradition, with intrigues of lovers and their mistresses, with magic, religion and superstition. They were, in short, the result of the necessity of the people to produce an art based on their own background and containing compensations growing out of their common life. When the works of the scriptores classici become increasingly remote and unrewarding, then scriptores proletarii must arise to supply the demands for that satisfaction that art alone can give.

The romancers, then, are closer to life and to spontaneous creation than their classic superiors, in spite of the fact that they do not bother with realism, that they indulge in the freest kind of fantasy, that they disregard probability and logic, and that they frequently allow their characters to lapse into the most wooden of types. In romanticism we see a return to feeling as a guide rather than form and precedent. As some one has said of it, if it ignored the classic unities of time, place and action, it supplied a new unity of compelling interest. This it achieved not by taking pains, but by sheer inward vitality. It is the democratic as opposed to the aristocratic art, a democracy of the imagination bordering at times on anarchism.

Between these two doctrines of classicism and romanticism, the history of the arts, controlled to be sure by the history of the life about them, swings back and forth, if not always in world cycles, at least in small waves within virtually every period. It is apparently nature's habit to effect progress in this manner of alternation, for even plant growth is seen to take place, not in a straight line, but first on one side and then on the other. The unfortunate aspect of the pendulum method, however, as it applies to culture, is that at each extreme a residue is thrown off that exhibits a deplorable hardihood, and manages to set up a tenacious existence in an orbit of its own, stolidly unaffected by the life around it. Thus in the twentieth century we are still faced with accumulations of Renaissance academism which clutter our educational systems and hang on the neck of our art criticism with the stubbornness of the Old Man of the Sea.

With the great dawn of the Renaissance there comes a mighty swing back to classicism. This is a strictly aristocratic movement patterned on inaccurate but idealistic visions of the classicism of ancient Greece and Rome. An awkward, wealthy, blousy upper class, weary of the age-old domination of medieval mysticism, has caught sight of an orderliness of mind and a personal elegance that once were the prerogatives of its forebears, and it sets out to attain them for itself with a fervor that is, amusingly enough, very like the exuberance of romanticism.

As a matter of fact, the impulse of the early Renaissance, like that of its correlative movement in the North, the Reformation, was essentially romantic. Though it lacked the genuinely democratic basis of romanticism, being wholly a movement of the ruling classes, it partook in a degree of the same quality in that it was a breaking away from superimposed codes of thought and practice for the attainment of individual expression. The particular manifestation of classicism against which it rebelled was that of the medieval religious system which dominated all thinking and made every man no more than an insignificant cog on an ominous wheel of dubious function. This system, in its turn, had once been a truly romantic movement in the basic sense of the word, for primitive Christianity was a mass demand for spiritual democracy, a demand that grew upwards through the ranks of society beginning with the slaves. Only with the crystallizations of ecclesiasticism did it pass into sterility and formula.

The ultimate weakness of the revolt of the Renaissance nobles lay in the fact that it had no such solid groundings to support it as either the early Christian movement or medieval romanticism had had; it never succeeded in getting down to bedrock, but merely substituted one type of classicism for another with no loss of authoritarianism but only a transfer of authority. The more durable results of the Reformation, for all that it, too, lapsed into petty bickerings and the establishment of many little orthodoxies, are perhaps attributable to the greater depth of its romanticism, that is, its superior democratic impulsion.

But the Renaissance was a movement of that element of society that Servius Tullius had denominated classici, and its ideals for the liberation of the individual from medieval suppression stopped with the restoration of a cultural life conforming, logically enough, to Aulus Gellius's category of classicus. The new vision had no meaning whatever for the common man.

To insure no relapses into medieval crudeness, academies were set up in every walk of life, with codes and rules for virtually everything, under official authority of the ruling sovereign. A select list of Greek and Roman masters became the standard for all style, and imitations and restorations of ancient culture were as exact as current scholarship allowed, which in many instances was undoubtedly very inexact, indeed. As Cicero was the model for all contemporary prose, so the original academy which he had headed as the last of a long line of scholarly succession from Plato, was, in spirit at least, exhumed as a model for the standardization of all cultural activities. Apparently Erasmus was the only devoted advocate of a broadly revived Greek and Roman scholarship who dared to criticize the fashionable apings of the day, and when he raised his voice to declare that "we must adapt ourselves to the age we live in, an age that differs completely from Cicero's," he was shouted down with abuse. To be sure, much of the ancient reviving was so copiously adapted to the age, however unwittingly, that even Erasmus, if he could have viewed it with sufficient perspective, would not have found the imitation too exact, for all the slavishness of its intention.

There can be no doubt that the impulse of the early Renaissance to abandon the sprawling remnants of decadent medieval romanticism and return to orderliness and intelligibility of form was a healthy and a creative one, a swing toward the center of balance after the pendulum had touched one of its extremes. But it was soon to swing to the other extreme and achieve a lifeless standardization, the only value of which lay in its unavoidable tendency to produce still another swing toward the center.

The ebbing of the Renaissance was followed by a movement that was in its turn quite as great a rebirth. Already in the baroque period emotional feeling had begun to make itself felt as against the restraints of classicism, and in the rococo with all its futile and meaningless elaborations there is an indication at least that fantasy and caprice have refused to be held down any longer and have got out of hand. The full revolt against classicism, however, does not make itself felt until the momentous eighteenth century has got well under way, but its roots go back at least as far as the philosophers of the Reformation who saw the essential nature of the individual man to be of supreme importance. On this basis all the revolutions of the century—political, social and artistic—were fought and won. The model for action was now no longer what the Greeks had done or what the scholars made of their doings, but nature itself as each man was able to know it without benefit of authority.

The new romanticism of the eighteenth century at best, however, was certainly far from realistic, for it dealt, as its medieval forerunner had done, with adventure, high emotion, fantastic and even supernatural extravagances; but it was concerned fundamentally with the emotional experiences of men, exaggerated and distorted though they might become in the process. Eventually, the tangible past, as opposed to the Olympian world of the classicists, became a living field of interest, the Middle Ages themselves assumed a new value in retrospect, becoming at last almost as much a source of material as Greece and Rome had been for the classicists. Their tales were refurbished and retold.

The personal passions of love and hate, of heartbreak and revenge, replaced the heroic aloofness of the old routine.

The Romantic Revolution, as it has been called, did not reach its climax until the early years of the next century, and within a generation afterwards it had spent its force. The clearest statement of its credo in its final period is to be found in the young Victor Hugo's preface to his play, *Cromwell*. Nineteenth century romanticism is seen much more markedly than that of the century before to present two complementary faces. In the first place, it represents, as it did in its earlier medieval manifestation, as definitely a Christian viewpoint as classicism represented a pagan one. Christianity itself, however, had undergone many changes, owing largely to the rise of Protestantism, and romanticism accordingly had a different philosophic flavor. It is now concerned deeply with personal morality and virtue, with the duality of good and evil and the consequent conflict in man, with the superiority of the soul over the grossness of the flesh. It indulges in flights of fancy over disembodied spirits, and voices a persistent yearning for higher ethereal spheres. It is easy to see how this approach, sincere and convinced though it might be in its beginnings, would slip easily, in its decadence, into sentimentality and sanctimoniousness.

The other face of the movement is its regard for nature with a particular emphasis upon pictures of folk life and peasant custom. To our taste as we look back at it, it seems prettified and superficial, but against its own background it had a certain lustiness which offset the contemporary concern for the more attenuated and unearthly qualities of the spirit. Rousseau had seen the two aspects as one, the simple passions of men related inseparably to the environment of nature, but the vigor of the romantic-democratic eighteenth century revolution had begun to wane, and passed steadily into greater and greater artificiality, ending in an atmosphere of trivial and saccharine insincerities which completely denied the vitality and the power that underlie true romanticism.

From this cursory summary, though it is chiefly along lines of literary development since both classicism and romanticism are literary terms, it is possible to sketch in a background against which these two antithetical approaches begin to assume their respective identities. Romanticism in every case precedes classicism, for it deals with content and substance where classicism is concerned with form and surface. It is matter where classicism is manner. It is spontaneous and demands participation of its audience, where classicism is reflective and invites observation. It is in effect emotional where classicism is mental; it induces excitement instead of balanced admiration; it is energetic and exuberant where classicism is poised and orderly; it seeks to awaken sympathetic experience instead of that combination of aesthetic responses that is generally described as beauty. Romanticism delights in things discovered, classicism in things made. Classicism is inevitably the development of material that has been uncovered by romantic impulses, for these are the forces that delve into experience and unearth its truths. No art movement, accordingly, ever begins by being classical; classicism is a second stage, a selective and refining stage.

The true classicist necessarily has a keen sense of style; that is to say, he is alert to the limitations of his chosen method of procedure, and deliberately pits his skill against his self-selected obstacles. If he is able to do this and take pleasure in it, he may succeed in achieving a high degree of effectiveness, and his technical adeptness becomes rather like the brilliant playing of a game. If he chooses to employ well-established forms such as the sonnet or the sonata, or well-established vocabularies like that of the academic ballet, he invites an easier response because his audience is familiar with the rules of the game and better able to applaud him when he scores. This intellectual framework exactly suits the temperament of those artists who are innately reticent, however deep their passions, and who seek restraining forms in order that, as Theodore Watts-Dunton said with reference to the sonnet, "the too fervid spontaneity and reality of the poet's emotion may be in a certain degree veiled, and the poet can whisper, as from behind a mask, those deepest secrets of the heart which could otherwise only find expression in purely dramatic forms." It is not an exploratory or an adventurous approach, but in those rare instances in which the artist's formal skill is animated by his awareness of the style he is embarked upon and is illuminated by the glow of living feeling, it can result in exquisite moments of contemplative beauty. But the pitfalls of sterile academism are many and deep along its way.

The approach of the romanticist is along the path of nature and subjective experience. He works not by rule but by revelation, trusting to his sensitiveness to himself and to his fellows to guide him to the adequate communication of emotional adventure. His peril is "self-expression" carried to the borders of emotional debauchery and resulting in formlessness and incoherence.

Modernism

MODERNISM (or what we call modernism today, for it is an inclusive term) has arisen to save him from these perils, since its characteristic drive is toward functional form. In modernism, as in classicism and romanticism, we are faced with a movement that is in no sense arbitrary but has manifestly grown out of its environment. Indeed, it is inconceivable that it could have come about at any other period of history, for it is directly related to the development of the machine, of power, of technology.

Contrary to the common assumption, it has not merely taken over these developments by contagion and mechanized itself; to read no more than that into its origin is to miss one of the salient aspects of its nature. That it has profited by the efficiency and the essential economy of the machine by which it is able to accomplish large ends with small means, is undeniable, but there is a deeper relationship to be sought. It is in a sense a repetition of the process by which romanticism came to birth in the Middle Ages. Then the classic culture had become so remote from the common man that he had no art and was forced to make himself one. Now something of the same sort had happened; technology had destroyed the current concept of art, which had been built up for many generations on the ideal of representationalism. Verisimilitude, the be-all and the end-all of art for so long, had ceased to be the business of the artist at all; it was accomplished now with genuine efficiency by any number of recording devices. There was no longer any sense in the artist's attempting to evoke wonder by his camera-like eye or his phonograph-like ear; he was clearly outdistanced, another victim of technological unemployment!

This mechanical inferiority to the machine, however, served to reveal to him the possibilities in his own medium, and he awoke to see that what was valuable in art was its very incapacity to represent nature with this infallible accuracy. If he compared his paintings, for example, with their subjects, he could not fail to see that where the camera could only picture them as they were, he had actually pictured them as he saw them, which was not the same thing at all. Among the personal limitations that kept him from mechanical perfection were taste, selectivity, and subtle psychological quirks in his mentality that somehow projected themselves upon the canvas in spite of him. Here lay a virtually unused power of interpretation. He had touched, indeed, upon the principle of abstraction, the principle by which the essential qualities of an object or an experience or a concept could be abstracted from the mass of irrelevancies surrounding it and given more value than nature itself had given them. Here lay the complete answer to representationalism, the complete defiance of the machine in art.

His goal now, far from being the reproduction of the already familiar in the common daily round for no other end than the pleasure of recognition, became the production of the unfamiliar out of this same round, utilizing the pleasure of recognition only as the taking-off place for an expedition into untried emotional fields. Instead of dealing always with the objective surface of life, which has long enjoyed the title of "nature," it was now possible for him to deal with essences, to penetrate ever deeper into the subjective roots of experience.

The process of abstraction renounces all obligations toward fullness of detail, fidelity of proportion, and outward considerations of verisimilitude. The artist retains from the realism of his subject matter only those dominant elements that accord with his intention, and these he makes more vivid, more intense, larger than life, stripped clean and taut and naked. From the standpoint of literalism, this is nothing less than distortion, but since nothing could be farther from his mind than to produce a facsimile of anything, there is no real distortion involved. He is not mutilating outward reality; he is creating a new and independent object known as a work of art, an expression of his mind, in which he uses certain aspects of outward reality merely as a base of supplies.

These processes make the artist of necessity something of a technologist in his own sphere. The easy approach to composition which allowed early romanticists to relax and lean on nature is closed to him, and it is incumbent upon him to find active and vital forms in which to demonstrate his dynamic inventions. For this he must look not only to what he has to say, but also to the means, the materials, the medium, in which to say it. If he were trying to create an illusion of nature, instead of to produce a self-acknowledged work of art, he would minimize these matters, and do everything in his power to make the spectator believe that he was not in the presence of materials, means, medium, at all, but of nature itself. But he is making something called a painting, or a sculpture, or a dance, and in each case the materials with which he is working will have something to say about how he handles them. In his pursuit of functional forms, therefore, he must know first of all the nature of his materials, whether they happen to be sound, color, or movement, before he can shape them according to their inherent laws into being the outward body of his intent. They must collaborate on a virtually equal basis with his personal perspective on his subject matter in the determination of the shapes, the manner, the degrees, of his abstractions.

With the gaining of this point of view, he has found a new freedom. As a painter he no longer tries to make flat surfaces give the illusion of three dimensions, as a sculptor he quits forcing stone to pretend to be flesh, as an architect he abandons the practice of disguising steel structure as Gothic masonry, as a dancer he no longer hides behind the attitudinizing of a Greek god or a fairy prince. Movement, steel, stone and pigment are all seen to have unsurpassable qualities in their own characters without having always to be made to masquerade as something else, to represent objects instead of presenting concepts.

If the abandonment of representationalism has more importance for the romanticist—that is, for the artist who is concerned with expressing something—than it has for the classicist, whose art has no direct concern with life experience to begin with, nevertheless the modern accent on functional form presents the latter also with a new range of activity. It allows him to abandon traditional procedure and to let his materials lead him into new structural fields by their own natures. Compositions in pure color, line as line, mass as mass, sound as sound, are eminently practical with no expressional intent whatever. Of the dance, of course, this is only partially true, for the body cannot be separated from implied intent. Even here, however, experiments have been made in which the body is completely disguised within architectural constructions, though whether this still remains within the category of dance is open to question.

The modern classicist may or may not go as far as Stravinsky advocates, but he will at least recognize the essence of the neoclassic doctrine when he reads in the composer's autobiography that for him "music is, by its very nature, essentially powerless to *express* anything at all, whether a feeling, an attitude of mind, a psychological mood, a phenomenon of nature" but that "its indispensable and single requirement is construction." He may be undoctrinaire enough to dissent from this dictum in the belief that it is impossible thus to have pure construction suspended, as it were, in mid-air, and that there must always be something specific constructed. Nevertheless, he will have a marked sympathy for Stravinsky's further statement that "one could not better define the sensation produced by music than by saying it is identical with that evoked by contemplation of the interplay of architectural form." Again, it is doubtful that a few stray beams tastefully arranged in space without function could be called architectural forms, but the general meaning is clear.

As in every genuinely creative period, the germ of life is in the romantic section of the modern field. By having evolved a solid approach to form that is at one with the very basis of

romanticism, modernism has effectually prevented the fulsomeness and rant that have frequently characterized romantic revivals, and has turned the seething energy of the romantic impulse
into channels of restraint and intelligibility. The resultant approach has sometimes been called expressionism, and it would
be difficult to devise a more fitting label.

Modernism is in every respect an unsatisfactory term to apply
to so definite a manifestation, for it is in no sense descriptive.
Certainly expressionism is not the first manifestation of modernism in history, but is only the form it has taken in our day.
Indeed, modernism in the large sense is that tendency in any
period which first senses and makes tangible the new directions
of its time before they have become an accepted part of daily
life. It is that trend which runs counter to the inertias of the
day, whatever they may be, and is prophetic of the next level
of artistic awareness. It is thus manifestly impossible to tie down;
sometimes it is classical in tendency, sometimes romantic, and
sometimes, as at present, it cuts squarely across both fields. Obviously, no matter what form it takes, it is inevitably strange and
unpopular in the days of its ascent.

The ability to make independent judgments based on immediate personal response is essential to the enjoyment of modern
art, for it relies on no teachings or academies, but deals with
absolute values in a thoroughly direct and even pragmatical way.

If such a digression as this does not dissolve all the mysteries
of Taglioni's romantic-classicism or Isadora's modern-romanti-
cism or Jooss's classic-modernism, at least it prepares the ground
for their discussion when in due course the occasion arrives.

Part Two

THE DANCE IN ACTION

Chapter Five

WHY WE DANCE AND HOW

꧁꧂

SUCH styles and aesthetic approaches as we have been discussing exert their influences upon the dance in a marked degree, but they do not in themselves constitute any natural divisions into which it falls. Its several branches are determined upon premises perhaps more specifically functional, certainly more inherent in its particular nature.

Before we examine these branches in detail, it is necessary to see what their basis of division is, and in general to clear the ground of certain old misconceptions about why we dance, which crop up like weeds in our inherited approach to the subject. Unless we watch ourselves closely we are likely to slip into the habit of associating the dance exclusively with joy, and as a result of that initial misstep we may find ourselves demanding next that it be graceful and pretty, and from there it is only a matter of inches before we shall have slid back into complete Victorianism and missed the point altogether.

This joy analogy is very close to the popular conception that the artist, when he finds himself in the presence of something of breathless beauty, hastens to record it so that the world may share its loveliness, a conception that is more fanciful than real. In the presence of breathless beauty, the artist, perhaps more than the average man, simply indulges himself, and there is an end of it. What sets him on to creative work is the vision of potential beauty in places where it has not been achieved, the need for fulfillments and realizations.

All art, with the dance in the forefront, is a matter of compensation. It deals not with what we already have, but with what we lack. It is not concerned with recording things as they are, but with remolding them "nearer to the heart's desire." But if this seems to give the impression of a farsighted, philanthropic unselfishness, let it be added straightway that such is not the case in any sense. The contact with art gives pleasure, it is true, and in the long run succeeds in raising the level of the world's behavior, but these are by-products which play no part in the fundamental motivations of the artist. He is concerned with personal, amoral, functional results exclusively. He is driven to create art; it is not a matter of choice with him, but as much a response to inner necessity as eating, and has in it no more regard for what the effect will be upon the world at large.

Because he is one of the most valuable of citizens through his ability to see more deeply than the average man into the potentialities of living and to point out the way accordingly for a general enrichment of life, he is not necessarily therefore the most noble and self-sacrificing, even though he is frequently forced to forego many of the amenities of gentle living because of the low financial rating that the world sets upon his work, from time to time. He is simply fulfilling the urgencies of those particular balances and unbalances of his personality that are called his talent and over which he has scarcely more control than over the color of his eyes. As some people are shorter or taller than others, more even-tempered, stingier, he is equipped with a greater margin between his vision of what is emotionally attainable and his ability to attain it. He is impelled, in other words, to create more and greater compensations for himself in order to maintain his equilibrium.

As we have already seen, art has necessarily the element of communication in it, that is, the artist addresses himself to others and demands and expects response from them. Though he is giving something forth, he is not doing so without expectation of reward. This may assume any one of a variety of forms, not all of which by any means are lacking in nobility and honor, for all the emphasis that has just been placed upon the absence of altruism in their motivation. Perhaps, to be sure, he desires nothing but praise and admiration, that is, an acknowledgment by others of the superiority he believes himself possessed of; perhaps his desire is a shade more profound and manifests itself as a seeking for substantiation of his vision, for a corroboration that amounts almost to collaboration with his audience; perhaps it assumes the still more dynamic form of an effort to convert his audience to his outlook, not for the sake of proving himself especially gifted in having such an outlook, nor just to obtain confirmation of its rightness for his own assurance, but to enlist support for it in order to leaven mass thinking and ultimately change the course of events. All these things, as can readily be seen, are of grave importance to the artist himself, irrespective of what their importance may be to any one else.

But not all branches of the dance are art, by any means, any more than all men are artists, though there is a certain kinship with art in all dance as in all men. A man, to employ a crude parallel, is rather like the boiler of a steam engine, which, if it does not find an outlet for the steam that is generated in it, will burst and destroy itself. That this force is employable to push a piston back and forth and hence to operate all kinds of useful mechanical devices is certainly no part of the boiler's concern. Men have similar safety devices; one of them is play, which is relatively equivalent to merely letting the steam escape, and the other is art, in which the escaping steam is turned willy-nilly into productive channels. Like most analogies, this one holds good only to a point, but it will serve.

As has already been stated more than once, men have inherent potentialities which must be used if they are not to atrophy. When the immediate circumstances of life offer no opportunity for their use, a set of especially created circumstances must be set up which will offer such an opportunity. In a general way of speaking, compensation for those denials and suppressions which occur in the life of the outer man—the thinking and acting man—take the form of play, while compensations for suppressions which occur in the life of the inner man—the man of feeling—take the form of art. Such distinctions cannot be made with any finality, for life experience does not divide itself into clearly differentiated departments like this, but combines elements of emotion and of action in every experience.

In the same degree, it is impossible to make hard and fast divisions in the types of dance, but it is possible to allow the natural characteristics of the several motivations for dancing to form their own classifications of sorts, however indeterminate the boundaries between them. Indeed, much of the confusion that prevails in looking at the dance grows out of the neglect of just such classifications, and we frequently find one type of dance condemned because it does not fulfill the functions of some other type. The oneness of all dance lies in the fact that in its every manifestation it consists of movement arranged in form to provide compensation for suppressions and unfulfillments in life experience. Within this unity it falls into three major divisions: recreational, spectacular and expressional.

Ritual and Play

THE recreational dance touches the subject at its most elementary level, before it has in it any of the qualities of art as such. It is practiced wholly for the benefit of the dancer himself and gives no consideration whatsoever to possible spectators. The forms in which we know it chiefly are the folk dance and the ballroom dance, but these do not in any sense comprise its full range. It extends from the simplest manifestations of spontaneous high feeling, such as the proverbial jumping for joy, to the most elaborate rituals of primitive peoples for religious or magical purposes.

In this latter category it becomes clear that we are dealing with something a little more profound than what we are accustomed to call play, but in its elements it is substantially the same. It is re-creation, the restoration of the individual to normal and harmonious functioning, and the extent of its formalism and solemnity varies with the degree of the individual's experience of the abnormal and inharmonious. These re-creational, restorative qualities remain in the dance throughout its higher classifications even when it moves into the realm of art, nothing being taken away by the translation to more complex spheres, but other things being added to this irreducible base.

If kicking the heels in the air for sheer high spirits does not in itself constitute dancing except in an embryo sense, any more than the random play of children does, it makes a considerable contribution ultimately. Such behavior as this, indeed, is the germ of the whole matter; when we bristle with rage, or start with fright, or resort to gesticulation when at a loss for an adequately expressive word, we are practicing the beginnings of dance. As a rule, however, the concept of dance is a somewhat more organized and sustained emission of movement.

It is best exemplified on the recreational level in primitive cultures, where there is no art in the present-day meaning of the word, its elements not having been isolated and developed into a separate compensatory division of culture, but remaining inseparable from the social and religious aspects of living. Here all dances are seen to fall into three loose groups. The first consists of dances of simple play, conviviality and eroticism; the second of what might be termed rituals of tension, and the third of rituals of release. The first group is so closely paralleled in our own so-called social dancing as to need no further explanation.

The second group is religious or magic in character. Basically these dances are manifestations of communal fears and uncertainties, for there is as yet in society no scientific approach, and birth, coming of age, sickness, death, the growing of crops, rain, fertility, and the powers that control them all are mysteries. Many of them are personified, and their favor sought as if they were human beings with unpredictable moods; many of them are considered as the bounty of unseen deities who must be cajoled or of ancestral spirits whose wisdom must be faithfully obeyed. Accordingly there are ritual dances for the bringing of rain, for insuring the success of the hunt or the battle, for healing the sick, for keeping the dead safely interred so that they will not return from the grave to do injury to the living, for separating the youths from the mother-period of their childhood and initiating them into the father-period of their adulthood, and for protection against every contingency that might possibly affect the well-being of the tribe. Obviously these are not pleasure dances. Sometimes they are of so violent and hysterical a nature that they induce bleeding at the nose, swooning, or trancelike forms of autointoxication and ecstasy. They are done, nevertheless, for the exclusive satisfaction of the dancers, and if they are far from being playful they are compensatory, restorative, re-creational.

The rituals of release are the natural complement of these rituals of tension. They are dances of relief from fear, celebrating victory over an enemy, peace with a hostile neighbor, a successful harvesting of crops, rain after a long drought, a good kill. They seldom manage within their ritual range to work off the full excitement of the situation, but lead eventually into the wildest of play and orgy. Thus the circle is completed.

There is little of all this that has come down to us in the direct line of art. The essential unity of living in primitive society is followed in the evolution of culture by a long period of analysis and departmentalization, and the elements that are found in such rituals as have just been considered are developed separately as religion, philosophy, science, politics, economics and art. In our own day we are beginning to see the signs of what may prove to be the next sequential step, namely, the synthesis of these several elements by processes of conscious integration, and it is possible that the unity thus achieved by conviction will be of a more substantial character than the instinctive unity of primitive life.

With the growth of intellect and rationalism and their inhibitory effects upon free motor response there has come a slackening of the habit of venting our emotional overcharges through direct action; the few survivals of older practices in our Western civilization are to be found chiefly in backward communities where such sects as the Holy Rollers and religious revival meetings in general still induce exhibitions of hysterical leaping and shouting, though these have nothing of the dignity of ritual. Feeble traces of ancient ritual are to be found in some of the folk dances that are to be seen nowadays, chiefly the fertility ritual of death and rebirth, but they have long since lost their conviction and have lived only as the empty shell of themselves in certain devices of form which they have evolved and which have been perpetuated for their own sakes, quite unmindful of the emotional stuff they were designed to contain.

That portion of our emotional overcharge which we have not learned to shunt into intellectual paths, we vent either directly in play as primitive men do, or else through the vicarious channels of art. Our artist-dancers serve to epitomize the tribe, presenting our rituals of tension and the release they demand, and in proportion as we are able to identify ourselves with their presentations of experience, we are able to find compensation for our personal overcharges and unfulfillments. Thus the roots of expressional dance are found in this lower stratum of recreational dance. The other arts, to be sure, also find their roots here, but through various processes of crossbreeding with intellect and objective materials, they develop forms ever farther removed from their simple origin.

The recreational dance, then, is entirely for participation and not at all for spectator interest; it is not art but play. This applies even to those elements which it has contributed to art, for they are the play elements, the re-creational elements, which go back for their effectiveness to personal experience. It is futile to look for spectator pleasure in folk or ballroom dance, for that is not the function or the intention of either.

Influence of the Spectator

THE presence of the spectator in the dancer's consideration leads at once to the threshold of art, though not necessarily across it. The performance may entail nothing more than an exhibition of personal skills, or it may become the medium for the loftiest and most profound communication. The threshold of art, however, is a tenuous barrier indeed to locate, especially in the dimly lit territory where the dance begins to have spectator interest. Once it has got well within this territory, however, it divides into two sections, one which is purely spectacular, that is, which concerns itself not with what it says to the spectator, but with what it looks like; and one which is expressional, that is, which is concerned not with what it looks like, but with what it says to the spectator.

The spectacular dance is inevitably classic in the sense that it does not create its materials directly from experience, but adapts materials already so created with an eye to either their formal qualities, their surfaces, their sensational appeal, or their aesthetic values. Its range is obviously a wide one from the many grades of refinement of the tap dance, the acrobatic adagio, the erotic "fan" or "bubble" dance, through simple storytelling, to the subtle and abstract beauty of the so-called classic ballet at its height. Generally speaking it takes what is functionally only a means to an end and makes it an end in itself.

It is not difficult to trace to the recreational dance at least three major sources of the materials of the spectacular dance. In the first place, there are the skills which are manifest in simple play—leaping, skipping, running, kicking, and similar natural activities which the earliest of human experience has already in its background. These, developed by use and growth, elaborated both rhythmically and dynamically by heightened exploratory interest, made the subject of contests, easily assume acrobatic dimensions and the brilliance to attract spectators. They may even be actuated by the most intense emotional excitement and become an extension of the body beyond itself into a kind of defiance of human limitations. Irving K. Pond, in his illuminating comparison of dance and architecture in *The Meaning of Architecture,* declares tumbling as it is practiced at its best by, say, the Arabs, to be "an exalted form of the emotional dance." Here certainly is a fruitful source of non-representational movement that is capable of awakening a keen sympathetic response in the onlooker. It is eventually the source of the vocabulary of the academic ballet.

Another rich lode is to be found in quite the opposite direction, namely, in man's innate faculty for imitation, based on that important branch of our perceptive equipment, "inner mimicry." These natural mimetic tendencies are given emphasis by primitive man in many of his rituals. Because of his belief in magic of a certain species, it is necessary for him, for one thing, to be able to impersonate with great accuracy the animals he is preparing to kill, thus identifying himself so completely with them that he is able to control their behavior. This is not so strange a belief as it may seem at first sight. When a man has experienced the effect of the dancing of others upon himself, and has felt himself compelled by the persuasiveness of forceful, rhythmic example to fall in and imitate their actions; when furthermore he has found that he can exercise the same power upon others by his dancing and force them to fall into his patterns, it is not unnatural for him to believe that the animals in the forest will be unable to resist these influences. He performs, therefore, with as great accuracy as possible, the behavior he wishes them to imitate. The matter of intervening distance is not important to him, for when he is drawn into the dance of others there is no physical contact between him and the dancers. The same conditions, then, prevail between him and his animal quarry. It is not human force but a supernatural, magic power that controls the situation.

If a dancer exhibits particular gifts for reproducing the exact characteristics of an animal, he is more than likely sooner or later to be admired for his talent quite apart from the purpose for which he has exercised it in the beginning. Exact representation becomes thus the source of entertainment to the onlooker, through the pleasure of recognition, and a large body of art is born whose only function is just this. It is a craft skill, perhaps, rather than an art, but it never fails to elicit applause from the admiring spectator. On its basis, also, a form of simple storytelling with suitable characterization becomes possible, and the foundations are laid for what is called realistic drama. From this same source of mimesis more important results are developed in the expressional arts, as we shall see in a moment.

The third spectacular development from elements of the recreational dance concerns itself with form. Actually the beginnings of form, or more specifically of pattern, enter into the dance as soon as it assumes any social aspects, that is, as soon as more than one person is concerned in the dancing. The pleasures to be derived from dancing together have their basis in the fact that each participant enjoys the sensation of sharing in a joint movement of greater power than any he could make alone. On this simple principle rests the chief power of the dance as an instrument for securing group solidarity, for it reveals the strength and superiority of the group as no amount of mere reasoning could do. To achieve this end, however, there must be a substantial measure of uniformity of action; that is, the dance of several individuals cannot consist of random improvisations by them all. If there are to be improvisations, as in many instances there are, they must be incidents against a constant background, or the mass sense will be destroyed and the effect of the collaboration lost. Thus elementary formal practices, modes of joint procedure, enter into the picture very early. Innovations are accumulated as time passes, semihistorical legends force their specific re-enactment into certain rituals, and before long there have grown up numerous formal routines of action.

When the individual rituals gradually lose their efficacy as faith in them lapses, these routines of action do not necessarily lapse with it but frequently survive, sometimes with new significances poured into them from outside sources but just as often not. They have simply become too habitual to be abandoned. From this passing of original meanings out of developed routines have grown many beginnings of spectacular art forms. A striking illustration is seen in the ancient ritual of defensive abuse which is found in countless forms in primitive cultures. The function of the ritual is to deceive those evil forces which might attack and destroy some cherished object or person, into believing that such object or person is essentially valueless and not worth attacking. In the exercise of this ritual the thing to be protected is made the butt of all kinds of ridicule, vilification and invective, and in the process much imaginative and witty invention is allowed to find itself. Long after the basic idea of defensive abuse has ceased to be believed in for its own sake, we find the routine of its practice kept alive and elaborated for the sake of its intrinsic qualities in the genius of Greek comedy. Another illustration is seen in the wearing of masks. Originally a ceremonial method of identification with beings of a sacred or powerful nature, it easily becomes a practice of art on the basis of the impersonality and symbolic abstractness of its representational power.

The dance abounds in such experiences, especially in the Renaissance when its spectacular development reaches its apex. Lorenzo de' Medici transforms the whole habit of masking into an art form; the morisco, once of ceremonial origin, becomes the central dance in early Renaissance ballets, the ritual of mumming loses its cosmic powers and contributes the forms that once contained them to the development of a spectacular dance art, and similar transmutations are seen on every hand.

In this process, whether applied to specific movements, mimetics or forms, the principles of classicism are at work; subjective impulses are scrupulously ejected so that what they have created may remain as objective material, subject to adaptation and manipulation for entirely aesthetic ends.

Communication

THE expressional dance proceeds on exactly the opposite course. It attempts to prevent the loss of the subjective impulses of the re-creational dance, and to make them a basis for direct communication with the spectator. For this end there must be certain adaptations in the objective direction, as a matter of course. In the first place, the use of these impulses must be taken out of the field of transient and uncontrollable inspiration, out of the virtual possession and hysteria which often dominate them in primitive society, and brought within the bounds of voluntary manipulation. In the second place, they must be rendered subject to the response capacity of the spectator instead of being solely for the emission of the dancer's inner overcharges. What the expressional dance retains at all costs, however, is its definite relationships to life experience. This is the source of contact with the spectator, for it seeks not merely to win his admiration for skills and his pleasure in designs, but to lead him into vicarious participation in the dancer's movement and its emotional associations.

But if the process stopped here, it would manifestly accomplish nothing except the production of a pointless stirred-up state, the revival of experiences already familiar, and no pleasure beyond that of recognition. It is the dancer's purpose, however, to use this revival of the familiar merely as a starting point, a point of meeting between artist and spectator, from there to lead the experience into newly imagined fields, into developments which life has not yet provided but which seem to the artist to satisfy his necessities and to assuage his need for deeper satisfactions and fuller utilization of his inherent capacities than practical conditions make possible at the moment. He is concerned with what the regular order of living never satisfies— the desire to know the meaning of life and his relationship to it. In this concern he is not only carrying on the motivations of re-creational rituals, but is marching in the same path with the contemporary scientist and philosopher, and emotionally clearing the way for them.

The expressional dancer's materials are created, like those of the recreational dancer, out of direct experience, but the element of objectiveness that inheres in the conscious processes of the artist gives them a higher concentration and a focus to the ends of clear communication. The mimetic faculty is employed not to reproduce actuality as an end in itself, but only to provide a means of meeting the spectator where he is in the world of actuality. Once this is done, representationalism is abandoned for those abstractions and distortions that will lead away from the actual into the conceptual. Obviously abstractions and distortions depend upon the soundness of the perception of actuality that underlies them, for one cannot abstract or distort without a norm to begin with.

Crystallizations of vocabulary or of forms work against the efficacy of the expressional dance and tend to transform it into merely spectacular material denying its nature and function. As a matter of fact, however, in the contemporary field of the spectacular dance are to be found countless instances where movements that have evolved out of the original creative processes of expressional dancers have been taken over purely as objective vocabulary by dancers who see in them only decorative or virtuoso values. In the contemporary ballet as well as in revues and night clubs, it is a common occurrence to run unexpectedly into movements that have been taken over bodily from Wigman, Laban, Graham, Humphrey, and put to alien, though frequently effective, use for their surface qualities alone. The effect of this upon the fuller general understanding of the creative dance from which such borrowings are made, is not a happy one, for it tends to cast over it the shadow of that very standardization that it has arisen to deny. Nevertheless, just as cubism and surrealism have been taken over by the window trimmers and the scales of Debussy and Schoenberg have been adopted by the dance bands, the surface aspects of the expressional dance as it has been developed since Isadora Duncan have been converted into a species of spectacular dance adapted to revue purposes, and sometimes called with becoming frankness, "commercial modern." The contemporary field is seen to contain several such crossbreedings, but they are generally easy to recognize and make for only minor bewilderments.

Chapter Six

RECREATIONAL DANCE

꙲꙲꙲꙲꙲

BEYOND the simple offices of maintaining the life routine, there is no activity that identifies us so closely with what we might call the basic man—that universal and timeless creature who is eternally "primitive" under the skin—as dancing merely for the fun of it. It is play in perhaps the least rationalized form practicable for social use, and in it, if we see it in its essential nature, we are able to find release for many of our repressions and return to the arbitrary disciplines of the social scheme refreshed and healthy of mind.

It is not the simplest thing in the world, however, to see it in its essential nature, for these arbitrary disciplines and this social scheme are not penalties laid upon us from without, which we would instinctively resist, but are actually the result of our own progress along certain lines, and we are loath to set them aside even for brief moments. As a result, recreational dancing, one of the most truly useful of human activities, is condemned by the moralist in us, despised by the intellectual, and censored from both sides until it frequently loses most of its function.

What we call modern civilization has concentrated on the development of the rational man at the expense of the man of feeling, and when this poor, submerged creature attempts to raise his head, there are cries of "Reaction!" and "Decadence!" to greet him. It is the great hope of our time that we shall before long be able to convince the rational man that his attempted exclusion of the man of feeling from the business of living is itself the height of irrationality, and that we shall begin to see man whole.

There is no better place to start this transformation than in the field of the recreational dance, whether in the ballroom, on the folk-dance green, or in artists' studios where laymen's dance groups meet under one pretext or another. Even the most rational of men, once lured into experiencing the pleasures of spontaneous movement in the relatively uncensored forms of true recreational dancing, will find that he has entered into a territory from which it is difficult to retreat. If he sees things in the art dance that appear incomprehensible, it is easy to blame the situation on the natural eccentricity of artists and let it go at that; but if he finds himself actually doing such things spontaneously, there is nothing at all incomprehensible about them, and even the activity of the artist becomes clear. There can be no more propitious approach to the dance in all its forms, then, than through the channels of recreation.

As has already been pointed out, recreational dance on our level of civilization is of more limited scope than that in simpler societies, for magic, religious and social rituals have largely disappeared into various scientific, intellectual and artistic departments of our more disparate life. What remains to us of recreational dancing is comprised in the so-called ballroom dance, which is erotic; the revived dancing of folk dances, which is convivial and gregarious; and the many but still unorganized layman's approaches to the dance, which are essentially creative, for all that they are not deeply communicative, and function in the semiartistic realm of self-expression.

This field of play is so closely related to the field of art that it is not surprising to find many of the same conditions prevailing. As in art, there is here that perpetual swing from extremes of feeling to extremes of restraint, and it is quite possible to find exactly the same forces of expressionism and aestheticism, of romanticism and classicism. The same general cycle of development also prevails—a formless and virtually chaotic emotional release, opposed by a steadily increasing pressure of decorum and formality, which brings about ultimately the suppression of impulse and the substitution of arbitrary routine; then a revolution abolishing all restraint, and the process starts anew.

It is perhaps easier to see these forces at work in our own day if we first observe their operations against something of the perspective of the past. Though in the present century polite society has been successively shocked by the appearance of the Grizzly Bear and the Bunny Hug, the shimmy and the Charleston, the Lindy Hop and the Suzy-Q, it is not, as some of the gloomier Jeremiahs would have us believe, because these are decadent days, but quite the reverse. As far back as we have any definite data on the subject, the uninhibited recreational practices of the unpolished and unpresentable classes of society have found their way from time to time into the ballrooms of the polished and presentable and have saved them from dry rot and utter decay. With luck, there will continue to be a similar infusion of shocks in the well-ordered ballrooms of posterity, for the vital elements of the social dance inevitably come from below. Today the most alert and progressive of our ballroom teachers make a practice of visiting the inelegant halls where sailors from foreign ports go to enjoy themselves, or where Negroes from the Deep South or the West Indies give free rein to their motor impulses, for here are to be seen the creative forces of play in full vigor. If the dances thus discovered need to be toned down and dressed up for polite consumption, at least there is less bowdlerizing necessary nowadays than formerly, and in that we cannot fail to see progress. In such slumming expeditions, these teachers are not only proving their sensitiveness to the sources of their art, but are also carrying on a tradition that is as old as the profession of dancing master itself. Their fifteenth century prototypes went in exactly the same way to the dances of the much despised peasant for their basic materials, recognizing instinctively, however little they admitted it, that no matter how much inventive genius a deviser of social dances may possess, there must be a groundwork of natural motor impulse to build upon, and this cannot be invented.

The Renaissance and After

BALLROOM dancing as we know it had its beginnings in the Italian Renaissance, where we might logically expect to find them. Before this, dancing for pleasure had been fairly spontaneous, and whatever conventions it acquired grew up through practice rather than through arbitrary rule. The courtly circles of Italy, however, turned their backs completely on this simple approach and developed official dancing masters to invent and teach socially acceptable forms. Five hundred years later we find ourselves still trying to keep alive this tradition, though like so many other traditions of the Renaissance it runs directly counter to the needs and tendencies of these times.

In the fifteenth century it was a progressive step, attuned to the imagination of the period and its ideals. With the breaking of the domination of the medieval church, which had submerged the individual entirely in its gloomy system, the man of the Renaissance found himself suddenly a personality, a separate being. Now that he had achieved this emancipation, what was he to do with it? What was he to make of himself, now that he was mentally his own master?

Personal achievement was clearly his necessity, for inherited social position and nobility were impossible for him, both practically and philosophically. As far back as Dante, nobility was seen to be not a matter of caste but of individual attainment; but even if this theory had not been thus a matter of inner conviction, it would eventually have had to be established to conform to actualities. The ruling princes of the Italian Renaissance, indeed, could lay no claims whatever to noble birth, and whether or not this circumstance was a leading influence in developing the humanists' philosophical scorn for hereditary caste, at least these self-made princes found it an eminently convenient theory. The pursuit of a self-achieved nobility accordingly became a dominating interest.

The ideal of individual freedom was a fine one, to be sure, as far as it went, but it is important to remember that the manner and measure in which it was attained had nothing at all of the democratic aspect, which our own form of idealism might lead us to assume for it, and not a great deal even of the basis of that inherent personal merit, those moral and intellectual accomplishments, which Dante had advocated. Position was purchased or stolen. Condottieri took high rank by force. The great house of Sforza was founded by a condottiere who remained just that to the end of his days; the great house of Medici was founded by a money lender, and long maintained itself by the not too scrupulous practice of this business. Titles and high positions were generally bought and paid for, in a society which was parvenu in a larger sense of the word than we can easily grasp.

Naturally, it despised the crude impulses of the old order from which it was trying to free itself, and had the most profound contempt for the common people who were still content to indulge them. But with the foundations of medievalism destroyed, with nothing to inherit either physically or philosophically from the immediate past which might aid in the acquiring of a noble way of life suitable to the newly envisioned free individual, where was there a guiding principle to be sought? Since it was the church that had been responsible for the mental servitude against which the present rebellion was directed, it was only logical to turn for guidance to the conditions that existed before the church arose. In the life of ancient Rome, now glossed over with the passage of time, there was seen a pattern for the culture which the new society so sorely needed. It is sometimes said that the Renaissance grew out of the classic revival, but the reverse is nearer to the truth.

However that may be, when Constantinople fell to the Ottoman Turks in the middle of the fifteenth century, large numbers of scholars who had maintained something of the classical culture there, sought refuge in the West, and there was an enormous upsurge of Roman and Greek ideals. It found its way even into the dances of the ballroom; Fabritio Caroso in the sixteenth century, for example, tells of inventing dances to fit the meters of Ovid.

But the dancing master and his work of refining and ennobling the social dance had come into being before this, which was perhaps fortunate for him. If he had not thus got himself and his art well established at an early period, they both might have experienced a vastly different fate when the antique revival rose to its full influence, for did not Cicero, that master of masters among the ancients, declare that nobody danced unless he was drunk or crazy? Or were the motor instincts of the Renaissance gentlemen perhaps stronger than their intellectual ideals, after all? It must have required some strong impulsion to bring about the ignoring of a precept by the great academic master. Nevertheless, the education of the gentleman, designed to make him amenable to the ways of noble society, included swimming, running, leaping, and wrestling, the knightly skills of riding, tilting, fighting of various kinds, the gentler arts of music, poetry and languages, and a special emphasis upon dancing above all.

The dancing master, when he first appears on the scene in the fifteenth century, is definitely preclassic, and for all that we can do little more than guess what his immediate origin may have been, he seems to be a reasonable outgrowth of the medieval dance in its later developments. These developments had been rich and various through the momentous centuries of the Middle Ages. The consecrated rituals of primitive society had been transformed largely into superstition and witchcraft, thanks both to the influence and the opposition of the church, and occasionally had boiled over into morbid mass manias as in the hideous outbreaks of dancing madness induced by the horrors of the fourteenth century with its plagues and disasters. In another manifestation it had become merely an exuberant pastime, leading more often than not to sexual indulgence, quite forgetful of the magic significance of fertility rituals that once underlay it. In still other developments, it had become a ceremonial social form, involving the masking and mumming and dicing of ancient rituals but now devoid of any specific significance except the honoring of a chosen individual.

The peasant, rising through these centuries from feudal serfdom to a large measure of independence, frequently assembled with his fellows and danced for fun, kissing and courting, or competing with his rivals in the height of his leaps or the skill of his capers and galleys, little knowing that in centuries to come these were to be dignified as cabrioles and entrechats in the

spectacular ballet. On festival occasions he joined in dances that
had been done for ages with magic purpose, but he knew only
that they were said to bring luck. The higher he leaped, the
taller the grain would grow. Sometimes in these festivities a
king was chosen and a queen to go with him, sometimes he
donned his wife's clothes for the occasion, sometimes he and
his friends staged a mimic sword fight—in all these instances
perpetuating ancient fertility rites of whose meanings he was
probably quite innocent. Frequently the company divided into
couples and executed dances of wooing, with a semblance of
elusiveness on the part of the girls, but eventual yielding. Sometimes he blackened his face with soot, little aware that since
this was once, like all other masking, a process of identification,
he was actually identifying himself with fire and performing a
ritual of purification. Perhaps he wore bells at his knees to
frighten away evil spirits. With his companions he participated
in processionals around trees or maypoles, or in serpentine paths;
he joined in circles with hands held, in double-line dances in
which he faced a partner-opponent or a potential sweetheart; he
spun his girl to the point of giddiness, lifting her high in the air
time after time until they both fell on the ground from ex-
haustion.

He did not have to mind his manners, and for that his social
betters despised him; but his compensations, in all conscience,
were fuller than theirs, as they were forced tacitly to admit when
they went to him for the basis of their own dances.

With the establishment of towns which began late in the
eleventh century, new forces arose to color the dances. Agricul-
tural rituals lost meaning, to be sure, but they had given birth
to many dance forms which were transplantable. Some of the
burghers amassed great wealth and established virtual courts of
their own, bringing at times a fine elaboration and generally

heightened social dignity to the dance. The roots of the great "third estate" were planted and a potent social class was born, with a way of life of its own.

Chivalry, also, brought vital changes to the dance. Particularly after it had passed from its earlier stages of military and religious orders and had degenerated into a sentimental code dominated by *courtoisie,* its mark was seen upon the practices of high society in the ballroom. Women were now extravagantly honored (at least in theory), and a new type of courtship dance came into being in which the frankly erotic pursuit of the peasant gave way to a coy and superficially respectful symbolism. More and more the essence of life experience was extracted from the dance, and its underlying meanings and purposes allowed to remain only well below the surface.

In the ghettos of medieval France and Germany there grew up the institution of the Tanzhaus, a building where the people assembled for ceremonial dancing on the Sabbath and feast days, and for weddings. In time the ceremonial character of the halls gave way in large measure and they became more frankly centers for recreation. Where at first there was strict segregation of the sexes, now mixed dancing grew apace, and persisted in spite of the best efforts of the rabbis to control it. Regulations were made to restrict such dancing only to close relatives, but devious methods were evolved to evade such restrictions. There has been little research on the subject, but it seems possible that the Tanzhaus may have made a greater contribution to later dance developments than it has been credited with. In the fifteenth century, when professional dancing masters make their first appearance in the courts of the Italian Renaissance, a number of them are Jews. This may, of course, be nothing more than coincidence, for Jews were active in the arts in the early years of the Renaissance, but if so, it is a striking one. Curt

Sachs notes, incidentally, that the only dancing master to whom any reference has been discovered in the Middle Ages was a rabbi. It would be interesting if we could find in the Tanzhaus another direct influence in the polishing and the orienting of the social dance of the Middle Ages toward its Renaissance goal. If perhaps in the rabbinical efforts to regulate and elevate the style of dancing some official position of supervisor had been created, we would have the quite logical beginnings of a profession such as we find later in Italy. This, however, is pure speculation.

From all these medieval sources we see preparations for the refinements and social controls of Renaissance dancing that are quite apart from any early influences of ancient Greece and Rome and tend, indeed, to protect the dance from the possible depredations of Ciceronian classicism.

Certainly if the life of the Renaissance was violent and indulgent and recognized no law but force, this was a pattern of behavior consistent with its overthrow of ecclesiastical domination. Its pattern of cultural practice, however, was anything but indulgent. Here it more than compensated for the complete license of its personal conduct by setting up a system of academic codes confining its creative activities in fetters which made the restrictions of church dogma seem liberal by contrast. As we have already seen, it was the substitution of one classicism of approach for another, avoiding at any cost the return to the impulses of basic man for guidance. These impulses were, indeed, anathema, in theory if not in practice.

Guglielmo Ebreo, one of the most celebrated of fifteenth century dancing masters, voiced the accepted ideals of the dance with vigor and clarity. In a paragraph which Otto Kinkeldey has translated in his invaluable little brochure, *A Jewish Dancing Master of the Renaissance,* Guglielmo writes: "The art of dancing is, for generous hearts that love it, and for gentle spirits that have a heaven-sent inclination for it rather than an accidental disposition, a most amicable (*amicissima*) matter, entirely different from and mortally inimical to the vicious and artless common people (*mecchaniche plebei*) who frequently, with corrupt spirits and depraved minds, turn it from a liberal art and virtuous science, into a vile adulterous affair, and who more often in their dishonest concupiscence under the guise of modesty, make the dance a procuress, through whom they are able to arrive stealthily at the satisfaction of their desires."

From the life of the times, it is difficult to deduce that either the satisfaction of such desires or even dishonest concupiscence under the guise of modesty was especially condemned in itself; rather we see the now fully developed tendency to separate dance from life impulses and make of it a liberal art and virtuous science requiring a heaven-sent inclination, an elaborate set of rules, and a whole profession of dancing masters to keep it from lapsing into its vicious and artless native state. Here, indeed, is a contempt for the natural man as profound as any the medieval church ever inculcated.

To be sure, certain dances persisted in something of their natural state; there were the saltarello and the piva and the quadernaria, lively peasant dances a trifle polished up for refined society, along with the more dignified bassa danza. But the favor of the dancing masters was reserved for their own highly developed form of the bassa danza and for the ballo. These were both composed dances frequently of the greatest elaboration, each separate composition with a title of its own. The bassa danza was fairly slow and made use, as its name would indicate, of steps in which the feet remained always close to the floor. By way of variety, a bit of the gay and more elevated saltarello was likely to be introduced in the course of the dance, but never to such an extent that the general air of the whole was affected. The ballo was quicker in tempo and made free use of saltarello, piva and quadernaria steps, in which the feet were lifted higher from the floor, even to the point of leaping.

Because of the complication of the figures in both types of dance, a good memory was considered one of the principal requisites for a good dancer. To make matters even more involved, bassa danza, piva, saltarello, and quadernaria could all be performed in each other's style, there being five ways of dancing both the bassa danza and the saltarello and four ways of dancing the piva and quadernaria. (This, to be sure, presents a fairly familiar pattern to our own day when the waltz step is frequently fitted deliberately to the fox-trot; nor would it have been altogether strange to the last generation which put the steps of the galop or two-step to the waltz and dubbed it appropriately the "ignoramus waltz.") In order to perfect one's sense of measure, Guglielmo advocated dancing deliberately out of time and defying the musician's best efforts to bring one back to beat, or having the musician play persistently offbeat in his effort to make the dancer violate the measure.

Basse danze were composed for one or two couples, or combinations of one lady and two gentlemen or one gentleman and two ladies; balli added further arrangements involving in some cases as many as ten dancers divided into two lines of five, men and women alternating in each line. Sometimes partners held hands, but very frequently they did not touch each other.

In such dances as these it is at once apparent that recreation in the simple sense of play is far from the dominating motive. Actually, objective invention, technical analysis and formalization, pride of craftsmanship, and personal vanity are leading rapidly toward the field of the spectacular dance. Cornazano, a colleague of Guglielmo, in his treatise on how to dance, specifically instructs his reader-pupil that (in the translation of Kinkel-dey again) he "should have such . . . grace of movement as will render him pleasing in the eyes of the bystanders."

In such a situation as this, when the recreational dance has ceased to fulfill its recreational functions and begun to prink itself up for the bystanders, we are justified in looking elsewhere for evidences of a kind of dance that will fulfill these functions. And we are quickly rewarded in this instance, for dances of a simpler and more elemental character are found not only to sur-vive among the corrupt and depraved common people, but also to be indulged in copiously by the generous natures and gentle spirits whom Guglielmo so ardently admired. Baldassare.Casti-glione, whose *Il Cortegiano,* written in the early years of the sixteenth century, was the "golden book" of Renaissance man-ners, makes it clear that certain dances were suitable for public practice and certain others were definitely not. Among these latter were two dances with marked spectacular possibilities which contributed greatly to the development of the ballet. They were the brando and the morisco, the former at this time still a peasant circle dance with the joining of hands in a chain, and the latter an ancestor of the English Morris Dance as we know it today. These, said Castiglione, might be done in the privacy of one's own room, but not publicly unless the dancer wore a disguise. Then, even if he were recognized, it would make no difference, apparently because he would have indicated his awareness that what he was doing was below his station.

Here we find the dominant cycle of social dancing in its rela-tions to spontaneity and formalism established in its complete-ness. To be sure, all through the Middle Ages there are records of dances disapproved in public and much enjoyed privately, but the profession of the dancing master and his codes of correct usage bring the cycle to a kind of perfection that it has not previously attained. When we have grasped the order of this cycle we have grasped the major process of development of the social dance, as true for our own time as for any other. The great currents of history cut across it continually, but if they alter its surfaces from time to time, they do not affect its general character.

The changing relationships between the social classes and the growing industrialization of the economic order produce ever new patterns which inevitably affect the recreational habits of all levels of society. The steady rise of the bourgeoisie from the establishment of its towns in the eleventh century to the climactic series of social and political revolutions in the eighteenth, the less spectacular but no less momentous climax of the "industrial revolution" in the nineteenth century, and that movement correlative to both of them as a kind of mental overtone, the "romantic revolution," which came to flower in the eighteen thirties, all found their reflection in the ballroom. With court life on the one hand and folk life on the other steadily declining, the rise to a position of dominance by the industrial city obviously demanded a different approach to dancing. Nevertheless, the same round of development continues to prevail by which the spontaneous dances of the lower classes pass through the formalizations of courtly society and eventually disappear as recreation altogether, either through sheer decay or by being professionalized.

The growth of interest in spectacle in the early Renaissance leads to the court ballet in France and finally to the professional theater. In the ballroom, the two major elements of eroticism and conviviality perpetuate themselves in constantly renewed forms of the couple dance and of the group dance respectively. The innate desire for liveliness in the recreational dance manifests itself increasingly and is restrained only by being sublimated into ever greater intricacy and elaboration.

The galliard, a gay and strenuous after-dance of the type which customarily followed the grave dances by way of variety, survives its short-lived companion piece, the stately pavane, and sweeps everything before it. The brando, despised by the dancing masters and the courtiers in Italy and proscribed by Castiglione, becomes one of the most popular and varied of dances in the French court under the name of branle. The courante is meta-morphosed from a rollicking peasant courtship dance to an intricate form very much admired by Louis XIV.

Greater metamorphoses than these, however, are to be noted. The zarabanda from Guatemala is transported to Spain where it is declared to be the most immoral and reprehensible of all dances. By the time it reaches the French court in the seven-teenth century it has become a solemn and dignified affair with little trace of its origin, and finally passes out of the field alto-gether into the theater and the musical suite. In its native land, where it was not subjected to these polishing processes, it is still performed today after a fashion, having become less a dance than a drunken carouse. It is interesting to note, however, that without the forcing of courtly academism it still survives, and even in its decadence, which is a natural one, it retains the element of emotional release which first gave it birth. The chacona, also from Central America and similarly pronounced obscene, skims through the ballroom briefly on its way to the formal ballet, where it becomes an elaborate and stately pro-cedure climaxing the evening's dances with the leading stars as its chief performers.

From the whirling dances of the countryside comes the volta, bringing to the upper circles at the end of the sixteenth century a dance in which for the first time in polite society the partners' position, to the horror of the conservative, is face to face and with their arms about each other.

The minuet, adapted from the peasants, begins its life at court as a lively couple dance, slows down to become the most difficult and rococo dance of its day in the late seventeenth century, and appears again in the nineteenth as a sickly travesty of itself, frequently performed as a group dance in square formation like the quadrille. To make up for the intricacies and the super-elegances of the minuet, the group dances of the seventeenth century turn to England and its lusty and varied country dance.

A century later when the waltz comes out of Germany in something of the same style as the earlier volta, it occasions even greater horror than its predecessor. It is, nevertheless, an undeniable expression of the romantic revolution, and prevails in spite of the fact that it is considered shameful and danger-ous in many circles until well into the nineteenth century. The polka begins as a couple dance with many figures, but soon discards its elaboration and sweeps the ballrooms of the world with its energetic peasant succession of slide, change, leap, hop.

In the delightful textbook of Allen Dodworth, that arbiter of ballroom dancing in New York in the late nineteenth century, we find the following dances described as being currently done in 1885: the galop, polka, waltz, quadrille, lancers, minuet, Vir-ginia reel and cotillion or German—most of them with many individual variations. By the turn of the century, there is a de-cided diminution of interest in the "square" dances that spells their eclipse, and by 1910 there is virtually nothing besides the waltz in a somewhat routine and dispirited shape, its crude but lively offshoot, the Boston, and the two-step, which is merely the old galop under a new name. The cotillion is still danced, but this is not really a dance in itself, but a method of introduc-ing waltzes and two-steps by ingenious devices involving favors and various kinds of game playing. The ballroom, indeed, is moribund.

Ragtime

AT this juncture the "ragtime revolution" burst upon the scene, and things were destined never to be the same again. This momentous overturning was but one aspect of a great movement, which is essentially a rebirth of basic man. It was the popular expression, the manifestation on a mass level, of that general cultural development that we call, with remarkably little descriptive imagination, modernism; a renascence in the full sense of the word, whose scope and vitality have still not been recognized as they deserve to be.

Like all insurgencies from below, it required a generation or more to work its way up through the levels of society to the top, there to be subjected to oppositions on the one hand and glib acceptance on the other, both presenting threats to its progress. For years it had been germinating in those shadowed territories of the social world where "nice" people did not travel, waiting to give unwitting confirmation to the fact that all the signs and portents, appearing in more respected sectors of culture, were indeed prophetic of human progress and not merely sporadic exhibitions of dilettantism. Indeed, the vulgar monopoly of the ballroom by Turkey Trot and Grizzly Bear, Bunny Hug and Kitchen Sink, and countless other defiances of formalism, was the only uncontradictable proof that the twentieth century renaissance had its roots in elemental common experience and therefore was capable of enduring.

Long before the tempest broke, even back as far as the eighties and nineties, there had been magnificent iconoclasms in the arts and sciences, but only in retrospect has it become possible to see that in their diverse departments they were heralds of the same repudiation of artificial codes and the same return to function.

In the dance there was Isadora Duncan, casting aside all precedent but that of man in his environment; in painting, Cézanne, with his persistent striving for realization of the eternal in nature; in music, Debussy, putting above all technical considerations the inner life and emotions of a musical work; in the theater, Stanislavsky, seeking to unite the actor's art to inner experience instead of to systems of gesture; in stage design, Craig and Appia, both turning away from surfaces to structure and function; in architecture, that prime functionalist, Louis Sullivan and his more brilliant disciple, Frank Lloyd Wright, delivering the building arts from the icy grip of eclecticism; in psychology, William James, bringing the inner man and the outer into a closer unity than theory had ever before acknowledged, and Pavlov, uniting psychological and physiological processes with his principles of the conditioned reflex; in aesthetics, Lipps and Groos and Vernon Lee, discovering in their several ways the validity of motor response and inner mimicry; in folklore, the beginning, first in Sweden and then in England, of serious attention to the study and preservation of man's simplest record of his emotional life, the dance.

If the ragtime revolution in the ballroom differed in surface from these imposing manifestations, it did not differ in kind; it was equally a return to simple function. Because it was on a less well-mannered plane, it did not wait for time to prove its value, but barged ahead without apologies. No more dull two-stepping, no more monotonous waltzing with all its original ecstasy long since dried up and blown away, no more silly cotillion devices; the dance was restored to something of its native honesty of purpose, kicking up its heels with exuberance, and embracing its partner with a frank admission of its erotic interest. No longer was movement restricted to the feet and legs, but the torso was also brought into action. True to Delsarte's doctrine of fifty years earlier and to Isadora's more recent findings, the ballroom dance demonstrated that the body could not be freely expressive with this vital central section rigid and inactive. Learning to "rag" was not easy for a generation that had been taught to dance with its feet alone, nor was watching its mobile shoulders easy for the squeamish, who fairly shrieked their protests. The natural man in the ballroom, indeed, was as much anathema in the twentieth century as he had been in the fifteenth, and the same forces arose to oppose him. This time, however, the victory was his, at least for the moment.

In the summer of 1910 the Grizzly Bear was the rage at Newport, followed the next summer by the Turkey Trot. That year the first Junior Cotillion of the season at Sherry's enjoyed the largest attendance in its sixteen years' history; it was not the cotillion, however, that was danced, but the "new dances." At a ball of the National Arts Club, the Turkey Trot, the Bunny Hug and their ilk were forbidden, but most of the eight hundred dancers retired to the corridors and did them anyhow. A society leader stated publicly that these dances were "graceful and pretty" (in which she was less accurate than liberal), and enrolled for lessons. Another society leader predicted that the Turkey Trot would undoubtedly supplant the Boston Dropstep in popularity. Social workers protested vigorously, and were especially horrified at a movement called the "shiver" in the Turkey Trot. They demanded a standard of propriety, and in this a large section of the dancing teachers joined with them. Some teachers even volunteered exhibitions of just how unseemly the dances were, and advocated measures quite as stern as Guglielmo Ebreo might have advocated five hundred years earlier.

From Paris in 1910 there had already come reports that the Argentine tango was to supplant the Boston Double Dip, and

before long it crossed the ocean along with a dozen or more
other dances using the rhythms of Latin America and claiming
one country and another as points of origin. Eventually we
even got as far afield as alleged revivals of an old French sailors'
dance and an ancient Chinese ceremonial. (Who nowadays
remembers the rouli-rouli and the ta-tao!) But the tango was
far too complicated to compete with the native dances on any
equal basis and soon its name was unofficially but popularly
transferred without any reason at all to a fairly mild development of the new dance type more accurately called the one-step.
Its only conceivable relation to the tango is that it introduced a
few figures, such as the ubiquitous grapevine. Only the more
temerarious attempted these foreign importations, but every res-
taurant and café had exhibition dancers to perform them and
to add innovations of their own.

It was one such pair, Mr. and Mrs. Vernon Castle, who eventually brought order out of the chaos without too much loss of
the essential vitality of the movement. In their adaptations, they
actually justified the society leader's earlier pronouncement of
"graceful and pretty." Castle was a genius at invention, and in
this period when a public had been released from years of
monotonous routine, the more new steps that were to be learned,
the better. The polka was brought out of the cupboard. Even the
old five-four time of the Five Step, introduced in the late forties,
was revived as the Half-and-half, and virtually nothing was left
untried.

Castle's contribution, however, was a more significant one
than merely the revival of old dances and the refining of crude
new ones. He was anxious to retain for the ballroom dance that
spontaneity which justifies it as a truly recreational medium,
and he is said to have so heartily disliked repeating even his
exhibition routines that he improvised them a great part of the

time. To be sure, his inventions and improvisations, like those of his colleagues, were immediately seized upon and taught as routines, and it is the unfortunate truth that his emphasis upon individual creativeness received little or no attention.

This very emphasis, however, is the heart of the matter. It is not necessary for the ballroom dance to be vulgar or uncouth in order to serve as a means of release and refreshment, but it is necessary for it to be spontaneous, creative, expressive in the wide use of the word. If decorum should have to be sacrificed once in a while for the sake of these other things, by all means let us sacrifice it.

No doubt the passage of time, even without the intervention of such a cataclysm as the World War, would inevitably have diminished the fine frenzy of the new movement. Certainly it allowed the cohorts of conservatism to mass their artillery, if not for an actual counterrevolution, at least for a strong defense. There is today a general subservience to the leadership of England in the ballroom and there the dance is rather consistently academized. In a country where there is still maintained a formal court life, it is only natural that the ancient habiliments of courtliness should likewise be preserved. When communities of a totally different social climate adopt them, however, they lay themselves open to suspicions of provincialism. Those who have once tasted the delights of truly improvisational dancing will inevitably find the English manner stilted and lifeless. When the recreational dance has become a matter of strictly routined practice, with its every move established by code; when it is subjected constantly to competitions for cups with questions of professional and amateur status, it is difficult to consider it as recreation at all. It would seem to be rather more in the nature of a spectacular skill, to be taken up as an avocation at the very least.

Ideally, if the recreational dance is to serve its true function as part of the social scheme, it needs to be developed with only such restrictions as grow inevitably out of the current modes of dress, limitations in the amount of space available, and the fact that since many dancers are on the floor at the same time, the music must be followed instead of led. The teacher who can impart within this framework the principles of soundly produced and controlled bodily movement and encourage the pupil's faculty for free expression and invention becomes an educator in the best sense of the word. The practice of selecting or manufacturing a new set of routines to be taught and made fashionable each season may be commercially rewarding but it makes small contribution indeed except to regimentation and snobbishness.

At present, our apparent reluctance where our creative powers are involved leads us to draw upon two chief sources for our material, in much the same way that the Renaissance drew upon its peasantry. These are the North American Negro and Latin America. In neither case is this material transported over the racial barrier without serious loss, but it brings a certain vitality, at least, to what would otherwise be a distinctly anemic field. The miserable thing that now masquerades under the name of the tango is a standing warning of the ultimate fate of importations in the Latin-American style. The shortcomings of the Lindy Hop and other Harlem developments when performed by white dancers, if not quite so marked, are still far from negligible when compared with the marvelous verve and even the great racial beauty of these dances at, say, the Savoy Ballroom on a good night. The Negro, indeed, has discovered for himself a rich and admirable recreational dance, and his contribution to our own development along these lines has far greater potentialities than have yet been realized. Before we can avail ourselves of them, however, we must quit trying to imitate him and undertake rather to learn from him, for it is not his routines, but his principles, that we need.

Precedent has proved that this method of made-over imitations will not meet the issue, and the same proof is establishing itself again at the moment with considerable vividness, to the accompaniment of that remarkable grandchild of ragtime known as "swing." The recreational dancer is no more interested now in such aspects of "grace of movement as will render him pleasing in the eyes of the beholders" than he was in the fifteenth century when he donned his mask and fled to the unseemly peasant dances, or in the early twentieth when he drove the cotillion out of the ballroom to make room for the Turkey Trot. The accepted routines of today may differ radically in form but not at all in essence from their predecessors, and the "jitterbug" has arisen to say so in no uncertain terms. He alone has caught something of the contagion of the Negro's spirit, and his argument is all the more eloquent because he is not trying to combat anything, but is simply turning to his own devices of spontaneous and improvisational recreation.

Until the underlying impulses of this highly significant movement have been recaptured in the more organized sphere of the social dance, we shall not have succeeded in realizing the full values of the ballroom as a recreational center. If ragtime pointed the way, swing has emphasized it. The tenor of its message would seem to be that the recreational dance of today is not called upon to teach manners and morals, as if it were still trying to adapt itself to the social ambition of the Renaissance; it is called upon only to provide a framework for the spontaneous release of those exuberant and creative impulses that gave birth in the first place to the couple dance. These involve fundamentally a recognition of the enjoyment of men

and women in each other's company, and include not only the
lyrical and the passionate aspects of courtship, but also the high-
spirited cutting up that belongs equally to this frank and healthy
boy-and-girl relationship.

Folk Dance

To be sure, social dancing as a whole embraces far more than
the polite manifestations of eroticism which have dominated the
ballroom for so long. In its historic pattern, its broader sociabil-
ity has been expressed in rounds, in longways and square dances
involving the participation of groups of varying sizes. If by the
end of the nineteenth century these forms had virtually disappeared in sophisticated circles, they had not done so in rural
communities where the necessities of conviviality are still maintained.

One of the most interesting developments of the modern social
dance is the rediscovery of these group forms as a lively recreational art for sophisticated city dwellers. Though the folk dance
movement gained ground steadily from the early years of its
organization in the nineties, things have taken a new turn in
more recent years, and about 1930 the practice of folk dancing as
a living art, instead of merely an ethnological study, among
people of metropolitan sophistication, began to assume significant dimensions. To speak of this movement as a revival is to
risk offending the scientific folklorist, who argues with complete authority that most of these dances have never left off
being done. Nevertheless, for that cross section of society that
has recently begun to practice them for the first time, it is literally a revival of something out of its background and beyond
its personal experience. In the long view, this kind of dance is
an essential element of man's age-old and indestructible basic

cultural structure, and it is therefore not the dance that is being revived so much as the men who are making their renewals of contact with it.

The whole trend is clearly a part of the modern renascence. It is the effort of a routinized population, caught up in the mechanisms and intellectualisms of a system that virtually transforms daily activity into a code apart from normal living in the manner of a huge academism, to find access to the realm of actual function. For this there is, of course, nothing comparable to movement as a medium, and merely to repeat the movement patterns in which simpler and more natural people have objectified their moods of conviviality and exuberance is to get by contagion something of their freedom and essential humanity. It is futile, of course, to try thus to assume a "simple life" that does not belong to us, and to use folk dance in this way is only to make it objectionably quaint and affected. In the final analysis we must evolve our own simple life without attempting to go backwards, in either time or progress, to conditions that do not exist. The very machinery of the power age from which we tell ourselves we must escape will itself make possible the leisure and the energy to achieve this kind of life, once an equitable adjustment of its great productivity has been made.

These revived dances, however, are not dated forms but living practices, to which men have contributed through the ages every movement, device and figuration that has suggested itself to them as natural and sociable. On this groundwork there is not only room but an invitation for other men in other worlds to make further contributions. When the urban sophisticate touches the folk dances, he inevitably commits a desecration of sorts, for these are not his natural means of expression and no matter how much he may respect them, the moment he attempts to put them into practice he begins to overpower them with his alien enthusiasm. It is eminently right that he should do so, for their value to him is infinitely less as dead mementos than as live recreational patterns. As the unfortunately short-lived Big Apple demonstrated, these patterns can be expanded to include all kinds of creative contemporary material, urban as well as rural.

They are, indeed, so common to nature that it is stretching a point even to call them traditional. Surely walking and running and skipping and hopping and turning are not to be put into any such oppressive category; and if formations of groups in circles or in facing lines or in sets of facing couples had not been evolved centuries ago they would have had to be evolved today, for they are inevitable. Similarly, swinging partners, the grand right and left, "sashaying" down between the lines, "do-see-do," promenading, and all the other figurations that have acquired (and lost) fancy names in their passage through courtly ballrooms, are not just perpetuated because they are older than history, but endure of their own vitality because they are basic and natural.

Within the extensive range of this almost instinctive material, there is great leeway for creativeness if there is a good "caller" to order the proceedings and a good musician to keep the phrases moving. It is probably impossible to get closer to group improvisation, which in its fullest sense, of course, is practically out of the question; and when compared with the pitiful stereotypes of ballroom routine with every step decreed by this season's dancing masters' convention, it is magnificently spontaneous and free.

To release the social dance from a total preoccupation with sex is a healthy thing. Though the courtship dance has an ancient and honorable function (and these dances contain their share of it), there are other functions for dancing, as well. In modern city life we are constantly being thrown with crowds which are not unified groups but, on the contrary, haphazard aggregations of individuals bent on separate and often conflicting purposes and paying no more attention to each other than absolutely necessary. Meeting each other thus en masse under conditions of stress and with a mechanical undercurrent of rivalry, has bred in us an unhealthy defensiveness against social gatherings, and has set up a kind of compensatory habit of isolationism that has kept us from knowing each other as fellows and neighbors. We can accordingly make good use of those large group dances of our ancestors in which they acquired a sense of social solidarity, and apparently we have discovered that this is so. We have found the satisfactions that belong to forming part of a common pattern and of participating in a group movement far more powerful than anything we could possibly make alone. All these things that have played important parts in primitive civilizations are found to have basic values for our own as well—to belong, in fact, to the essential nature of man.

Amateur Activity

RECREATIONAL dancing includes still another major subdivision and one that lies quite outside the boundaries of what we call the social dance. This consists of the extensive practice of the dance in its art aspects by those who have no thought whatever of making a career of it, but who find here a release for their creative impulses and their leanings toward art. The idea is more than familiar in the other arts, with amateur dramatic groups, "little theaters," church choirs, glee clubs and choral societies in virtually every hamlet. In the preradio era, a piano in the parlor was second in importance only to a range in the kitchen in the majority of homes, and there are still multitudes of people who study some musical instrument merely for their own pleasure.

In the dance, it is this more individual approach that is most in evidence, for groups comparable to the choral society or the dramatic club require more organization and a wider recognition of the dance as an amateur art than have yet been found practicable on any great scale. In the former German Republic, however, this type of activity reached a high degree of development, and lay-dance choruses were to be found in virtually every center.

The beginnings that have been made in this country are nevertheless notable. A tremendous amount of attention is being given to the development of the creative dance in general education, where the particular requirements of the lay dancer are being more and more fully understood and adequately met. This development extends all the way from the primary grades up through the college years, and has begun to bear fruit even beyond. There are, for example, increasing numbers of dance clubs organized each year by graduates of various colleges who wish to carry on the work they have begun as students, and here we find a parallel of sorts to both the amateur musical and dramatic groups with which we have been long familiar and the admirable German lay-dance choruses.

The chief centers for amateur activity at present, however, are the studios of professional dancers, where there are always to be found nonprofessional students attending classes eagerly. In the tap dance schools, which literally teem with them, it is easy to see the connotations of simple amusement, but the more serious types of dance, though they are more arduous and less superficially rewarding, offer other and deeper compensations. Here are to be found the release that comes through strenuous technical training, and the creative pleasure of dancing as part of a group and at times functioning as its choreographer. Logically enough, large numbers of young dancers of this type are to be found in the field of the so-called modern dance where the creative processes are of first importance, but they abound also in studios of the highly professionalized ballet, of the Spanish and Oriental dance, and virtually wherever any kind of dancing is taught and practiced.

Several ostensible reasons are given for this form of activity; business girls sometimes claim that their sedentary occupations make them feel the need for exercise, and frequently there is talk of reducing surplus weight and of various generalities about health and beauty. Actually, however, whatever the rationalizations may be, its function is to supply channels for those impulses toward art which demand expression however little communicative value they may contain. This is in fact that recreational field that is best characterized as self-expression and that lies midway between simple play and art.

The professional artist-dancer, concerned primarily in perfecting his own art and giving form to those creative ideas that are clamoring for expression, is more than likely to find it an ordeal to work with these laymen for whom the mere establishment of contact with the creative process is quite enough and the goal is nothing more than personal release. For the educator, however, whose chief concern is with the development of the individual to his highest realization of himself, there is a medium here of deep-lying values. Clearly the lay dance belongs entirely outside the professional sphere, both technically and psychologically. As long as it remains even nominally within it, it is bound to labor under a burden of inferiority and struggling dilettantism, whereas in a world of its own it becomes an activity of free and fine accomplishment.

Chapter Seven

SPECTACULAR DANCE—THE BALLET

※≈≪≫≈※

THE great spectacular dance form of the Western world is, of course, the ballet; so much so, in fact, that the word ballet is frequently, though mistakenly, used generically to include all dancing that is done for audiences, even those types that are non-ballet or actually anti-ballet. Properly, the term ballet refers to a particular form of theater dance, which came into being in the Renaissance and which has a tradition, a technic and an aesthetic basis all its own.

Literally, any dancing performed for an audience is to be classed as spectacular in that it is done for the benefit of the spectator, and not for the benefit of the dancer as the recreational dance is done. Practically, however, it is necessary to make a distinction beyond this, for one branch of the spectator dance is designed to be watched objectively and another is designed to be participated in vicariously by the onlooker. The former is sensuous and intellectual in its appeal, and belongs in the category of entertainment, at its worst catering to sensation alone and at its best attaining high degrees of taste and subtlety and requiring developed criteria of judgment; the latter is more elemental, stemming from the same sources as the religious, magic and social rituals of simpler peoples, and having for its purpose the awakening of emotional perceptions. This second type is primarily expressional in its intent and makes the spectator actually a participant, in a sense; it therefore excludes itself automatically from consideration in the purely spectacular classification.

Such a division as this in the spectator dance is age-old. The relation of the ballet to it, however, is perhaps unique among the great dance forms of the world, for contrary to all precedent it grew up with secular interests exclusively. In early cultures, in which the dance is an integral part of group life and forms the medium for its rituals, it is customary to find its leaders among the priests and medicine men, and from this source deeply rooted in the lives of the people grow the professionalized dance arts. They are slow indeed in becoming secularized, but persist in dealing with subjects of sacred import, formal conventions and ceremonial practice, and frequently confine themselves to specific seasons of the year and to honoring certain deities. In the days of classic Greece we find professional dancers of both sexes entertaining the guests at dinner parties, but such secular dancing is done by slaves or low caste freedmen and is of distinctly low evaluation. When the great games, of sacred origin, are going on, the streets are lined with side shows of tumblers, jugglers, contortionists, and sword swallowers, but the rich and respected art of the choric dance in both tragedy and comedy takes place only in the celebrations honoring Dionysos.

To be sure, it was in the efforts of the Renaissance to revive this choric dance that the ballet found its specific directions, but these efforts were concerned solely with restoring the choric forms and took no notice of the ritual quality of the Greek dance. Dionysos had now no religious significance whatever, nor, indeed, could anything have been more remote from Renaissance thought than cosmic or mystic motivation for its dancing.

The turning to classic mythology was not a conversion by any means to the spiritual values that underlay it; it was simply the eager embracing of a glamorous hierarchy of symbols to make art about, replacing the perhaps more truly functional but hideously dull and domineering Cardinal Virtues and Cardinal Vices and their associated saints and devils, which belonged to medieval mythology.

Under no conditions could it be said that religion of any kind provided the historic pattern of creative impulse from which the Renaissance built its arts. It was surfeited with medieval religious domination and its arts sought not inspiration in it but release from it. Certainly what little it received from the religious developments of the Middle Ages in the way of artistic heritage toward the shaping of its dance art, it was quick to divest of its original character and transmute into secular and intellectual forms. Yet neither the ballet nor any of the other art achievements of the Renaissance could have evolved out of a period without a deep and compulsive drive, fundamentally as emotional as any primitive religious drive, however different in outward manifestation. It was, in effect, antireligion, the rejection of all mysterious forces controlling man without his volition. He was weary of servitude to that intangible thing, his soul, and its dubious happiness in a remote sphere; of his mind and his body he was intensely aware, and of their present fulfillments. In his emancipation, it was these he would cultivate. The refinements of the sensuous and the intellectual were his pleasure and his purpose. Whatever came to his hand he turned to these ends.

In his making over of old forms and redirecting of old impulses lay the sprawling elements of the early ballet. The pageantry and parading that the Middle Ages had so loved were stripped of whatever religious quality they may have had and made the occasion for sumptuous spectacle and artistry. What had once been a procession in honor of St. John, for example, now found itself a great aggregation of floats designed by the finest artists, depicting the glories of ancient Rome. The street carnivals and maskings were similarly polished, and the private masquerades of the ballroom were equipped with subjects, characters and a semblance of dramatic action.

Even the tournament which had been introduced into Italy from France was transformed into glamorous pageantry. Though it had left its native land as a game devised to be as nearly like actual warfare as possible to satisfy the belligerent tastes of knightly fighters who fretted under periods of enforced peace, it now acquired fictional subject matter, elaborate floats to bear its contestants to the lists disguised as Turks or Moors or what-not and accompanied by their trains of festively arrayed servants and maidens, and impressive processions before ever the jousting began.

Into the banqueting hall itself, after the custom of the Middle Ages, were brought floats representing castles, towers, forests or ships and containing companies of masked dancers. Here after a long and flattering set of verses had been addressed to the nobleman who headed the table, the dancers dismounted and performed moriscos suitable to the characters they represented— warriors, Moors, nymphs, tritons, nereids, or monkeys. At a famous dinner in Tortona, each course was introduced by a group of dancers, musicians and declaimers, representing appropriate mythological figures—Jason of the Golden Fleece presented a roast lamb, Diana a stag, Theseus and Atalanta a wild boar, sea deities the fish, Hebe the wine, and so forth, with suitable music, flattering verses and moriscos.

But eating and fighting were not the only social practices that were subjected to the incessant interruptions of these colorful artistic interludes. They found their way and were welcomed into other less likely forms of entertainment. Performances of the comedies of Plautus and Terence were adorned with any number of unrelated intermedia. Moors with burning torches in their mouths, satyrs with Pan as their leader, giants and monsters, groups of swordsmen, drunken cooks, were likely to appear in the midst of any comedy to perform moriscos. What is more, Isabella d'Este, that archetype of the great lady of the Renaissance, confessed herself frankly bored when there was too much Plautus and too little song and dance. In the pastorals Orpheus had no hesitancy in pausing to sing the praises of a noble churchman, and in the farces written in imitation of Plautus, despite the contemporaneousness of their characters and action, Jason might well appear at the end of an act to sow the dragon's teeth from which would arise armed warriors to offer a morisco.

The morisco was an ideal dance for these dramatic uses, for from its ritual days it had inherited masks, such accouterments as circlets of bells at the knees and swords or sticks, and a tradition of ceremonial sword fighting which gave it inherent dramatic color. Besides this, it was processional in form rather than rigidly figured, and presented therefore an easy adaptability. These qualities, no doubt, were what had disqualified it for purely social use, but along with the more closely figured brando, which employed pantomime so freely that it was similarly banned from the ballroom, it furnished the chief medium for those court festivities that leaned more in the direction of interludes to be watched than of dances for general participation.

Ballet and Opera

FOR all its uncontrolled enthusiasm, here was a glorious fecundity, and its lack of consistency did not go altogether unnoticed.

More and more there were stirrings to emulate the great art of the Greek theater with its unity of poetry, music and dance. In France, where all the significant developments in the ballet occurred when once it had been transplanted from Italy, a group of poets and musicians banded themselves together for this very purpose in the third quarter of the sixteenth century, and obtained letters patent from the king to form an Academy of Music and Poesy. Their practical efforts, it is true, were short-lived because of the religious wars, but the idea behind them remained to germinate. A few years later a similar group with perhaps a more fundamental grasp of the same problem began to function in Italy, calling themselves the Camerata. Characteristically enough, the fruits of this general movement were in France the ballet and in Italy the opera.

Actually all the diverse elements were not drawn together into any semblance of unity until 1581, when at the court of Henry III of France, Balthasar de Beaujoyeux, Italian-born valet de chambre to the king's mother, Catherine de' Medici, produced what he entitled "Balet Comique de la Royne" as part of a wedding celebration in the royal family. Here were the usual long harangues in verse, and the entries of floats bearing nereids and satyrs and the like who dismounted and danced, but a thread of dramatic consistency held it all together in a measure without precedent. This event dates the beginning of the ballet as a theatrical art form, and all those concerned in it were fully aware that it was a momentous occasion. They were convinced, indeed, that the choric drama of the Greeks had been restored.

As a precedent for future practice, however, it was totally impractical for it had cost 900,000 crowns. Something far more capable of frequent repetition, even though artistically inferior, was required to satisfy the prevalent passion of the court for entertainments of this sort, and for many years the custom narrowed itself down to a type of ballet made up of a number of entries each on a different subject, the whole perhaps being related to some common idea such as the seasons of the year or the parts of the world, and leading up to a conclusion with general dancing.

Meanwhile the opera was growing apace in Italy. The complete unity of music and speech which the Camerata had sought had resulted in the creation of recitative or musical declamation, but this had soon been embellished with the inevitable interludes—vocal interludes in the form of florid arias and dance interludes according to the venerable tradition of the morisco. Elaborate machinery for scenic effects further adorned the whole and helped to give it tremendous popular appeal. Its effect on the French ballet was at first merely to replace the spoken harangues with recitative and to increase the emphasis on scenery and mounting. Later the two forms were wedded by Lully, with opera decidedly the dominant member of the household.

Jean-Baptiste Lully, the leader of Louis XIV's musicians, was another of the expatriate Italians who have played such prominent parts in the ballet's evolution. In his combining of the elements of the Italian opera and the French ballet he achieved the finest synthesis that it had known in many a long year. Though it was actually the opera that carried the weight of the whole, as it would almost inevitably do in the hands of a musician and especially an Italian-born musician, the dance interludes were numerous, in every case justified by the action of the story and made to carry it along in something of a continuous line. This was a situation, however, which did not long endure, and the ballet, as it has had a significant habit of doing throughout its entire life, slipped away from the sustained dramatic line into its native field of decorativeness and abstraction.

But Lully was responsible for other changes that were perhaps more enduring and touched upon more fundamental issues, if less directly planned. By thoroughly unscrupulous methods (for he was as gifted in politics as in art) he possessed himself of the charter of the Royal Academy of Music and this he combined in 1671 with the Royal Academy of Dance which had been listlessly in existence for the past ten years. Within two years the joint academy was granted by the king the use of the theater in the Palais Royal, made vacant by the death of Molière, and the consequences for the ballet were very great.

The theater had been built approximately thirty years before by Cardinal Richelieu, who had given it a large and excellently equipped stage framed by a proscenium arch in the newly popular Italian manner, and had devoted the entire remainder of the hall to the audience. It had always been the practice in the court entertainments to employ the stage or platform at the end of the great hall in a fairly minor capacity and to bring the formation of the dancers into the main body of the hall. The king or the ranking noble and his entourage occupied a dais at the far end of the room and the rest of the spectators stood along the side walls, thus all but surrounding the performing area. In the theater of the late cardinal, however, all the ballet's action was now forced onto the stage with the audience directly in front. To be sure, dancing had been done on such stages before. Even in this very theater certain of the comedies of Molière had freely employed incidental ballets. Now, however, the whole art of the ballet was taken out of the ballroom and confined behind the proscenium arch.

Eventually this contributed to the first great technical innovation in the ballet's history, namely, the turned-out hip. As the body is articulated, the hip joint is of the ball-and-socket type and has considerable play, so that the leg may not only be swung forward and backward and raised somewhat to the side, but may also be rotated on its own axis. Such rotation is, of course, eminently useful in ordinary movement, but at this stage of the ballet's development it took on added importance. With the spectators all seated in front, it became necessary for the dancers to face in this one direction as much as possible, which was simple enough when moving forward and back, but which entailed certain obvious difficulties when it came to moving across the stage to right and left. If, however, the legs, instead of being kept in their natural position, were turned outward at the hip so that the toes pointed in approximately opposite directions to left and right, the difficulties were at once obviated, for such a position allowed the legs to pass each other without interference as the body was moved sidewards.

Again, if the leg in its natural position was raised forward, perspective foreshortened its movement so that it lost its design for the spectator directly in front of it. If the leg was turned outward at the hip, however, the same movement might be made to the side and seen in profile in its full outline while the dancer remained with his face forward. The dancer's range of decorative visibility, so to speak, was thus vastly increased.

To be sure, the principle of the turned-out hip was no new invention, nor were its full potentialities developed at once. With the passage of time, however, its values were increasingly realized and the degree of the turning-out was gradually extended from that which was familiar in Lully's day—that is to say, with the feet at little more than a right angle—to that which began to prevail in the highly technical period of the nineteenth century and continues to the present time—that is to say, with the feet making a straight line from toes to toes.

The ballet master in Lully's academy was Pierre Beauchamp, a man of apparently great gifts. Besides being a practical and imaginative craftsman, he was also a fine theorist and exactly

the type of man to head one of the countless academies of which
the period was so productive. It was the function of these
academies, according to what was thought to be exact precedent
from ancient Rome, to formulate the rules and laws for whatever branch of the arts or sciences they might represent, and
to enjoy a monopoly upon them in return. Beauchamp left no
documentary records of his activity in formulating the laws of
the ballet, but if the word of his contemporaries is to be credited,
he did a good job of it. The five basic positions of the feet,
which are still fundamental in ballet practice, were now established officially for the first time, though of course they had long
been in use. Also, a system of notation for dance compositions
was patented by him though it was developed by his contemporary, Raoul Feuillet.

The ballet had now definitely entered upon its professional
phase, the necessary impulses of amateurism in its best sense
having been outgrown. Women were admitted to its ranks on
a professional basis, and public interest quite apart from the
court assumed notable dimensions. When the king himself suddenly quit dancing, for reasons that have never been clearly
established, the amateur period received the coup de grâce, and
though the ballet remained an aristocratic art and depended
upon the crown for support, its progress was from now on in
the hands of professional artists.

Noverre

THE beginning of the eighteenth century saw the ballet in the
throes of the usual rigidities that attack academies in general
when the immediate necessities of their establishment have been
satisfied, and henceforth all creative efforts were to be directed
toward combating its immobility and pedanticism. Of such

efforts there were several that were significant and one that was epoch making.

With the elimination of the noble amateur there came also a marked tendency to eliminate the restraints of his etiquette as they affected the dance. Heretofore, all the dancing had had upon it the stamp of Guglielmo and his colleagues of long ago; that is, it was stately, elaborate in its ground plan, perhaps intricate in its footwork, but leaning still somewhat to the type of the old bassa danza in that the feet were never lifted very high from the floor. Even though Lully had considerably increased its tempo, taking away thereby some of its excessive dignity, he had done nothing toward directing it away from its concentration on ground plan. Now it began to concern itself with the restoration of all those leaping elements in the dance that had been so diligently suppressed by courtly manners, and against which, indeed, there was still considerable opposition.

This change of emphasis focused attention upon the need for alteration in the style of costume, at least for the women, to keep jumping steps from being both difficult and ineffectual. Marie Camargo, who delighted in technical skill, accordingly defied convention and shortened her skirts to the ankles. The standard dresses of the women, however, remained tremendously heavy and adorned with elaborate panniers. Enormous head-dresses, many jewels, gloves and hose, heeled shoes and masks completed what was virtually a uniform and heretofore an un-questioned one. The men were similarly encumbered by a costume which the Renaissance had patterned after that of a Roman general. It differed from the women's chiefly in that for the latter's panniers and train it substituted a short, widely-hooped skirt called a tonnelet, or little cask, and knee breeches.

A rebellion even more significant than Camargo's was that of her colleague and rival, Marie Sallé, who in dancing the role of Galatea in London discarded headdress, panniers and jewels and wore only draperies patterned after Greek sculpture over her corset and petticoat. This was a daring innovation, based not on technical necessities but on a desire for greater expressiveness and verisimilitude. It was not immediately accepted but it heralded larger reforms shortly to come.

Actually the great romantic movement was astir. That concern with man's essential nature against which the Renaissance had rebelled, was beginning to force itself into the realm of expression as the artistic voice of the rising movement toward democracy, in whose history it has always been a collaborator, however unconsciously.

Certainly the inspired spokesman for the romantic reform of the ballet at this time was politically no democrat. Jean George Noverre, protégé of Marie Antoinette, was arrogant, a snob and as much of a schemer as Lully had been before him, though not so clever at it. Kept out of the directorship of the academy and its performances at the Opéra until his ideas had already had so much influence that they had lost their novelty, he finally endured a brief and unhappy tenure there, allowed himself to be bought off with a pension, fled to England in fear of the Revolution, and died in retirement in France an embittered old man. Nevertheless he was the greatest genius the dance had yet produced as well as its most effectual reformer, and his *Letters on the Dance and the Ballet* published in 1761 constitutes one of the landmarks in its literature.

With regard to his romanticism it is essential that immediate qualifications be made, for in the light of what has happened in the world in the intervening generations, his steps in this direction seem less bold than they actually were in their own day. The full creative possibilities of movement in the dance were not to be discovered for nearly a hundred and fifty years and did not come even remotely within Noverre's range of vision. His reforms remained still in the academic realm; that is, instead of turning to self-experience for his materials he utilized what was already established in the accepted codes as his basis of operations. When he advocated going to life for movements and patterns of conduct, he clearly indicated that he was thinking only of the surface of life as revealed by observation. It was his ambition to make the ballet an imitative art; the concept of an expressional one could scarcely have appeared to him as a possibility. Yet in spite of these reservations which a true perspective make unavoidable, it would be difficult to overestimate the scope and depth of his reforms.

The "ballet d'action," the form he initiated, gave the dance for the first time an independent place in the theater. Though it was to retain its function of supplying interludes for the opera, it had now a sphere of its own as well, in which aria and recitative did not interfere. It told a unified story of sorts, patterned after the tragedies of the theater, of Corneille and Racine, and its action was unfolded in pantomime of dramatic intelligibility, with formal dances only where they might be conceived of as logically occurring. Masks were dispensed with in defiance of tradition so that the face might assist in the projection of the dramatic mood. Tonnelets and panniers and headdresses were likewise relegated to the discard for the sake of realism.

That this realism was not too radical, however, we can scarcely fail to grasp when we recall the costumes of which he was so proud in "La Toilette de Vénus." Similarly, though gesture should spring from feeling and mood and not from rules, and though dancing masters should observe the life movements of workmen and soldiers on the march, etc., still when emotions were depicted, they should always be the emotions of refined people, for others might disgust the spectators. Dancing, like poetry and painting, "should be no other than a faithful likeness of beautiful nature"—and obviously nature became beautiful only when censored and polished.

In the divertissements in the opera he was incensed at the inviolable routine by which certain dances, with their particular specialists performing them, came in each act, growing to a grand climax in the elaborate chaconnes and passacailles. The ballets in the opera should be made to advance the story, he maintained, instead of having no relation to it whatever beyond the negative one of an interruption. In both these opera divertissements and the ballet d'action, the use of symmetry for its own sake, of standardized and overfamiliar material, of meaningless but decorative movements of the arms and legs, of a corps de ballet without characterization and a share in the plot, were all ruled out by his system.

Though he demanded technical excellence, he was not interested in it as an end in itself, but quite the contrary. "Children of Terpsichore," he imagines a savior of the dance as saying, "renounce cabrioles, entrechats and overcomplicated steps; abandon grimaces and study sentiments, artless graces and expression; study how to make your gestures noble; never forget that it is the life blood of dancing; put judgment and sense into your pas de deux; let will-power order their course and good taste preside over all situations. . . . Renounce that slavish routine which keeps your art in its infancy. . . . Be original, form a style for yourselves based on your private studies. . . ."

It was his mission "to unite action with dancing; to accord it some expression and purpose," and in these things he unquestionably succeeded, taking the ballet so far from the classic ideal that had dominated its early beginnings in the ballrooms of the Renaissance that it has never turned to it again. His pupil, Dauberval, continued his gospel, passing its theory on, in turn, to his pupil, Salvatore Viganó. The latter took it to La Scala in Milan and developed it dramatically farther than Noverre had ever dreamed of doing, and finally achieved such a concentration on its pantomimic elements that his critics declared it had no dance left in it at all.

The Romantic Era

MEANWHILE, new forces of democracy and romanticism were working still other changes in the ballet. In subject matter and characters, approximations to ordinary contemporary life were being made. Though they remained, in all conscience, far-flung and exaggerated according to our standards, they frequently dealt with lesser personages than gods and heroes or even kings and dukes. The ancient line of pastorals with its sentimental shepherds and shepherdesses had never really died, and now it was turning naturally to the simple folk of this newer day, making picturesque romances among peasant lovers, or between peasant maids and noble lords, and generally painting an idyllic picture of the countryside which no doubt the farmers would have been hard put to recognize.

During the French Revolution, still other types of contemporary characters were to be seen—sans-culottes, soldiers, priests and nuns—in works glorifying liberty and equality, extolling the American Revolution, dramatizing the age of reason and its destruction of the symbolism of the church. Reforms in costume were carried considerably beyond Noverre's ideal of the demands of realism. Even the heroic and mythological characters, of whom there were still scores surviving, now began to wear apparel of some archeological accuracy. The painter David, a leader in the neo-classic resurgence at the end of the century, had persuaded his friend Talma, the actor, to forego the old Renaissance-Greek-Roman uniform in favor of something nearer to historical truth, and the result had been so successful that the ballet also had been persuaded to lay aside forever its traditional garb in favor of robes and tunics of classic simplicity. But this was to be a brief dispensation, for soon the neo-classic rage subsided, taking with it once and for all the gods and heroes of Olympus. The flowering of the Romantic Revolution had arrived, and the dance could not possibly remain unaffected by it.

For the ballet, however, it was a revolution only within the boundaries of its own academic foundations. Though there were manifold changes in all directions, the essential approach to movement through the channels of the traditional technic was unquestioned. The basic vocabulary with its brilliance of style, its personal virtuosity, its idealizations, was turned to new subject matter which involved new aesthetic, philosophical and moral premises, with no disturbance at all, unless a notable increase in its range and powers to meet new demands could be called a disturbance.

The tenor of these days was a kind of anti-Renaissance, discarding the worship of principles that were supposed to have arisen in antiquity, such as the classical unities of time, place and action, and pleading, as Victor Hugo wrote, for "the liberation of art from the despotism of systems, codes and rules." Such a convention as verse, constituting an art medium, a texture, was not under attack; and the traditional technic of the ballet fell into a similar category. It was the arbitrary limitations on the use of these textures that the romanticists rebelled against.

Art, said Hugo, should combine the tragic and the comic, the sublime and the grotesque, as human nature combined them. It should mirror the conflict set up in man by the two elements struggling within him, one striving to tie him to the appetites and passions of the body, and the other striving to lead him to the higher realms of the soul. The pendulum had swung away from the extremes of Renaissance paganism, past the truth of man's essential nature as it had been seen by the great thinkers who had followed in the wake of the Reformation, and back to a kinship with the Middle Ages. For all the substantial accomplishments of the transcendentalists, this nineteenth century duality was, indeed, scarcely more than a watered version of Gothic mysticism.

In the ballet, supernaturalism reigned. Where once nymphs and fauns, satyrs and dryads, naiads and nereids, had marched and countermarched in intricate formations, now disembodied spirits rose from their graves to lure young mortals to a romantic doom, winged creatures of the woods perished for love of handsome youths, and an ethereal host, compounded half from faerie and half from the Christian graveyard, suffered and sacrificed for love.

It is no mere coincidence that in this time of aspiration, of yearning for heavenly realms, of symbolic interest in creatures of the air, dancers for the first time in their history rose upon the points of their toes. Gravity had been defied in increasing measure ever since the ballet was first turned over to professional dancers with a pride in the height of their leaps, but now it was actually denied. If the triumphs of elevation had previously seemed not only more practicable but eminently more suitable for men, now the women were able to outdo them, and in a manner intensely feminine, by an illusion of suspension in air, of fragile and unearthly lightness.

There is no record of who introduced this innovation, and this is not to be wondered at when we realize that it was in no way comparable to the elaborate and sustained use of the points that we know today. It consisted in the beginning of no more than an occasional rise to the tip of the toe for a brief instant. Not until its continued use and desirability had led to the development of a reinforced slipper was its sustained and truly brilliant employment made possible. It is a great temptation to believe, even without an atom of proof, that it was Marie Taglioni who introduced the use of the points. Not only was it quite in keeping with the wistful lyricism of her style, but her father, who was her chief teacher and choreographer, was keenly aware of the possibilities of this style and had devoted himself to developing it along its own characteristic lines. Certainly "La Sylphide," which he created for her, was the first of the supernatural romances and might well have utilized this illusion of supernatural elevation.

However this may be, "La Sylphide" introduced a new style of ballet which was widely copied and a new style of costume which immediately became popular. This latter consisted of a simple, tight bodice without sleeves, with wings attached at the shoulders, and a voluminous skirt of filmy white tulle in countless layers reaching halfway between knee and ankle. It was designed by the painter, Eugène Lamy, as suitable garb for an aerial heroine, but it became as much a uniform as the old panniers and masks had once been. Stripped of its wings, and with its skirts shortened to sometimes little more than a puff of tulle about the hips, it has endured to our day as the standard "ballet skirt."

Up to this time, men had been the principal stars of the ballet, possibly because they had had the advantage of a more spectacular technical style with which to meet the competition of the personal charm and seductiveness of their feminine colleagues. Now with a newly developed spectacular style for the women which did nothing to destroy their native allure but actually enhanced it, the men were outdistanced. They became, in fact, little more than a necessary evil, and were frequently despised whole-heartedly. Not until the Russians, many years later, revealed again the possibilities of the masculine element of the dance, was the male dancer's position restored to anything of its former dignity.

The glorification of the ballerina was a characteristic feature of the nineteenth century ballet. If the Taglioni type of heroine represented the aspiring, spiritual branch of Hugo's duality, the voluptuous and earthly branch was by no means neglected. Its outstanding representative was the beautiful Fanny Elssler, who eschewed the airy and supernatural world for one of more substantial pleasures. Quite consistently with the democratic interests of the romantic movement in its larger aspects, the folk practices of the simple man of the countryside became the subject of increasing attention. This fitted well with the already existent type of ballet that had come down with many modifications but still in a fairly constant line from the pastorals. It was here that Elssler shone. It was her delight to transfer to the stage (though in terms of her academic training, of course) all the color and fire that belonged to peasant dances, especially those of Spain and the Slavic peoples.

Out of these contrasting types of Taglioni and Elssler, the ideal of the ballerina has grown, and she remains today alluring and voluptuous, but at the same time ethereal, elegant and remote.

Fokine

WHEN the fire of this contagion from the Romantic Revolution had spent itself, the ballet was left with little to engage its attention except its greatly increased technical powers. These it proceeded to use to steadily declining purpose, finally betraying them into gaucherie and inefficiency. The latter half of the nineteenth century saw the ballet in France and Italy, its ancient seats, slip into the most lethargic and unworthy condition in its history, a state which may well prove to be the end of its Latin line.

Its next manifestation of creative vitality was to come from the hinterland, from Russia. There the rich Slavic plasticity of temperament, touched by the vigor of the North people and the mysticism of the East, together with the best of training from the more experienced West, made for a combination of resources that awaited only the appearance of a personal genius to bring it to flower. That genius was Michel Fokine.

Meanwhile, however, from another quarter of the hinterland, America, had come the long-delayed fruition of the Romantic Revolution to the dance. Isadora Duncan had rejected not only the traditional costume, music, scenery and storytelling of the ballet, but also its entire academic system of movement, and by going back to the spontaneous nature of man for her basic approach had brought upon the art of the dance the only real revolution in its history. Fokine's re-creation of the ballet was certainly not inspired by her, but it was just as certainly affected by her. In her freedom of the body, her innate eloquence, her musicality, were re-enforcements for his own ideas in these directions, even though the essential subjectivity of her creative method was so far outside the framework of his approach as to be scarcely noted.

In every way Fokine's reforms were much nearer to Noverre than to Duncan, though he went immeasurably farther than Noverre had gone. Expressiveness was his great goal. Like his predecessor he urged "the children of Terpsichore" to "renounce the slavish routine" which kept their art in its infancy, and to go to nature as their model instead of to the classroom. The traditional academic technic he considered indispensable for training but not sufficient in itself, since it ignored all natural movement and did not even teach the dancer how to walk, much less to move in the styles of other races and other times. Also, it was for him merely classroom training and not to be used on the stage as vocabulary, except, of course, where period style required, as in his own "Les Sylphides," an idealization of the dance of Taglioni's day. The constantly turned-out hip was for him ludicrous because inexpressive. Similarly, dancing on the points of the toes, which had degenerated into a mere acrobatic stunt, should be reserved for those occasions when it was appropriate and symbolized the lightness and the ethereal moods of the supernatural creatures who had inspired its original creation. He was distressed by the fact that the dancer was being taught in general to use only his legs, ignoring the rest of the body, when his ideal was that the whole body should be not only in movement but expressive. For him every ballet required a new technic, suitable to the period and the country in which its action occurred. It was ridiculous to see Greeks, Egyptians, Spanish and Russian peasants dressed in the conventional ballet skirts and dancing in the academic manner even to the use of the points.

The first of his five cardinal rules was that no ready-made routines should ever be employed, but every work should evolve its own movements and patterns according to the style and flavor of its locale and subject matter. The second rule insisted that extraneous passages either of dance or pantomime should be avoided, so that there should be no specialties, no mere divertissements, but only a dramatic sequence of expressive action. The third rule cast into outer darkness the old-fashioned and quite unintelligible system of pantomime by gesture of the hands alone and replaced it with the complete eloquence of the entire body at all times. The fourth rule brought the corps de ballet into the dramatic logic and expressiveness of the action instead of allowing it to serve only as conventional decoration and background. The fifth rule demanded a unity of purpose and a complete collaboration between the dancing, the music and the scenery and costumes, abandoning the then current practice of considering them as independent departments which might well (and frequently did) have no contact at all with each other until the dress rehearsal. Obviously such a fantastic practice was only possible where costumes were standard and unvarying, where music was nothing more than the requisite number of counts at the required tempo, ordered in advance. Now designers were to be free to evolve settings and costumes with some archeological and ethnological flavor as well as artistic quality, and musicians, scenarists, and choreographers to work together in the creation of a theatrical unity.

To be sure, the new ballet was not designed to be realistic, but to establish nevertheless a fundamental rapport with nature, and to be credible within the framework of its necessarily artificial conventions—the presentation of dramatic action as movement to music, the stylization of movement, and the idealization of its treatment both of what is beautiful and gracious and sensuously stimulating and of what is grotesque and comic.

Fokine's contributions to the repertory have been incomparable in range and quality, and if his later works have not produced the sensation of his earlier ones, it is not because his powers have declined but simply because the iconoclasms of his theory have become the accepted standard. In "Petrushka" he carried his doctrine of expressiveness to perhaps its most complete fulfillment, for here he went beyond the bounds of merely ethnographic style and developed a succinct and vivid treatment of psychological types. Since his three chief characters were puppets, he allowed their mechanical quality to accentuate the main features of their personal natures and to achieve thus a strongly marked individuality. Petrushka himself is an introvert, moving always in upon himself; the Moor is an extravert, moving in large outward gestures; the empty-headed and unfeeling Ballerina is made to burlesque the rigid and meaningless routine movements of the old-fashioned academic dancer. Though this was fantasy, it brought realism closer to the ballet than it had ever come before.

This work suffers gravely in contemporary presentations, even more perhaps than some of his other early works, which have likewise been performed steadily for the past thirty years and are indubitable classics. Lacking in most instances his personal direction and in every instance dancers at all comparable for his purpose to those of the magnificent Imperial Russian Ballet for whom he composed them, they are sometimes mere travesties of themselves. Whether they can ever again have justice done them is open to question, for nowhere outside Russia is there sufficient subsidy for the ballet to make possible that breadth of education which fostered the art of Fokine and his colleagues and which his ballets demand. In Russia, however, his reforms have not taken root as they have in Western Europe. When he was struggling to introduce them there, he was met on every hand by academic opposition and bureaucratic conservatism, and it was only when Serge Diaghileff secured permission to take the company out of the country for an annual season that his theories were allowed free rein.

Diaghileff, however, was by no means wedded to Fokine's theories as such, and very shortly the association was broken; but not before history had been made and the ballet restored to the status of a major art.

Nijinsky and the Diaghileff Period

THE chief ornament of the company Diaghileff sponsored was, of course, Vaslav Nijinsky. That he was a dancer of unmatchable gifts is beyond question; his contribution to the art of the ballet as a choreographer, however, is an issue that will never be solved. Of his meager output of four works, only "L'Après-midi d'un Faune" survives and in a thoroughly flaccid and meretricious form. His colleagues, for the most part, have considered his choreography as only the premonition of his subsequent madness, but if he was actually far in advance of his time this would have been said of him anyhow. Of recent years a fanatical cult of young people who never saw either him or his works has grown up to canonize him, largely, it is to be assumed, on the basis of the morbidly romantic character of his personal life and tragedy.

One thing only seems true beyond cavil: his choreography for the "Sacre du Printemps," whether the product of incipient insanity or of that genius which is proverbially close to it, was an epochal creation, hinting for the first time at the possible basis of a truly modern development for the ballet which has still not been fully achieved. In its day there was no general sensitiveness to such a movement in the ballet, and it was so radically different from even the great reforms of Fokine that it would have been a miracle if it had not caused passionate opposition.

Its chief innovations were two: Under the specific influence of the eurythmic teachings of Jaques-Dalcroze, it sensed the formal aspects of Stravinsky's complex musical score in terms of movement, arriving thus at an architectonic quality that no previous ballet had had. Though on the one hand this was musically derived and on the other its sequential procedure was primarily determined by a literary-dramatic program, it was nevertheless a definite step in the direction of absolute dance form. The second and perhaps the more extreme innovation was the departure not only from the academic approach to movement, a practice which Fokine had already made acceptable, but also from any objectively existent style whatever, in favor of a completely invented vocabulary. It is impossible to determine whether this was deliberately planned as a reversal of all academic practice—the toes turned inward, the emphasis on heaviness and angularity, the denial of the flowing line—in order to present the primitivism with which the subject dealt as antipodal to the refinements of tradition, or whether it was an impulsive, spontaneous, motor inspiration, influenced only subconsciously by a desire to destroy traditional conventions of movement. If it was the former, then it was still essentially objective, applying the academic method in reverse, but using it nevertheless as a guiding principle; if it was the latter, it bore a closer relation to the subjective method of Isadora Duncan and was accordingly far more radical, though less significant within the historic framework of the ballet.

In any case, it could scarcely have come about if Fokine's "Petrushka" had not preceded it. This is not to accept by any means the argument that is sometimes advanced that it was only an adaptation of the grotesque, turned-in movements of Fokine's puppet hero; there is a deeper relationship than this to be implied. Petrushka was said to be Nijinsky's favorite role; it was created for him, and certainly nobody else has ever been able to touch its possibilities. In it for the first time he was subjected to the experience of movement created to accord with individual psychological characteristics, and characteristics, furthermore, which in the interest of dramatic truth demanded a breach of all the self-contained logic of the academic canons. The awakening of a new logic by means of which inner impulse was united to outward expression independently of code, may well have lit the flame which both brought this particular performance to its state of incandescence and transformed this peculiarly sensitive boy from merely a brilliant technician and interpreter into a potential creator. All this is simply further speculation added to the mass that already exists, but it comes perhaps nearer to the truth than those theories which can accept as coincidence the manifest likenesses between the Nijinsky of "Petrushka" and the creator of the "Sacre du Printemps."

During the World War and after, Diaghileff's ballet entered upon a period of financial stringency, nervous experimentalism, makeshift and decline. Of the original company which had introduced a new art to Western Europe, only Diaghileff himself remained, and he was neither dancer, choreographer, musician nor designer.

These were years in the world of art in general when experimentation and the seeking of new directions were rife. The modern movement in music, painting and stagecraft had but just attained its majority, and in its wake fantastic cults, born unmistakably of the war, arose in rapid succession. Perhaps because their more substantial predecessors had been scorned before they had come to honor, everything new was treated with at least tentative respect, for an eager advance guard was determined, apparently, that nothing hereafter should go unnoticed, however ridiculous it might seem.

Diaghileff, discoverer of new talent, prophet of new directions, allowed most of the movements of the day a hearing in his ballets. The basis of the repertoire consisted of those more conservative works which were composed along the general lines determined by Fokine's reforms, but the progress of the period as a whole was definitely away from Fokine's romanticism and toward a characteristically postwar neo-classicism. Choreographic materials and designs were used less with relation to the realisms in which they might have originated than to the reactions they might be counted upon to produce in the spectator. This was an about-face from the borders of expressionalism toward which Fokine had led and a return to pure spectacularism. The unifying element that held all the diverse experiments together was the diligently maintained code of the academic technic, but this was used merely as a familiar and tangible constant, something to cling to in an unstable time. Its inherent nature and its value accordingly as a guide to the ballet's next step forward were not seen, as indeed they still are not.

Diaghileff was now supreme, and however open-minded to other people's ideas he might be, the final directions of the company were ultimately his decision. It is of the utmost importance, therefore, to realize that he was not a dancer, but only a connoisseur, perhaps equally interested in music and painting. It was this fact and this alone that led to his missing the opportunity that was his to create a new and truly functional ballet along the lines of modernism.

A cardinal principle of functionalism, as we have already seen, is a knowledge of the nature of materials and the application of that knowledge in the evolving of structures. In the dance this means abandoning the reliance on imitations of nature, on musical forms or dramatic sequence, and allowing the structural forms of the dance to grow out of the inherent qualities of movement. For the ballet, a frankly spectacular art not concerned with expressionalism, a resort to life movement with its emotional origins in the line of the modernism of Isadora Duncan and Mary Wigman, was as unnecessary as it was impossible. All that was required of it was to return to its own medium, its own material, so that it could replace its reliance on music, décor and representationalism with a functional basis of dance. Lip service aplenty was done to the old established academic code, with a fine air of loyalty but no realization whatever that here was the all-important foundation upon which the truly modern ballet might (indeed, must!) be built. It was blandly accepted simply as a source of vocabulary and a means of training.

There is no question that in these exciting days even the flightier legion of modernist cults, dada and vorticism and the rest, were rejoicing with their betters in the emancipation of materials and the new vistas of functional form that were opened up by the perception of their inherent structural qualities. The ballet admitted them all; it welcomed painting as painting and music as music, but never so much as thought of the possibility of dance as dance. As a result, no structural basis for building the ballet in its own terms as an autonomous medium was evolved, and alone among the arts it failed to attain the new levels of freedom and integrity of form made possible by the principles of modernism.

How great was Diaghileff's personal responsibility for this is difficult to judge; his own genius ran in other lines, and perhaps the concept was never presented to him by any of the dancers about him. Certainly if he had chosen a different path he would have had no difficulty in finding artists to follow him, as indeed they followed him in the path he did choose. The Swedish Ballet, organized by Rolf de Mare with Jan Borlin as its choreographer, adopted his point of view and practiced it, if anything, more violently. Cubism, constructivism, surrealism; the sophisticated simplicity of composers like "Les Six"; dada scenarios, colloquial subject matter tending in the popular cynical direction of an almost morbid triviality, all led the way and the ballet meekly made suitable adaptations in its academic idiom of movement and followed.

Three choreographers contributed mainly to these years: Leonide Massine, who as a mere boy had joined the company when Nijinsky left it, and had grown up under Diaghileff's careful tutelage; Bronislava Nijinska, sister of Vaslav, who had danced in the original company that came out of Russia, left when her brother did, and returned after nearly a decade as chief choreographer; and George Balanchine, who, having begun his training in the Imperial school before the Revolution and finished it there under the Soviets, finally left Russia because his artistic divagations were rather too extreme for acceptance.

Massine, not inherently of classic bent, followed mainly the pattern of the ballet d'action as Fokine had developed it, though with major differences in texture. With tastes less lofty and a style less noble, he turned largely to genre subjects, with a predilection for humor and a racy, sharply defined and frequently ingenious vocabulary. In his more daring moods he ventured into many avenues of experiment linked with the contemporary approaches of the advance guard to modern painting, music and stagecraft. On him fell the burden of carrying the company through its most perilous years, and his clear head and excellent craftsmanship served Diaghileff valiantly. It is nevertheless true that only in recent years, since he has served himself rather than any other master, has he begun to find himself as an intrinsically important choreographer.

Nijinska's accomplishments were by far the most impressive of the period, partly, to be sure, because of her exceptional gifts and her wealth of experience, but also partly because of her essential independence of Diaghileff. In "Les Noces" to Stravinsky's music, she persuaded both him and the composer against their will to allow her to produce a masterpiece, coming closer to the tectonic integrity of the dance in the true spirit of modernism than anything else had done since her brother's "Sacre du Printemps." It is, indeed, one of the great works of the repertory. Even her far less vital ballets inspired by the decadent spirit of the postwar period, such as "Les Biches," manifested a fine and authentic individuality of style and a gift for genuine inventiveness against the background of the ever present academic vocabulary. Though her repertoire as a whole has perhaps been uneven, she is easily the most significant of all the post-Fokine Russians, and the one who has come closest to sensing the basis of the new classicism that must sooner or later constitute the ballet's modern epoch.

Balanchine was an out-and-out experimentalist, able to play brilliantly with surfaces and to achieve endlessly novel effects against a background of fine musicianship and substantial technical craftsmanship.

With the death of Diaghileff and that of Anna Pavlova, which followed shortly, the Russian Ballet came definitely to the end of its cycle of establishment, though certainly not to the end of its sphere of influence. Its principles were familiar more or less all over the world, and for this not Diaghileff but Pavlova was mainly responsible. If she led the art of the ballet forward in no aesthetic sense, her contribution was perhaps even more important in that she served as a counterbalance to Diaghileff. His activities narrowed the field of interest more and more to a cult of balletomanes, generally fanatical, frequently neurotic, while she toured the world with her company year after year, nosing into out-of-the-way communities where there was no aestheticism whatever and little sophistication, and extending the range of an aristocratic art over a broader and more democratic field than it had ever before dreamed of invading. That this tended to lower her standards of artistic perfection, at least in practice, cannot be denied, but the trail she blazed economically is one which the ballet must follow today if it is to exist financially.

Artistically Pavlova was perhaps nearer to the ballet of Taglioni than to that of Fokine, though she was his devoted advocate and in the fullness and integrity of her emotional line deeply indebted to him. Her greatest distinction, however, lay in the exquisite perfection of her intuitive style, through which the academic code was illumined and glorified, maintaining its essential classic purity but kindled by the inner warmth of romanticism.

The Contemporary Field

IN its present period the ballet has entered upon a phase of decentralization that should mean new life and health for it. If most of its activities are directly influenced by its great Russian epoch now past, there is a strong consciousness of national environment in many of its newer manifestations that can scarcely fail to enrich and invigorate it.

In the direct line from Diaghileff, two companies of increasingly international personnel (for all that the non-Russian members are equipped practically automatically with Russian noms du théâtre) divide the world territory between them under Russian direction. At the head of first one and then the other of them, Massine has been phenomenally productive, and though not all that he has done has been by any means of unequivocal excellence, he has nevertheless reached his top form as a choreographer. In his turning for inspiration to the symphonies, from Beethoven to Shostakovich, he has oddly enough come nearer to a genuine modernism than in all his years of experimenting with up-to-the-minute insurgencies. Though there is, to be sure, little reason for grafting a gratuitous visual program upon these purely musical works, a mirroring of their forms has at least served to give some shape to the ballet. If this is only a reflected shape, and not the substance of the ballet's true body, it nevertheless takes it one large step away from stylized representationalism and within hailing distance of abstraction. It is perhaps pertinent to remember that before the expressional dance found its basis for autonomous form, Isadora Duncan turned to this same source for inspiration and support.

The symphonic ballets are not even in quality; sometimes they are mathematically thought out and complex, frequently they contain long passages that seem to be nothing more than marking time until the music has finished, sometimes they are equipped with programs that tend to nullify their very virtue of abstraction. On the whole, however, they may be taken as an indication of a transition to a more fundamental structural approach, which, if it materializes, will be of the utmost importance. "Choreartium," set to the Fourth symphony of Brahms, is perhaps the most clean-cut, compact and formally successful of the series.

Ironically enough, Massine's finest work by a wide margin charts no new courses. It is "Nobilissima Visione" (retitled "Saint Francis" for America, presumably in consideration of the national illiteracy), which is a deeply serious chronicle of the life of the saint of Assisi couched in highly stylized medieval movement. With a magnificent score by Paul Hindemith and fine settings and costumes by Pavel Tchelitchev, it is one of the few great ballets in the contemporary repertoire.

The dangers that exist for these companies that tour for all but a few weeks in the year, playing daily and sometimes twice daily, are ominous. With no resources for the development of artists, such as the old Imperial Ballet had, no leisure even for self-development for those dancers who might choose to study something besides technic, no opportunity to gain perspective on one's own performances or to grow in the subtler perceptions of a role, little time, indeed, even for adequate rehearsal, the picture is a dark one. A new work of any depth and style, however brilliantly alive at its première, is almost certain to return at the end of the season bedraggled and mechanical, with other new works treading on its heels. This is the major peril that faces an art cradled in court subsidy when it is forced to adapt itself to the exigencies of commercial survival.

In Paris, Serge Lifar, the last of Diaghileff's protégés, has brought the ballet at the Opéra to a stronger position than it has occupied there for many years. In this conservative stronghold he has issued a manifesto that contributes substantially to the theory of the modern ballet, yet unborn. In it he demands that the dance be the center and controlling force in the ballet, that music and décor be subsidiary to choreography and subject to the choreographer's will. In his ballet, "Icare," he has even gone so far as to reduce the music to the status of the German modernist's percussion accompaniment.

The logic of this argument is irrefutable as far as it goes, if the ballet is ever to find its own structural basis for composition; and the nonballet division of the dance has already demonstrated its practical truth. But Lifar's creed contains at least one notable omission that destroys the validity of the theory as a road to that abstraction without which the ballet can never be free; he makes no mention at all of representationalism and the domination of the dance by the patterns of dramatic sequence. For this reason, if for no other, his heresy has failed to justify itself in practice. It is significant, however, that he has been able to go even as far as he has gone, and there is a kind of magnificent justice in the fact that the ballet has made its most potent gesture against music in the very institution where Lully united the two arts with bonds of steel.

In Russia the ballet has gone its way as if there had never been any Fokine or any Diaghileff, for in this instance, once again, prophets were without honor nowhere but in their own country. On the surface, even the Revolution wrought little change in the ballet's course, besides the temporary interruption of its activities and the introduction of new revolutionary subject matter. The theaters and schools of the old regime passed over into the control of the new and the academic tradition went with them. Even much of the repertoire dating from the mid-nineteenth century survives, and perhaps more fully than anywhere else in the world. Technically, however, the dancing has attained extraordinary acrobatic brilliance and has willingly sacrificed something of its finesse to meet the needs of a tremendous new audience drawn from every walk of life. Deep and fundamental changes are undoubtedly brewing beneath the surface and the future is charged with interest accordingly.

In England an unofficial but nonetheless national ballet is well on the road to being. In its beginnings a decade ago, it was compounded of a long-standing love for the Russian Ballet, many of whose important figures have settled in London; a good deal of the set tradition of the adored Cecchetti, which would have an obvious appeal for the English respect for authority; and a remnant of the old Diaghileffian advance-guardism, all carefully assimilated, analyzed, reduced to a system, in the typical English manner. Its most important development, and one from which much may be expected as time goes on, was the establishment in 1931 of the Vic-Wells Ballet and school, thanks to the initiative of the Dublin-born dancer-choreographer, Ninette de Valois, and the far-seeing courage of the late Lilian Baylis, manager of the Old Vic and the Sadler's Wells Theaters.

The clear-sighted and capable Miss de Valois, already the dean of British choreographers, is its director, and associated with her is Frederick Ashton, a marked contrast to her in every respect but that of competence.

The picture in America is not nearly so bright. The futility of hoping for any such establishment as the Vic-Wells in New York is made clear by a glance at the record of the Metropolitan Opera House, the logical home for such an enterprise. Besides bringing Pavlova and Mordkin to this country for several seasons beginning in 1910, and sponsoring two financially calamitous tours of the Diaghileff company during the war, it presented a total of eighty-four performances given over to the ballet during the entire twenty-seven years of Gatti-Casazza's directorship, and forty-two of these were of "Coq d'Or" in its half-ballet and half-opera form after the model of Fokine's original. During the first three years of Edward Johnson's directorship, the story, if not much happier, was at least quite different, for George Balanchine and his American Ballet were installed and fairly active. This was a clear case of cross-purposes, however, for the blood of La Scala in 1890 coursed through the veins of the Metropolitan, and by contrast there appeared to be no blood at all in the anemic aesthetics of Balanchine. The next season saw a return to the status quo ante Balanchine, which seems likely to prevail.

Some of the other opera companies—notably Chicago's where Ruth Page and later Catherine Littlefield have produced new works each year—have much better records, but their seasons are too short to make for any kind of establishment. Accordingly, the ballet in America depends upon itinerancy and private financing. Miss Littlefield and her Philadelphia Ballet and Lincoln Kirstein's Ballet Caravan are the only organizations now operating on anything like a nationwide basis.

With a background markedly less propitious than even England's the American ballet has thus far made little actual headway, though it is certainly not without its accomplishments. It has produced a number of promising young dancers, some of whom have changed their names and cast their lot with the traveling Russians. In the matter of choreographers it has been less successful, having so far brought to light only one genuinely distinguished talent. This is Eugene Loring of the Ballet Caravan, who, though he has actually turned out very few ballets, is unmistakably an artist of independent mind and creative ability. A comparison of his work in its present stage with that of practically any of the accepted choreographers of the day at a similar point in their development, gives him both added stature and increased importance for the future. At present he has shown no interest in formalism or pure abstraction, but has worked from a dramatic basis in terms of a highly adapted representationalism, in which a keen feeling for character, visual effectiveness and theatrical vitality in the best sense have combined to produce a continually fresh and pungent idiom.

The Ideal of Ballet Aesthetics

THE most advanced word that has yet been spoken with regard to the still unrealized modern ballet is contained perhaps in Lifar's "Choreographer's Manifesto." Though it is incomplete, it at least has had the courage to attack the problem boldly. As the modern dance of the non-ballet type has done before it, the ballet must inevitably cast aside, at least for a period of self-discovery, all its accumulation of "aids"—music, décor, drama—and concentrate on its own nature and essential medium. This medium is obviously the academic code of abstract movement, which it has built up over the centuries and from which throughout its history it has never totally separated itself. It is this that needs to be examined from a fresh perspective as something besides traditional mumbo-jumbo, for here, indeed, lies the root of the ballet's aesthetics.

Unless it is willing to discard this code entirely, it must necessarily find its fullest powers in the character of a classic art instead of dallying with romanticism. The classic approach alone allows for an objective vocabulary and an objective mode of procedure, and the academic code itself is incapable of being expressive of human emotion or even imitative of nature. Both ecstasy and mimesis are ruled out of its principle and its historic practice. In its beginnings it was evolved quite coldly, albeit from living sources, by experts who were seeking elegance of carriage, graciousness of gesture, and a general refining of movement away from crude, everyday utilitarianism, for the achievement of an idealized deportment. Ecstasy is patently out of place in such a program, and mimicry focuses on the realistic instead of on the ideal. Such was the basis of the court dance, and even when dramatic action of sorts was introduced into it, impersonation was symbolic rather than realistic, and pantomime was removed as far from nature as possible, taking at most only the outline of nature's gestures and giving them shapely and balanced contours until they became decorative even if unintelligible. Because of the essentially realistic character of pantomime, which makes it resistant to the abstractions of design, it was separated necessarily from the formal element of dancing and confined to sections of its own like recitative between the arias of an opera.

Throughout the development of this system of idealized movement, especially after the ballet was professionalized, its range has been increased by the gymnastic skill of individual executants, by discoveries of new means for enlarging or refining its spectacular appeal, by practical necessities of the stage, but never by the infusion of natural gesture. Its codification has been intellectual and based on geometrical-aesthetic principles, disregarding the nature of the body's movements in life and compelling it to conform to the desired scheme of practice by extending itself or even at times violating itself. It is thus purely an artificial system, in the literal meaning of the word, designed for aesthetic results alone.

Every effort to introduce realistic life impulses (and there have been many) tends to destroy its classic purpose and to nullify its abstract effectiveness. The system itself has always resisted these inroads and at the first opportunity has reasserted itself to the discomfiture of its reformers. The greatest of these, Michel Fokine, understood that to accomplish his richly conceived romantic ends, he must take drastic steps to subdue this traditional force, and we find him urging the dancer to leave the academic vocabulary in the classroom and follow nature. In the creation of his magnificent theatrical synthesis he took the ballet, indeed, as far away from classicism as it can go without ceasing to be ballet altogether. The next step would necessarily have been to leave the academic vocabulary out of the classroom as well and turn directly to subjective movement. (To be sure, in his "Les Sylphides" he also took the ballet nearer to pure classicism than it had been for many years, as if to indicate that his major interest in going the other way was prompted by conviction and not by an inadequate grasp of traditional principles.)

In this direction of synthesis, Fokine has brought the ballet to the ultimate goal that was sought first in the Renaissance, and it would seem that there is nothing more to be added. At the opposite end of its scale, however, it finds itself capable of being not just one element in a synthesis (albeit the dominant one), but self-sufficient dance. In the logic of the aesthetic scheme un-

derlying the academic code it has inherent autonomous potentialities; it is not merely a means for doing something else—for
training the body or for interpreting music or for enacting a
drama—but an end in itself. As André Levinson, its most able
modern aestheticist, said of it, "the technique is no supplementary reinforcement to [the dancer's] art . . . it is the dance itself." Its substance, the basis of its classicism, is its technical
material, or more accurately, its technical approach and the theory inherent in its academic code.

It is not thus restricted by any means to "school figures," to
jetés and brisés, entrechats and cabrioles. These, indeed, are
quite meaningless in themselves; their only function is to illuminate the idealism that underlies them by manifesting its law
and logic. The average dancer, unhappily, rattles through them
as thoughtlessly as a child through its prayers, perhaps mainly
because in our day they and the system they stand for have been
nothing but a kind of language in which to express something
else. Yet the most elementary steps and the most hackneyed
combinations can be touched into life and beauty by the dancer
who relates them to their central scheme of aesthetics and makes
them simply the means for bringing it into visible action.

With a sense of the unity and the supreme consistency of this
central scheme, invention becomes easy and logical but no longer
a pressing necessity for its own sake. In the great poetry, the
great painting, the great drama of the world, the same simple
emotional relationships are invoked time after time, finding
fresh validity in every new circumstance; there is no necessity to
seek always for psychopathic variations in order to prevent the
old sorrows and angers and hatreds and loves from becoming
banal. Similarly if the principles of the ballet's aesthetics were
better understood and more intuitively sensed by its practitioners,

there would be less need for the constant searching out of outré attitudes and contortions for novelty's sake.

The vocabulary, however, is by no means set and closed, for all that its principle is absolute. The sharper dynamisms of to-day, the increased grasp of beauty in the mechanically functional line and force, the better understanding of the values to be found in dissonance, and the steadily growing gymnastic prowess of the dancer are capable of evolving a wealth of new vocabulary while still not only remaining within the classic principle but even strengthening and revivifying it.

The theory of this geometrical-aesthetic basis involves something quite apart from the arrangement of lines and masses in patterns of purely visual decoration, simply substituting arms and legs and torsos for so many sticks and globes. The body is incapable of translation thus into lifeless mechanics, but even at the height of its abstraction it remains always a living body. Here, indeed, is the very heart of the ballet's aesthetics, the source of its drive. It is a glorification of the person as person, the presentation of its ideal essence freed from the encumbrances of a rationalistic universe of cause and effect, a pragmatical universe of organic drive and utilitarian function. It exemplifies the personal achievement of abstraction, of transcendent self-containment. In its idealization of the body it strips away all necessity for practical accomplishment, turning certain of its conformations to uses more harmonious than the functional processes that have shaped them, and superseding where possible even structural elements which have been bred by utilitarian demands alone. Its idealization, like all other idealizations, struggles constantly to resist being drawn unwittingly into assent with the arguments of that realism which it is its whole purpose to supplant. It does not explore the body's possibilities for life movement, therefore, but concentrates on adapting it to the specialized system of movement that is established for it. In this, to be sure, it is not unique; all the classic dances of the East have long done this, with differences in result comparable to the differences in ideals, but with no difference in process.

This does not argue for either mechanical dehumanizing or stereotyped uniformity for all dancers. Indeed, if the true nature of the theory is understood, these common faults among dancers and misapprehensions among spectators cannot possibly come about. Even so astute and sensitive a critic as Levinson falls into the first trap. In his lively essay on "The Spirit of the Classic Dance," after arguing the necessity for the dancer's being trained along lines contrary to the habits of ordinary life, he writes: "You may ask whether I am suggesting that the dancer is a machine? But most certainly!—a machine for manufacturing beauty." This could be true only if it were possible to conceive of a machine as having a consciousness of its selfhood and a will to archetypal perfection. The precision and the abstraction in a machine's movements, in which there is no choice but to be precise and abstract, deny the essential vitality of the ballet, namely, the personal achievement of these ends. The machine's movement is merely motion; the ballet's movement is motion dictated by taste and selectivity.

As for regimentation, the employment of a common code of movement does not necessarily make all dancers alike any more than the employment of a common language makes all speakers alike. In the latter case there are differences in the quality and pitch of the voice, in the inflection, in the choice of words, which make it impossible for any two speakers to be identical in speech. In the use of the ballet code, the same kind of differences exist, some of them innate in the body and unconscious, and some deliberately and imaginatively assumed. The existence of a specific code actually heightens these differences, serving as a standard of reference against which individual variations are made doubly vivid. The process is automatic and involves a peril as well as an opportunity, for the routine practitioner, who has not the artistry to use the system to his own ends, will inevitably allow it to use him and to expose him in a mental nudity which is all the more revealing because he is unaware of it.

The greatest differentiation is naturally between the dance of men and that of women. Their employment of the same code of movement automatically accentuates their divergences and aids in the idealization of the essentially feminine and the essentially masculine. Again there is a peril involved, and here a more serious one for the health of the art as a whole. With the dancer who is not an artist and the spectator who does not consider that a limitation, it is easy for the glorification of sex to become immediate instead of ideal. At times in its history the ballet has been forced by the insistence on pulchritude and coquetry out of the category of art and into that of polite pandering.

The accent on this element in the last century, with the critical writings of Théophile Gautier as a high example, produced a serious situation for the male dancer, who was jeopardized not only in prestige but also in the maintenance of the virility of his art. The approach to the academic code itself was made predominantly feminine, and even today with men and women taught in the same classes where the women are vastly superior in numbers, there is likely to be a feminine color to the proceedings. This puts upon the classic male dancer the stern necessity of alertness to dominate the system and use it to his own ends instead of unwittingly letting the softness and the curves of his colleagues' technic use him.

The system, indeed, is not inherently feminine in any way, but totally impersonal, an abstraction against which to emphasize the idealized male as well as the idealized female. It reaches its

height in this direction in the classical pas de deux, which is in
a way the epitome of the ballet. In it we are shown first the static
qualities, so to speak, of the medium and of the dancers in relation to each other—balance and line, the strength and stability of
the masculine and the lightness and delicacy of the feminine, not
in terms of free mobility but sustained and supported. Then follows a section for each dancer in which the idealized masculine
and feminine are seen separately in full and free range. The
coda, continuing the aspect of free and unsupported movement,
climaxes the sequence with a passage of brilliant interplay between the sexes. (How seldom do we see a pas de deux danced
with any such realization of its potentialities! It is generally reduced to a kind of contest in which the partners vie with each
other for the approval of the spectators.)

Just as the masculine and feminine qualities add their especial
flavors to a common code of movement, so individual personal
qualities can be made to illuminate it. This potentiality can be extended actually into the territory of impersonation and dramatic
action. Such a divagation might be forever unnecessary for
dancers whose greatness of spirit, depth of penetration and personal grasp of style were so rich and imaginative that they
could give us ever new and engrossing glimpses of themselves
in idealization, but such genius is scarcely to be expected in any
large numbers, and the perfect classic dancer is perhaps the
rarest of all creatures. It becomes essential, therefore, to broaden
the scope of the ballet by giving the dancer synthetic increases
in personal range. As his natural character affects his manner of
exemplifying the standard code, so an assumed character can
also be made to do. Thus the ballerina says, in effect: "If I were
a gypsy or a peasant maid, a butterfly or an odalisque, this is the
particular flavor my arabesques and my pirouettes would take
on." She is not pretending to be the peasant maid or the

odalisque, nor is she costumed with any realism that might deceive us into thinking she is; she is only showing how such a personality might utilize the established principles of the academic code to project its own idealism and how these principles would react to such use. The personality and individuality of the ballerina herself are thus by no means submerged in such an assumed role, but are actually enhanced by it.

Dramatic situations provide similar occasions, and their selection by scenarist and choreographer, if the true quality of the classic academic ballet is to be maintained, will be dictated not by verisimilitude or psychology or dramaturgy, but by their ability to produce illuminating results upon and by means of the basic code of movement. Emotional situations are not meant to be truly touching or felt sympathetically in any degree, but are designed to be understood and admired in terms of their sensitive and subtle variations on the classic theme of idealized abstraction. Credibility is not an end to be sought, but rather an enemy to be combated, for if it arouses sympathetic response, it only blinds the eye to the dancer's purpose and true art. Logic, the self-contained and impeccable logic of the system, is of supreme importance, but credibility on an emotional or realistic level is a drug to deaden the kind of appreciation that is needed. The ballet, indeed, is neither the actor's medium nor the storyteller's.

Certainly it is not the painter's medium or the musician's, either. It is not a spatial art in the sense of being concerned with the dancer's relation to his environment; it is a timeless and placeless idealization of him and of him alone, against a background of infinity, if you will. Since he must dance upon a stage, there must be décor of some sort, but its proper function is to minimize itself completely and concentrate on maximizing the dancer. As for costume, he is assuredly no couturier's mannequin; his apparel must exhibit him, not he the apparel. There can be no equality of collaboration here; the dancer is king or bondsman.

The situation is much the same where the musician is concerned, for as the décor is the spatial setting of the dance, so the music is the temporal setting, and nothing more. It is as inappropriate to ask a choreographer to create a dance to fit a ready-made score as it would be to ask a dramatist to write a play to fit a series of ready-made settings and costumes. It is not the dancer's business to exhibit the music, but the musician's to exhibit the dancer. Again, there can be no equality; the dancer is either supreme or subordinate.

Theory of Technic

WITHOUT some sensing of these matters, the technic of the academic ballet inevitably becomes nothing more than a collection of arbitrary and lifeless acrobatics, and as such it is frequently taught and even more frequently practiced. When its underlying aesthetic intent is apprehended, however, it falls into an easy and vivacious order. If idealistic abstraction is its soul, its body may be said to be dynamic equilibrium. The dancer becomes a sensuous and sentient object maintaining balance against all hazards, inviting and even extending these hazards far beyond the margin of safety and meeting them effortlessly in evidence of a dominion over the inertias and circumscriptions of realism. Heaviness, effort, the overdramatization of difficulties conquered, are essentially vulgar and mark the parvenu in this glorified company.

Verticality is the keynote of the entire procedure, both theoretically and practically. The mechanics of the situation demand a strong vertical axis upon which to erect a postural norm. Both for facility and for effectiveness this axis must be as narrow and as concentrated as possible, in order to bring into immediate range that field of instability which provides the dancer with his challenge and his victory. Thus the position that may be considered as the postural norm is that in which the dancer stands in readiness for the majority of his exercises; his body is erect, turned out at the hips, his feet together so that the heel of each touches the great-toe joint of the other; his legs make one solid column with no space visible between them at any point; his arms curve downwards close in front of him with the fingers all but completing their circle. This is the narrowest stable base that he can maintain, and from it he is able to move in any direction at a moment's notice. Thus we see the turning out of the hip, introduced in the seventeenth century for the attainment of a broader front, serves also to produce a narrowing of base, bringing the vertical axis of the body straight to the floor through the joined arches of the feet instead of allowing it to divide into two lines as it would do if the feet were side by side.

Upon this clearly established verticality, every conceivable variation is played. The arms, besides superimposing arcs of travel, set up a series of concentric planes with the shoulders as a horizontal axis. In conjunction with the legs, they define also those vertical planes which the body sets up about its upright axis; and especially do they effect the torsions in those planes, as when the horizontal of the shoulders is made to cross the horizontal of the hips. The warp that is thus produced replaces the flatness and monotony of the single plane with an accentuation of the body's tridimensionality and the subtleties that inhere in it. It is also a manifestation of that mechanical principle of opposition that underlies not only the ballet's technic but the action of the body in life, and for that matter, of any other object that is subject to gravity. This principle demands that as weight is shifted to one side of a central axis, there must be a compensatory shift to the opposite side if equilibrium is to be maintained. This principle the ballet dramatizes continually, as it maintains its basic verticality against extensions and counterextensions of every variety.

In the pursuit of its fundamental idealism, it habitually transmutes mechanical function thus into aesthetics. The support of the legs is dramatized in countless ways, by freeing one or both of them for the creation of independent designs—crossing and recrossing in the air, describing arcs and circles, approaching the horizontal line of flight in various degrees—and restoring them to their supporting function always at the proper moment, being careful to maintain suspense but never to threaten disaster. Soft knees and ankles remove the harshness of the instant when contact with the earth is restored after a venture into the air, and allow the body to retain its volatility by providing a gently rebounding force from below to meet its gradually settling weight while it is still in descent.

The arms, whose practical necessities are smaller, indulge freely in design, sometimes emphasizing the contours of a large and general movement, sometimes creating a deliberate counterpoint. About the central straightness and vigor of the body, they set in motion circular forces, soft, effortless, elegantly controlled. It is here that the aristocracy of the ballet reveals itself—on those rare occasions when, indeed, it is present.

The parvenu in this ethereal world will expose himself most likely in the use of the torso. Mistaking its upright carriage for rigidity, he will allow it to become a heavy and solid mass carried about with no little effort by the legs. He will forget that the vertical axis of the body is slender and ideally no more a tangible thing than the axis of the earth. Likewise, he will take it for granted that his arms begin at the shoulders, instead of realizing that their point of origin is a common center at the central axis, where they are seen to form one continuous and integrated element, alive from fingertips to fingertips, instead of two rather superfluous appendages whose uselessness is obvious except in a world of eating and drinking and practical accomplishment.

The easy erectness of the trunk and the set of the head above it not only lend a nobility of style, but help to point that play between the shoulder line and the hip line which produces the opposition of planes. The direction of the line of vision is an important element in establishing the scope and the intention of a movement, and this brings the head again into a strategic position. With the sensitive dancer the face will also make a positive contribution, changing subtly and in perfect collaboration with the shifting aspects of the body, though without regard for psychological states of emotion or what is sometimes called expression. Certainly it will not reveal the effort or the physical strain that a mere human undergoes in creating this exalted abstraction of himself, but neither will it wear the hideous mask of a fixed smile.

The actual vocabulary of movement is elaborated from a simple set of five fundamental positions of the feet. These, executed with the hips turned out, place the feet first heel to heel in a straight line, then in the same straight line with a foot's length between them, then with one heel touching the arch of the other foot, and again in the same relationship but with one a foot's length in front of the other, and finally with heel to toe. In practice these are subject to alteration and variation in much the same way that vowel sounds are altered and varied in speech from their cardinal purity. There are five corresponding positions of the arms, others for the head and the hands, and eight directions of the body. Upon these foundations seven types of movement are executed—bending, stretching, rising, jumping, gliding, darting and turning. The five poses called arabesques, in which the line of the horizontal dominates, are largely, though not exclusively, used as climactic attitudes in which to finish sequences of movement. Another pose of similar function answers to the name of attitude, and is an adaptation of Bologna's famous statue of Mercury which Carlo Blasis introduced into the ballet in the early nineteenth century. From these comparatively few elements, an inexhaustible repertoire of combinations is to be achieved, and when the ballerina rises upon the points of her toes, she adds a new dimension which virtually doubles her range.

Such an art obviously makes large demands upon the spectator; it is an art, indeed, for the connoisseur. He must not only be aware of the aesthetic basis of idealized abstraction and be sympathetic to it, but he must also have at least a passing knowledge of the technic and vocabulary if he is really to appreciate its full values. As a result, the strictly classic ballet has had a consistently small audience throughout its life; that is its penalty for being classic. The impulse of contemporary modernism, with its seeking for basic materials and their autonomous formal tendencies, may or may not be capable of winning a wider appeal because of the essentially unifying effect of its processes, but whatever its effect in this direction, it opens a new world to the classic-academic ballet in so far as its individual integrity is concerned. This involves no restoration to some high estate from which it has fallen, but the attainment of a perfection that it has never before enjoyed. Its technic is incomparably more brilliant than it has ever been in the past, and there is now possible for the first time a perspective in which its basic drive stands out clearly and can be seen as permeating all its materials. As it has been progressively humanized, romanticized, democratized, it has won the world's favor, but at the cost of its classicism.

Whether this is desirable and in line with social tendencies is beside the question.

Most of the artists who are working in it are conceivably too close to it and to its immediate tradition to realize its possibilities along fresh lines. There is a trend at the moment, it is true, to return to classicism, but this takes the form in the main of a return to the nineteenth century, to the romantic period, in fact— which now passes current for classicism! It is apparently the habit of artists in general, when they sense that the latest great cycle of their art has spent itself, to attempt to go back to the great cycle immediately before that and take up the course from there. Classicism, however, is not to be found there. Blasis, the greatest theorist of the time, argues as a matter of course for synthesis, for music and drama. The course, indeed, must be picked up farther back than that, in no especial period but on the level of fundamental principles.

Perhaps we must look for new values to be discovered not in the line of the established companies at all, with the traditions of La Scala and the Maryinski, of Fokine and Diaghileff, ingrained in them consciously or unconsciously. It is not unlikely that the last word has been said in that direction, at least for a time, and that in some new field (perhaps America, though there are no signs of it yet) a free choreographer may be able to sense the classic basis of the art in its modern application, skipping over the whole long development toward romanticism.

Certainly, whoever he may be, he will have to be a courageous rebel, for the mere mention of such an idea is likely to produce foamings at the mouth in orthodox circles. He will have to be strong enough to face accusations of destroying progress and of trying to turn back the tide. Just as the modern expressional dance in its return to basic principles of life movement for its procedure has been damned for its alleged effort to revive primitivism, so the modern ballet will meet a bombardment when it returns to the basic principles inherent in the academic code. Actually, however, there is never any retrogression in a return all the way to fundamental principles; only by such action is it possible to learn how to go forward on a solid foundation.

Chapter Eight

EXPRESSIONAL DANCE

❧❧❧

Isadora Duncan

IT is not until the advent of Isadora Duncan that the expressional dance comes into being as an art. At least this is so for modern times. It may well have had a cycle of existence among the ancients from the time when Arion ordered the Dionysian dithyramb until the greatness of the Greek arts was lost in rationalism, but of this we can have no definite knowledge. It was glimpsed more than once as an ideal in the ensuing centuries, and thus by indirection wrought many changes in the history of the ballet. Indeed, it has been the lodestar of romanticism in the dance, but its full realization occurred only when Isadora discovered the "soul" and related movement directly to human emotion. This was a profound overturning, clearing away ages of accumulation of intellectual restraints and yielding the power of motion to the "inner man," which is what Isadora meant by the soul.

It was not an isolated phenomenon, however, for, as we have seen, the more progressive minds of the day in virtually every department of activity were similarly concerned. If Isadora was able to isolate the element of expressional movement, as such an element as radium is isolated by a Curie, it was no accident, no violation of orderly processes; it was simply that she was a peculiarly sensitive channel for an idea whose time had come. The gathering forces of the modern renascence were upon us.

To appreciate the impact of her dance is impossible for a generation such as ours which has been so largely influenced by it as to take it more or less for granted. It is perhaps something of an aid, however, to try to see it as for the first time against the picture of the ballerina of the day. With jewels in her pompadour, a coquettish smile on her lips, her torso encased in whalebone, an aura of tulle ruffles about her thighs, her shapely legs encased in fleshings, and box-toed pink slippers upon her feet, she displayed her pretty acrobatics according to the set routine of a decadent art, whose real possibilities (limited at best, because classically circumscribed) had been all but forgotten. Into the world of this animated artifact came Isadora, jewelless, corsetless, unshod, the free lines of her body and its bare flesh visible beneath a simple Greek-styled tunic, her movements without virtuosity of any kind, concerned only with eloquence, springing from life instead of from a fixed convention, and proclaiming the fullness of emotional conviction, with an elevation of style that transmuted its personal truth into a kind of heroic universality.

If Isadora dallied a bit with Greece, in the belief that the creative spirit and function of the dance had been lost since Hellenic antiquity, she reverted in fact to something far anterior to it, namely, to basic man. Unlike the artists of the Renaissance, she was not concerned with reviving the forms and surfaces of Greek art, but in discovering the deeply rooted principles which these seemed to indicate. Beyond the adoption of the tunic as a costume, she made no literal borrowings whatever, and this was so clearly the practical solution of the problem of apparel that if the Greeks had not provided her with its pattern she would have had to invent it herself. As for her concept of beauty, it was considerably nearer to that of the Pre-Raphaelite Brotherhood than to the spirit of the Greeks. She had, indeed, no objective model for her procedure, but turned away from all imitation and adaptation, to the very nature of man, in the purest application of the theory of romanticism.

This nature of man in the only form in which she could know it was manifestly the nature of herself. With a concentration that was akin to that of the Orient, she sought here "the central spring of all movement, the crater of motor power, the unity from which all diversions of movement are born," for the ideal of the dance that she saw was "the divine expression of the human spirit through the medium of the body's movement." This center could manifestly be no material entity based on mechanical principles, but must be rather a focus of mental and emotional forces. Through its dynamic agency the stream of "spiritual expression" must be made "to flow into the channels of the body, filling it with vibrating light."

With the accomplishment of this miracle, she restored the dance to life. The body was no longer merely an instrument for the articulating of arms and legs in design and imitative gesture, but a totality of spontaneous expressiveness. In the development of movement thus from an inner source, it was her ideal to find for every dance key movements, as it were, from which other movements would flow of their own accord in fulfillment of the initial impulse. Here was the discovery of the motor phrase, and the realization of the power of movement to evolve its own forms. This idea, and the even more radical one that the dance could achieve its own form only by these means, were among the earliest of Isadora's convictions, and she gave them voice as far back as 1903 in a lecture in Berlin. It was not to be her lot, however, to carry them to their logical conclusion in the achievement of independent dance form, for the source of her greatest inspiration was also in this direction her greatest handicap.

This was music. Upon it she relied almost as a drug to stimulate her to action. Only when she heard the earth rhythms of "attraction and repulsion, resistance and yielding" as they pulsed through the measures of Bach and Beethoven and Wagner, was there kindled in her a sufficient identification of herself with the elemental forces of creation to touch the crater of her motor power into fire. She did not "interpret" the works of these composers in any sense; she made no effort to parallel in dance form the ideas and convictions that they had expressed, for none knew better than she that they had done their work supremely well and needed no assistance from her in making themselves clear. Neither did she take their accents and figurations as a pattern to be retraced by her in floor designs and aerial convolutions. They were simply the motive power by which she was led to "recover the natural cadences of human movements" which had been so long forgotten.

Indeed, the use of such music was so little a part of her plan and purpose that she pronounced it "an offense artistically" and inexcusable except as a measure of necessity. From it, however, besides its major purpose of stimulation, she was able to acquire by contagion two vital truths about dance movement: first, that its activity lay in a realm of abstraction as far removed from representationalism, yet with its roots as deep in reality, as the realm of music; second, that it existed not as a sequence of bits and pieces, but as a continuum modeled and contoured by organic logic.

Because it had such power over her, and she had so surrendered to it, she was never able to free herself completely from its domination, although she clearly saw that such freedom for the dance was desirable and perhaps ultimately inevitable. She even created phrases and whole dances without music, but as a rule she rested her compositions upon its structures and allowed them to be carried along by its progressions. The achievement of autonomous form was for others to compass.

Obviously in an approach such as hers there could be no such thing as a vocabulary of movements; the body was not acting so much as being acted upon by inner compulsions. It was not concerned, therefore, with mechanical accomplishments as ends in themselves, but moved freely within its natural dimensions. These dimensions, it is true, were heightened toward natural perfection as far as might be, and a gymnastic training to this end was practiced, so that the body might be responsive, vital, a transparency offering no obstacles whatever to the "sentiments and thoughts of the soul" which it was called upon to express. The building of muscle, however, and sheer gymnastic skills were matters for the physical educator; after that came the dance.

Certainly there was nothing in her philosophy or her art, however, that denied the body after the prurient custom of the time. On the contrary, it was to her a thing of beauty and eloquence, and in a day when one scarcely dared even to admit having such an evil and vulgar thing, she preached a glorification of nudity. What she advocated was not the unconscious nakedness of the savage who knew nothing else, but the deliberate nudity, proud and aware, of the man who had learned what a magnificent instrument his body was. That she did not dance nude was no contradiction of her theory, for to have done so would have limited her aesthetically even if it had been practicable in a world of propriety; but her costumes were always the minimum required for her purposes, and the sense of the body beneath them was never absent.

It was, in general, this taking of the attributes and functions of the natural man which he used unconsciously and translating them into conscious practice—that is, into creative practice—that constituted Isadora's great achievement. Her dance was basically the very rituals of tension and of release by which the natural man sought compensations for the unbalances of his environment, borne across the border from the purposes of personal recreation to those of communication. It was the beginning of a new era, the discovery of a new world, for the dance; for the first time in centuries it was equipped to take its place among the major creative arts, and indeed, because of the primal basicness of its materials, a place at the head of them all.

It was, however, the beginning of an era and not the completion of one. Isadora's dance was necessarily still closely related to the re-creational qualities from which it arose. This was its greatness, but also its peril. In her own practice, because of her unparalleled ability to command the spectator to re-experience sympathetically every move she made, it was altogether great. She was able to transmute into pure revelation the joys and tragedies of her personal life, and those of the world as they touched her into sentience, but this was through a consummate individual art that transcended theory, great though her theory was. Her reach exceeded her grasp; what she could do she could not explain. In those who have followed her in the direct line, therefore, there has been no repetition of her accomplishment. The peril lies in the temptation simply to be, rather than to reveal. It is easy for the dancer to listen to music and allow it to stir him; to be concerned with a personal experience, rather than with communication; to be self-interested, self-expressive, and ultimately no artist at all. It is perhaps even easier to forget all expressional connotations and try to make a spectacular vocabulary out of the totally unsuitable surface aspects of Isadora's movement, in which there is no spectacular quality to be found. The result is inevitably a meretricious simplicity, an arch prettiness.

Mary Wigman

IT is not until after the war that the expressional dance enters a new phase and finds itself labeled as "modern." Just as an earlier day prepared the ground for Isadora, with a return to fundamentals as its drive, now Mary Wigman was the product of a time when these newly revealed fundamentals were being whipped into form. "Without ecstasy," she has written, "there is no dance. Without form there is no dance." But with the economical, organic, functional attitude which modernism takes toward the subject of form, what was demanded for the dance was not merely something to contain its ecstasy, but something to embody it. The materials of which it was made, in other words, must be allowed to externalize its subjective concepts according to the laws inherent in their own natures.

Rudolf von Laban had already formulated an analytical approach to dance in which the body's relations to the space about it were exhaustively examined. It was seen that the structure of the various members and the resultant types, directions and extents of movement possible for them, set up as the immediate sphere of a dancer's movement an imaginary icosahedron, with its various lines and planes. These dimensions and directions, however, were not ends to be sought, in any way comparable to the prescriptions of the academic ballet, but constituted only a summing up of all possible spatial and directional possibilities. The dancer's movement was predicated entirely upon an inward will to move, which determined all the aspects of his motor performance.

For Wigman, however, such unexceptionable reasoning dramatized itself emotionally, and space assumed definite entity, almost as a tangible presence in every manifestation of movement. As man and his environment interact upon each other, shaping and altering each other's character and destiny, so movement and its environment, space, interact, and the resultant is dance. The dancer, therefore, is no longer an ego in a vacuum, so to speak, but an epitome of the individual in his universe. He is continuously engaging the forces within him with those forces which press upon him from without, sometimes yielding to them, sometimes opposing them, but ever aware of them, and finding his identity only in this dynamic process.

Now for the first time the creative dance was brought within the range of form, for it was able at last to create something with an existence of its own. Heretofore it had been at best simply an emanation from a person, as when Isadora by her irresistible power to awaken sympathetic experience was able to project an emotional concept directly into the minds of her audience. Now it assumed the dimensions of an objective work of art, for it had entered into the full-bodied world of relationships. Instead of being lyric—that is, consisting of a simple outpouring of feeling of whatever depth and intensity—it became dramatic, presenting the conflict between two forces.

As has already been pointed out, it is not the artist's purpose merely to work his audience up into a state of frenzy, but to arouse a sympathetic emotional state about a particular experience or set of circumstances, conveying to him thus a specific revelation that will not leave him where he was before, but will change his feeling toward some aspect of life. Emotion is not enough; it must be emotion in relation to something, and part of the artist's responsibility is to establish this something with sufficient clarity to give direction to his emotion. With Wigman's sense of space as a tangible symbol of universal forces, the dancer is supplied with something outside himself, which he may shape to his purposes, and toward which he may direct his emotional reactions so that even his most subjective experiences become visibly externalized.

Here we find the dance recapturing the essential element from which the theater grew in the days of the dithyramb, and which is the heart and soul of the theater at all times. In that Bacchic religion from which the dithyramb stemmed, the god himself, as Jane Harrison has said, is the projection of group emotion. Thus drama was born in that prehistoric moment when the mass emotion of a group of frenzied dancers became so powerful that it seemed to be a force outside themselves and was personalized under the name of Dionysos; he was a symbolized presence of their awareness of external forces toward which to direct their emotional outpourings, hitherto only a focusless discharge. What we are held by in a dramatic performance is not beautiful words beautifully spoken, not an actor's exhibition of his personal charms, his voice, his enunciation, his emotional gamut, his technical skill; it is the relationships that are created in action before us between the human being and the forces of life about him, and between human beings and human beings, under the influence of these forces. These constitute the substance that the true theater art creates, the thing that was not there before, its entity.

With Wigman, dance creates a similar entity, and touches for the first time in many centuries its common ground with theater. Isadora knew that her dance was not of the theater, but Wigman's has acquired an extra dimension which allows it to stand alone, so to speak, upon a stage. As must be evident, this did not come about through trying to force it into the patterns which the theater has taken in its generations of development away from the dance. Certainly it has nothing to do with that degeneration of the conception of the theater which makes it a place for spectacle and exhibition, a show business in far more than the colloquial sense of that phrase. In the nature of the dance itself, movement in relation to space, she touched quite as a matter of course the element in which the theater exists, man in relation to his universe.

To grasp the full meaning of Wigman's use of space, however, it is essential to remember that it is not confined to the area and cubic content of the stage on which she is working, but accepts these only as a kind of gateway through which to enter the symbolic sphere of space as universe. In just such a way the great actor uses his immediate environment of wood and canvas and paint as a channel through which to bring into experience his larger and more significant universe. This has been, beyond question, her greatest contribution to the discovery of the dance and its unfoldment, and it is so great a one, indeed, that all future development must ultimately accept it and build upon it, as she accepted and built upon the revelation of Isadora.

It by no means comprises her total achievement, however. The whole spirit of modernism compelled her to go farther than this. If she knew that the dance consisted of two elements, subjectively created movement and symbolically materialized space, it became immediately incumbent upon her to learn the nature and character of these materials in order that the inherent, self-determined forms of the dance might be realized.

In her approach to movement, the physical training of the body as such is a thorough one, based on a natural gymnastic that will produce not a vocabulary or a style of movement or a self-existent virtuosity, but a perfectly functioning instrument able to respond to the demands made upon it. To a great extent, these demands are themselves a part of the training, for it is fundamental to the Wigman theory that emotion is not put upon the outside of movements already evolved, but that the emotion actually evolves the movements. Thus there is as much stress laid upon emotional training as upon physical, and more, perhaps, upon the production of movement from subjective impulses than upon either element separately. The full possibilities of the body have been explored and a range of movement has resulted that is extraordinary both in its eloquence and in its freedom from stereotype. The emotional aspects of dynamics have been sensed so fully that the dancer works consciously in various keys of tension, and becomes deeply aware of both extremes of the scale and of the basis of rhythm that lies in their alternation. The study of space in its significant aspects is in large measure inseparable from these studies of movement, for the one cannot exist without the other.

In her treatment of music, Wigman has again been completely radical. With such a clear vision of the creative sources of the dance and of the medium in which it exists, it is not surprising to find the domination both of musical formalism and of its emotional suggestion completely destroyed. Her very first dance was, as a matter of interest, without music of any sort, and frequently since then she has omitted all sound from the accompaniment of some of her compositions and of particular sections of others. In her theory of this much misunderstood relationship, she has once more uncovered principles which can never be denied as such, however differently they may be applied in practice.

With a realization of the fact that the dancer's music is essentially his own song with the percussive accents of his bodily rhythms, she has evolved the ideal type of dance accompaniment. Her music, composed either along with the creation of her dance or after the dance has been completed, is of greatest simplicity and frequently has no independent musical validity whatever apart from the dance. It employs almost exclusively nonorchestral instruments, matching the quality of the dance's tone with melodies on unsophisticated flutes, gongs, drums. The employment at times of the inappropriate and unadaptable piano, which practical necessity makes apparently unavoidable for the dancer, is the only exception to her complete musical logic.

With Wigman the dance stands for the first time fully revealed in its own stature; it is not storytelling or pantomime or moving sculpture or design in space or acrobatic virtuosity or musical illustration, but dance alone, an autonomous art exemplifying fully the ideals of modernism in its attainment of abstraction and in its utilization of the resources of its materials efficiently and with authority. This brings it, however, to no state of finality, no crystallization, but only to a complete statement of its selfhood, to a revelation of the principles upon which it may enlarge its borders and deepen its awareness of itself. New vistas are continually opening up, demanding that new elements be considered and new principles evolved for them, but this necessitates no invalidation of the old ones which have proved themselves basic.

These principles are entirely impersonal and of universal application. That Wigman, their first advocate and exemplar, has applied them in a manner purely personal, colored both by national cultural influences and by her striking individuality as person and artist, does not imply that they are thus wedded to her style and point of view, but indicates on the contrary, that they are amenable to the subtlest variations of temperament and artistic manipulation.

In her own dances, Wigman has reflected the general philosophical tendency of the German mind; they are dances of introspection rather than of action, concerned with revealing inward states of being. Because of the intensity of her own passions, the states of being she has visualized have been by no means static or remote, but vital, vibrant, stirring. From the tenderest of lyrical moods she has jumped to extremes of grotesque and demonic obsessions and back again to the restraints and nobility of tragedy. The magnificent aliveness and eloquence of her body, her profundity of emotional penetration, and her ability to communicate her perceptions in the unintellectualized realm of experience make her dancing a thing of constant evocation, and mark her as certainly one of the greatest figures in the modern arts.

That there are superficial aspects of her performances that do not translate easily is necessarily true, for all art takes on the colors of its immediate environment, and the more sensitively it is conceived, the more in need of translation it becomes. Such things as these, however, have to do wholly with national taste and background and do not in the least affect the substance of her art itself.

The theories that underlie her dance could not have been determined in advance by sitting down and taking thought; they are too patently subjective and subjectively arrived at. Nevertheless, with that devotion to analyzing and ordering principles into a consistent philosophy which is so typical of the German mentality, they got themselves somehow objectified and integrated so as to be systematically teachable. The genius of Wigman, to be sure, cannot be thus pinned down, but the laws which are seen to function beneath the surface of her dance can be and have been, and in that orderly methodology and its results lies a basis of continuity such as no amount of personal genius can guarantee.

American Tendencies

THE modern development of the expressional dance in America presents a completely different picture. It has achieved no comparable maturity of method, partly because it is younger by nearly a decade, and partly because the characteristic tendencies of the national mind have led it in other directions. Wigman is too nearly contemporaneous with the American leaders to have influenced them in any tangible way, even if they had not been traveling divergent roads. Further than this, their own prime necessity, as they were well aware, was to resist all influences from without and to find for themselves the principles that underlay the dance.

Isadora had provided a general groundwork for all such independent investigations and experiments, but of her personal approach not one of these young American dancers had any firsthand knowledge, for Isadora, rejected by her own countrymen in her early struggles, had devoted herself almost exclusively to Europe. The influences that they found about them, and which they had actually known in practice, included the ballet, which was academic; Denishawn, which was eclectic; "stage dancing," which was meretricious; and the rhythmic and interpretative schools in Isadora's wake, which were given over largely to illustrating music and to self-expression. In none of these, obviously, was there to be found any help toward the creation of a dance that would satisfy the generally unformulated demands of modernism that were inwardly so urgent. There was nothing to do but to seek for an entirely new basis for procedure, and with characteristic individualism, each dancer betook himself into his own retreat and devoted himself to this pursuit.

Certainly in this period there was no collaboration; on the

contrary, every dancer was so determined to arrive at conclusions that would satisfy his own particular requirements that he diligently avoided the experiments of his colleagues lest he should see something to disturb his own line of progress. Yet with all this conscientious independence, it is interesting to note that a certain dominant unity of spirit emerged, in spite of many differences. In the direction of their efforts, in their emphases upon particular elements of the dance, in their technics and their treatment of materials, the results they produced in their search for a basis for a modern dance differed only in minor respects from each other, but departed with marked unanimity from the results produced by Wigman in her similar search. Those matters which had led her to her greatest discoveries, the objectification of space and the evolution of a functional music, they were inclined to pass by, leaving the situation much as Isadora had left it. Their concentration, on the other hand, was on things that did not enter at all into Wigman's scheme, as we shall see.

In this essential divergence it is possible to see the effects of different national environments, the contrasts between an old civilization and a new, between what is peculiarly German and what is peculiarly American. Wigman's dance is a dance of acquiescence; the American dance is one of affirmation. Her compositions, she has said, "are nothing more than a confession of life brought into symbolic form . . . an acceptance of, a saying 'yes' to, everything that is alive and that will yield life." In her performance, her passionate desire is "to become one with these dances, to disappear in them, to live them." Nothing could be farther from the attitude of the American dancer; he does not accept life, but undertakes to shape it to his own ends. He is not content with experiencing and revealing states of being, but insists on dealing in states of action. He starts with a state of being, so to speak, and works toward the achievement of another, the actual process of accomplishment being the subject of his concern. He is less interested in being than in becoming.

There are, to be sure, copious instances in which this is not true; any number of dances in the American repertoire have been merely projections of introspective states, but these are not characteristic of its best tendencies, for it is not equipped to cope with such material. When Wigman deals with states of being, she possesses, in her materializing of space, the means for directing her emotional force to an outward object. The American dancer, however, lacking this means, at best achieves a kind of representational imagery, and at worst falls into an inherently psychopathic kind of self-expression. He is not by nature healthily introspective; he looks not into himself but rather out from himself.

This being so, it is curious to find that his movements are markedly closer and more held in than Wigman's, who, for all her introspection, allows her movements to range widely about her. Again, it is her use of space that makes the difference, for when she sends a movement outward she is clearly aware of its goal. For the dancer whose space is not thus emotionally delimited, an outgoing movement goes off into nothing and is functionless. No more apt example can be found than those gestures of generic "yearning" and undefined "giving" which take the arms of the "interpretative" dancer upward or outward into the realms of pure sentimentality.

The shaping force behind the American dance, the thing that makes it a dynamic art instead of a pictorial or a meditative one, that determines its purposes, its use of materials, its forms, its powers—and its limitations as well—is the traditional American approach to living. In this scheme of things man himself is the center of the universe, the master of his environment, conscious of his power and of its basis in the law of his being. That "natural law" uncovered by the great thinkers of the Reformation which makes life, liberty and the pursuit of happiness unalienable rights, led to the settlement of the land in the first place, to the growth of its institutions, and to the creation of a national mind from which its culture stems. Though demagogues have cheapened the expression of its idealism and copybooks have made it meaningless with repetition, it exists as a potent presence nonetheless. It is the foundation on which solidarity is built among a people without racial unity or any of the other timeless inertias of association to bind them together. Because it is in a sense voluntary, it has nothing of that resignation to control by destiny that belongs to those inertias that are produced by the involuntary workings of evolution.

Certainly the impulse of a civilization that has cut its way through wildernesses, both physical and mental, to shape its environment according to its own concepts, must logically carry into its arts something of this same desire to change the world. Isadora recognized the impulse in herself, and along with her visions of love and death, she danced continually the theme of social revolution and justice, in a manner that could be called only by the fearsome name of propaganda.

The American dance is never without propaganda, to use that word in its true meaning, for it finds its whole being in the presentation of its perceptions of man in new manifestations of his inborn dominion, with as great a power of persuasion as it can possibly summon. The impulse behind it is fundamentally the same as that behind those rituals of primitive men by which they seek to bring their visions of desirable goals into actual being by pre-doing them as dance. Even when it departs from its larger concerns with action, its simple statements are declarations of man's supremacy. Negations do not exist, for they are translated into affirmations by satire or burlesque or even by passionate denunciation.

The dance, bent thus on making a point, has no time for sensuous dallyings and ornamentation; it abstracts its material to the most pungent essences and presents it sparsely and directly. Such a method is eminently in accord with the simplicity of the characteristic American background, the great puritan tradition with its functional philosophy, its devotion to essentials and its abhorrence of waste and indulgence. When it grows from genuinely creative sources, the dance in these terms is capable of achieving heroic stature. All these concentrations have extended its movement to an intensity and a degree of sheer physical power that give it breathtaking possibilities, and when they are utilized for the externalization of emotional conviction, the result is of incomparable eloquence.

Such concentrations, however, have not been without their dangers. If they have served in one direction to open up fields of magnificent accomplishment, they have served in another to impede progress. In pushing states of action to ever more vigorous ends, the states of being from which they arise have been more and more forgotten. The subjective aspect of the dance has been taken for granted, while the principal effort has been directed toward the development of a greater physical range and a more extended structure for composition. The subjective aspect, however, cannot be taken for granted in any degree without a corresponding loss of expressional power. When technics are allowed to grow up in their gymnastic capacity alone and their link to emotional experience is allowed to lapse, what results is nothing more than a vocabulary of gymnastic movements. These may be strikingly spectacular for exhibition purposes, but they have nothing to do with the dance as a communicative art. Thus it is not unusual to find stereotypes of movement as artificial as those of the academic ballet, but without its central logic, appearing over and over in a dancer's repertoire, totally lacking in evocative power because not created in association with subjective experience. This is the major peril to the American dance at the moment.

Motivated perhaps by this same conviction that the dance is an expression of dominant action, there is a deliberate avoidance of the lower end of the dynamic scale. This works a serious limitation upon the dancer's range, and results in a marked overuse of tensions.

There is no doubt that the accent upon action and tension and structure, though rooted in genuine conviction of a fundamental character, was increased out of due proportion in the early period of the modern dance by a rebellion against the excessive neglect of these matters that was so long prevalent. On every hand the so-called interpretative dancer abounded, having got nothing more from the epochal revolution of Isadora than a belief that bare feet and chiffon scarves, coupled with a little Schubert, made up the formula for the dance, simply because it produced in the dancer a feeling of "beauty." Even in Denishawn, a company of vastly superior caliber on the whole, such things went on, for all that they were endowed with a sturdy showmanship that insured their theatrical effectiveness. Aesthetic dancing held the field with the soft gracefulness of its "free plastique."

To look at it thus, however, from the viewpoint of what has developed since, is to do it considerably less than justice, for it made a distinct contribution to the dance as a whole, and without it there would have been no foundation at all to build upon. In it were kept alive the materials of the expressional dance, even though it did not quite know what to do with them. Because it touched the level of personal participation, America began to dance for the first time, for the dance was seen to be capable of something closer to common experience than the spectacular gyrations of "toe dancing." This spark of creativeness, together with the employment of the natural movement of the body as a technical medium, gave the dance a foothold in the field of education, and no other single development in its history to date has been of equal importance with this.

When the impulses of the modern spirit began to make themselves felt, a major schism inevitably came about, and those dancers who were animated by the necessity for new methods along functional lines were compelled to break away from the inertias of the aesthetic dance that opposed them. Not unnaturally these inertias assumed for them something of the proportions of the Seven Deadly Sins, and all procedure was dominated by the determination to resist and destroy them. Perhaps the very fact that there could be no clean-cut break, no instantaneous transition from one method well established to another ill defined, added firmness to the rebellion during its formative stages. Those factors that seemed to stand in the way of the dance's full realization of its basic materials and structural foundation became anathema; every suspicion of factitious grace or fanciness, every hint of emotion discharging itself for no other end than the pleasure of the discharge, was quashed almost before it appeared.

Habits thus formed have largely persisted, though all these problems have long since been solved. The first period of the modern expressional dance, indeed, has accomplished its purpose magnificently. The second period must necessarily concern itself less with structure and body and more with form and spirit, less with objective goals and more with subjective processes by which alone these goals can be attained. That this period has already begun is amply attested by the bulk of recent activity, but that it has not yet reached its zenith is equally obvious from the evidence.

It remains for this period to establish not alone the elements which comprise the dance, but the principles by which it operates. The American theme of action must now be applied to theory itself, for as yet the production of movement out of subjective experience is left to inspiration and accident. Movements accumulated from these fortuitous moments of illumination, together with others ready-created out of gymnastic technic, comprise a completely static collection of stuffs, and no amount of separately conceived animation poured into them can give them the semblance of life. It is the process itself by which movement is evolved out of experience that is dynamic, and movement evolved by this process is the only substance out of which the dance can be molded. Unless it is thus alive, it is incapable of creating its own forms, and must submit inertly to being arranged in patterns manufactured for the purpose. Until this cardinal principle is established, instead of being merely taken for granted, there is no basis of continuity for the American dance such as there is for the German, and each succeeding generation must start again from the beginning.

Tremendous progress has been made in taking the dance out of the category of a lyric art, which is essentially a recital art, and making it an art of the theater. As we have already seen, the keynote of such a transformation is the establishment of relationships—oppositions, concords, adjustments—within the frame of the dance itself.

The American dancer has achieved these necessary relationships chiefly by means of group composition, though such achievement is by no means the automatic result of the employment of a group. When, however, two or more dancers are aware of each other, not merely as obstacles to free movement in the area that is available, but as the personification of emotional, dynamic tensions interoperating, the frame of the dance assumes an entity just as the frame of the drama does when actors set up emotional relationships between themselves.

Wigman, having touched the matter at the source in a manner that the American dance has not done, is able accordingly to make even her solo dances of the stuff of the theater; for the American dancer a solo, no matter how intense or how vividly characterized, becomes perhaps dramatic but rarely theatrical in the best meaning of the word.

An extended type of group composition has also been evolved that belongs distinctly to the theater in its manner of construction and unfoldment. It is totally independent, however, of conventional theater forms, of storytelling and pantomime, as well as of pure spectacle. Musical precedent is also abandoned; it does not lean on the structure of a symphony or put separate dances together after the method of a suite. Its material is the abstract movement of the dance, and it builds its episodes entirely according to dance logic. These episodes are organically related, and though they are clearly defined individually, they are in general quite inseparable from the whole.

In this same direction, important experimentation is going on toward the creation of a functional type of stage setting, neither decorative nor representational in intent, but devoted to defining and accentuating aspects of space and of the movement within it.

Undoubtedly the restoration of the ballet to public consciousness in America by the tours of the Monte Carlo company that began in 1933, served as a stimulus to this tendency toward theater forms. The spectacular pattern of the ballet, however, with its synthesis of independent arts, served in no sense as a model. All the experiments in the expressional dance were, and are, along modern lines, bent toward the discovery of forms out of the inner necessities of the dance, and with no thought whatever of trying to fit the dance into already established theatrical molds.

In the matter of music the American dance is in a notably unhappy state. Though it has put aside the old practice of dancing to music created to be complete in itself, it has substituted a practice that is only slightly better. The current custom is to have music composed to fit the completed dance, color and content being taken into consideration as well as rhythmic patterns, but in the great majority of instances this does not solve the problem at all. Music thus composed is more than likely to be not dance music, but still essentially independent music merely hampered by the limitations now put upon it by the dance.

Truly functional music for the dance, as we have already seen, demands a turning back of musical progress to a degree that the average musician would find intolerable, and in most cases, impossible. Its full mission, however, is to serve as a projection of the dancer's voice and rhythmic pulse; its purely musical requirements are nil and the farther it is removed from the independently developed mechanisms of musical structure and orchestral instruments, the more completely it will fulfill its function. There is a grave dissatisfaction with the musical situation among the dancers themselves, but few of them have gone into the matter deeply enough to see its solution.

From all this it is evident that if the American dance and the German were to combine their strength they would move the history of the art forward by at least a generation. Such a result, however, cannot be accomplished by the simple method of amalgamation. In so deeply subjective an art, progress must come through individual unfoldment rather than through objective assimilation. Of its three greatest needs, the American dance has in its own theory the basis for the supplying of one, that is, the creation of movement directly out of experience without resort to vocabulary, for that was Isadora's way. Its solution of the musical problem must come through courageous experimentation, and since it is already recognized as a problem, it is perhaps half met. When it finally discovers the principle behind Wigman's space relationship, it will no doubt be through some channel so entirely its own that there will be no superficial likeness at all between the two results. It is often said that the best way to learn anything is the hard way, and in a field so pragmatical as this, that is perhaps the only way.

Ruth St. Denis

Such a generalization as the foregoing must automatically imply a horde of exceptions. Indeed, an examination of the work and theory of every individual artist will reveal perhaps as many points of variance from it as of agreement with it. Yet since the American dance is not dominated by a single colossal figure as the German dance is, some contradictions must inevitably arise in any estimate of it as a unified expression. A unity of sorts it definitely possesses, however, with its roots in the great tradition of Isadora.

But Isadora was not immediate. When those dancers who are now the leading exemplars of the modern movement were at the beginning of their careers, she was as remote as Newton's laws of motion. What was immediate was Denishawn, built largely by Ted Shawn on the basis of Ruth St. Denis's significant art, the first great American dance company and nurturer of what was best in the native field. If the modern dance in its chief manifestations arose ultimately as a rebellion against its tenets and practices, these very tenets and practices nevertheless gave it the sustenance and support that allowed it to mature.

Their influences upon its evolution were positive as well as negative.

Ruth St. Denis, like Isadora Duncan, came into the dance at a time when it was at its nadir creatively, and, like Duncan, lifted it to new heights. Because her nature was the antithesis of Isadora's, her art was also antithetical. Yet as a product of the same forces in human thinking, it, too, was primarily concerned with getting away from merely sensuous surfaces and personal exhibition to underlying realities. Duncan sought these by yielding herself without reservation to the forces of nature within her, St. Denis by denying these forces for the achievement of a transcendental sense of the universe. Both trace their lineage back to the primitive dance of re-creation; Duncan's to that Dionysian outpouring of emotion which itself becomes the god, St. Denis's to the Olympian evocation of his presence by ritual and symbol. The former is purely ecstatic, the latter rather religious.

The East was the inevitable source of material for St. Denis, but her dances were not simply Oriental dances, as she was eager that people should understand. They were the medium for a spiritual idealism that found itself in closest kinship with the mysticism of the East but was entirely free from any specific commitments to it. In its deities and their symbolisms she found an objective basis for the presentation of her own concepts. If she put them to more serious philosophical and creative purposes than nineteenth century romanticism had put its sylphides and ondines, they were just as definitely made to serve as instrumentalities for entrance into a spirit world.

It is true that St. Denis reveled in the spectacular opportunities afforded by her choice of material, that she worked naturally in terms of characterization and representationalism, that she always managed to make even her most consecrated moments thoroughly effective from an audience standpoint; she was a natural child of the theater, colored both by the perceptive truths of Delsarte and the fustian of Belasco, able to dramatize her own experience, and almost to receive her most profoundly sincere and deeply rooted inspirations ready-framed by a proscenium arch. Yet with all this, she was not merely a spectacular dancer; the entire force of her electrical personality and all her dramatic instincts were directed to the achievement not of astonishment and sensation but of evocation. This was a new idea for theater dancing and an immeasurably valuable one. Movement became symbolic of something instead of being content with virtuosity.

It is safe to say that this whole Oriental cycle was compounded of a religious-aesthetic impulse so strong as to be almost an obsession, a wealth of dramatic instinct, and a great natural gift for dancing; it was, in other words, sheer inspiration brought to realization by its own force through channels that happened to present themselves. Certainly there was no technical approach to them; indeed, after more than thirty years of professional dancing, St. Denis has still evolved nothing in the form of a technical method. It was not the means that were important but the end. In the contemporary ballet it was personal charm and acrobatic prowess, not what one did with them, that mattered; with Loie Fuller it was the effect of light on moving drapery; but with St. Denis everything was bent to the expression of an idea. Only Isadora before her had ventured upon such untried ground, and she in a vastly different manner and quite outside the purlieus of the theater.

Of all this there was obviously little to teach, especially since St. Denis was well aware that she was an instinctive creator and not an analyst or an educator; but there was much to impart, and she has proved herself to be not only a personal revolutionary in the dance, but also one of the great inspirers in its history.

The Oriental cycle constitutes her chief contribution, less for its self-contained beauties than for the expressional emphasis that evolved out of its compelling idealism. It was not, however, her only major contribution. Out of her growing dissatisfaction with the futility of trying to pass on to pupils indiscriminately the substance of her Eastern dances as a kind of routine repertoire and an objective technic, there developed in her mind the concept of another type of dance that would be less wrapped up in her personal vision and consequently more adaptable as a general form. This concept owed its origin frankly to Isadora's use of great music, though it differed radically from Isadora's manner of using it. In St. Denis's plan, the music was not to be merely the awakener of motor impulses, but was to be "visualized," both according to its emotional content and after the specific patterns of its notes and phrases.

As a fundamental artistic method, there is nothing at all to be said in favor of such an idea, but as a transitional step in the growth of an art, it was of definite value. For the first time form began to appear as a possibility, apart from both the mechanical arrangement of spectacular elements in an effective routine and the mere reliance upon the natural sequence of storytelling. Though here it relied wholly upon the structure of music, from this it acquired, if only by contagion, a sense of emotional logic as a controlling element in form. It was led, also, quite automatically into the field of abstraction, a field rather far removed from the dramatic and representational field in which St. Denis had previously worked. New possibilities appeared for ensemble dancing, with impersonation and dramatic sequence giving place to something akin to orchestration. If for the uncreative dancer it was little more than a formula utterly devoid of artistic importance, it offered to the instinctively creative artist a method of procedure containing a certain amount of freedom and a fruitful field for growth. Essentially, however, it was limited, since it was tied to music even to the extent of trying to translate musical patterns note for note and instrument by instrument into movement, and when the modern impulse arose demanding that materials be studied and allowed to control their own forms, it was seen to constitute a serious obstacle. Nevertheless St. Denis is entirely justified when she claims that its practice marked the first step toward the characteristic American concert dance of today.

Ted Shawn's part in Denishawn was, of course, of quite a different nature from all these things. As St. Denis has written, she was its spirit and he its form. His share in shaping its course was perhaps of larger dimensions than hers, but it added nothing to the concepts or the evolution of that expressionalism with which we are here concerned.

Martha Graham

THE two chief streams of the contemporary American dance—though not, to be sure, its only ones—flowed in their beginnings through this major channel and have been in great measure shaped by it. They depart from it together on the basis of modernism with its demands for abstraction and functionalism and the absoluteness of the medium; they depart from each other on the basis of the means for attaining these ends, and this difference grows not from opposing platforms of theory, but from the governing condition that truly expressional dance varies by its very nature with every individual.

In common with every other manifestation within this field, therefore, the dance of Martha Graham and the dance of Doris Humphrey must be considered as purely personal emanations;

not in any petty sense, but on the principle that nobody can think another's thoughts, feel another's emotions, experience another's reactions, or express his own intuitions and convictions in another's terms. Most of the confusion regarding the expressional dance has arisen out of the failure to recognize this point, and out of the resultant effort to try to read into every work some standard code, or to find some "key" such as the credo of surrealism. The only key, as we have already seen, is to be found in sympathetic experience through inner mimicry and the complete abandonment of any intellectual effort to understand.

No dancer has suffered more from this erroneous approach than Martha Graham. Because of the distinctive quality of her dance, so unlike anything that has gone before, at least in the surface it presents, it has perhaps inevitably given rise to the belief that it is based on some involved philosophy or some esoteric theory of movement. Nothing could be farther from the truth, however, for it is simplicity itself. Its distinctiveness of quality arises from the fact that it is a faithful projection of Martha Graham, and she is an original. It is more accurate to consider her as such than as an originator, for she dances as she does because that is the only and inevitable way for her to dance. It is as completely natural to her as Isadora's quite antithetical way of dancing was to her; "it fits me," she has said, "as my skin fits me." She is not operating according to any theories of dynamic design or setting up any aesthetic cults; she is not concerned with proselytizing or establishing a system; she is simply dancing as she is compelled by her inner conviction to dance.

Graham's dance, at its height, instead of being studied and intellectual, as is frequently alleged of it, is supremely naïve, in the best sense of that word. It is the response of a sensitive and passionate nature to the life about it, and the aesthete who tries to make something else of it succeeds only in stubbing his toe and falling quite short of its essential greatness. Though she herself has spoken and written eloquently of it, she has never been able to formulate any objective theory for it, for the simple reason that it has none. "It is the affirmation of life through movement," she has said. "Its only aim is to impart the sensation of living, to energize the spectator into keener awareness of the vigor, of the mystery, the humor, the variety and the wonder of life." It is much better to let it go at that and quit obscuring the issue, which is, after all, the art itself and not the way the wheels go round.

The arresting quality of Graham's art, and even of her very presence on the stage, which makes it impossible to be indifferent to her, is the result of a dynamic equilibrium between inner forces. It is this that gives her movement its character and shapes its contours into a style so far removed from the generally accepted standard of what is natural. This movement is not concerned with general standards, but is the product of those elements that make up a specific nature. With her phenomenal sensitiveness to influences about her, whether they are conditions of living, works of art, the landscape, theories or people, there is a compensatory pull, of which she is well aware, toward integration, toward drawing together from all these dissipating tendencies those elements which constitute her individual being. Without this same integrating force she might easily follow the line of her inherent emotionalism to a dance of sheer Dionysian indulgence, and no doubt it is her knowledge of this that gives such weight and emphasis to her condemnation of mere self-expression and improvisation.

The growth of her art, indeed, has been the growth of this power to hold in check a veritable menadic strain which is instinct with destruction. It has not been an art of expansion, then, so much as an art of restraint. But these restraints are well below the surface; they do not consist of outward devices struggling with difficulty to hold a mere exuberance in bounds. Though her forms are taut and tense and her technic steely, the conflict they represent has taken place at a more elementary level than this, where force has been opposed by force in a commanding emotional counterpoise.

Nevertheless, as an element in this very conflict, the discipline of technic has assumed for her the character of an inner necessity as well as of an outward safeguard. She has made of it, indeed, something stronger than her will into which she can in a measure retreat for guidance and direction, both as a performer and as a composer. Nothing else can insure the repetition of a composition once completed and guarantee it against being carried away into new flights of creative emotion and improvisation. For the composer it becomes essentially a classic process, the setting up of a barrier, within which it is safe to roam without fear that a too great fervor may lead unwittingly into fulsomeness or incoherence.

For Graham in a singular degree the restraints of technic have meant freedom and a heightened expressionalism. The impact of her communication has been increased by being forced through the finely calibered apertures of her method. But there has been a negative side to the situation as well, for the weights on the classic side of the scale at times have become so heavy that the balance has been destroyed. Technic treated as "a cold, exact science" has sometimes been inclined to lose its character as a principle and has taken on rather the character of a vocabulary. Under such continual emphasis, muscular memory is likely to revert to technic instead of to subjective experience when dance associations are aroused, and to deny every demand of expressionalism. Under such conditions it may easily give emotional release to the dancer without conveying anything at all to the spectator, short-circuiting the dance, as it were, into as definite a state of self-expression as ever characterized the interpretative period.

Graham's dance is essentially dramatic, and this not alone in that it is rooted in a dramatic soil. The greater part of her repertoire actually touches on the field of impersonation, and here is perhaps the clearest answer to the accusation frequently made against her that she is exclusively concerned with introspection. Her dances, to be sure, are not based on that joint process of observation and interpretation which constitutes pure impersonation; there is just enough of observation in them to establish a contact with her subject, and from there on the process is rather one of identification. She becomes the symbol of the thing that she is touched by, and the intensity of the experience itself gives it a kind of incandescence. Something of this sort occurs in the majority of her most successful compositions—in "Primitive Mysteries," "Act of Piety," "Frontier," for example. In these she is certainly not undertaking any literal impersonation of an Indian, a ferocious bigot, a pioneer, yet just as certainly it is these objective concepts that have touched her into action.

Though the very nature of her practice results in the abstraction of all emotional experience, as well as of movement itself, into a high state of concentration, she has rarely dealt in terms of subjective abstraction, that is, in the direct formalization of personal feeling without recourse to this external identification. Her succession of opening dances has done so, but like all opening dances, they have been scarcely more than the projection of a mood of greeting in such terms that the style and technic of what is to follow will be more familiar. Except for the introspective "Ekstasis" and the dramatic and architectural "Dithyrambic," none of her compositions in this manner has achieved a success at all comparable to that of her more full-bodied works.

The nucleus of her art is her personal power of evocation, and this is a power too individual to be taught, to be transferred to others by contagion, to be captured in a technic or embodied in any set of specific movements. Her solo dances, accordingly, have been of vastly greater moment than her group dances, with the single exception of "Primitive Mysteries" which is a masterpiece.

In her kind of dance, which is almost as much an art of the person as Isadora's was, such matters as relationships in space are beside the point. Experiments in the use of décor, in the current trend toward extended forms of composition, in the functionless "constructions" of a tired neo-classicism, only serve to obscure the real quality of her greatness. Her openness to influences has frequently led her into such blind alleys as these, for apparently she has listened as wholeheartedly to dogma born of the atelier or the greenroom as she has to the potent rhythms of the Indian dance, the pulse of the American landscape, the underlying beat of a humanity resisting destruction. It is not her lapses, however, that are important, but the successful realizations of her genius, which have made her one of the great dancers of the world. Her range is wide and her sympathies warm and deep. Her satire is terse and withering, her tragic intuitions both stark and tender, her moments of lyricism vibrant and lovely.

Doris Humphrey

AGAIN we must shift to another world when we consider the art of Doris Humphrey, for she differs from Graham in almost every respect except the magnitude of her accomplishment. This difference is in no wise to be compared with that between

Duncan and St. Denis, yet it involves once more a transition from the Dionysian to the Olympian.

Humphrey is innately balanced; she does not attain to poise by pitting equipollent forces against each other in the dramatic way that Graham does, but exists in it naturally and without effort. It forms, indeed, the norm from which her dance deliberately departs and to which it returns. She is not at the mercy of outside forces, but rather challenges them of her own free will; it is she, not they, who is the initiator of the conflict. Her whole art is in a sense the creation of unbalances, patterned after those that appear in the life about her, in order that she may rectify them. It is thus that it establishes its contact with those processes of compensation for unfulfillment, those rituals in which the desired act is pre-done, which constitute the substance of all expressional art.

Here, as in every other instance of a creative dance, the philosophical tendency that dominates it, consciously or unconsciously, is exemplified in the technic. The beginning of Humphrey's independent career was based on that necessity which was in the very air to understand the material with which she was working. Like all her American colleagues, she took for granted that the substance of the dance was movement that emanated from inner impulse, and because the ability to produce it without effort constituted the very heart of her talent as a dancer, she did not question the processes involved. But it was essential for her to know something about the nature of this movement after it had been produced, and what forms it would naturally assume that would allow its inherent significance to communicate itself to others.

In Denishawn she had had a wealth of experience with traditional vocabularies, which were superimposed upon her own movement and used it only as a kind of motive power to project themselves. She had also dealt with arranging a more abstract type of free movement upon the patterns of music, for St. Denis had leaned heavily upon her assistance in the practical execution of her theory of music visualization. But these methods left the basic problems untouched. What were the intrinsic rhythms and phrases of movement like, divorced from these arbitrary controls? What, indeed, was movement itself like?

For the answers she turned, as others were also turning, to a study of the body; her efforts, however, were in the direction not merely of anatomy and physiology, but also, in a measure, of physics. Such a procedure would probably never have occurred to a dancer concerned only with the discharge of emotional tensions or even with introspection, but to one as alive to the dancer's relationship to the universe about him as Humphrey was, it was entirely logical. It was also logical that the balance of her own outlook upon that universe—her meeting of it on equal terms, so to speak—led to the discovery of a similar balance as the key to her technical approach to movement.

Certain self-evident principles emerged concerning the movement of the body considered simply as motion. One was that balance merely as the state of rest is the antithesis of motion, and that as balance is destroyed by any agency, the motion that results increases in speed and power until it is checked by the intervention of an equal and opposite force. The extreme of this increasing arc of motion is destruction in the impact of the two forces. Thus motion ranges between the two extremes of inertness and destruction, and this is the basis of its rhythm.

The body as an animate object brings this rhythm into action through its instinct for self-preservation and also through its powers of volition. In the experiences of daily life, the body is constantly making unconscious compensatory adjustments, meeting forces of unbalance in one part with equal and opposite forces in another. In its volitional use of this rhythm it enters into the field of dance, deliberately seeking unbalances which will extend experience far beyond the bounds of ordinary routine and countering them with a strength and alertness that proclaim man's mastery. To deny the perils implicit in such unbalance or the effort involved in the production of the counterforce is not only to deny nature but to destroy the dramatic quality that inheres in the simplest of movements thus created. To give free play to both elements is to discover the motor phrase in its most functional aspect, and to touch on the foundation of form. When the conflict between the two forces is not merely mechanical but is motivated by those intuitive perceptions that prompt the artist to create, there is the pattern of a dance art that is richly expressional, completely organic in form, and teeming with life.

In such a method, intellect undoubtedly plays a part, but certainly there is nothing cold or rationalistic about it. It is intellect constantly informed by emotion, the servant, not the master, of a total artistic personality. It has made it possible to think through many a problem of craftsmanship instead of muddling through, to erect a challenging standard of criticism, to sweep aside everything that smacks of evasiveness or affectation and to come frankly and directly to the point. Thus deeply visioned realities, born in that intangible realm of subjective experience where art dwells, are brought to the surface in forms of luminous clarity.

Though it is as a dancer that Humphrey has won her fame, and justly so, it is as a composer that she has led the dance forward into new fields of accomplishment. Indeed, with her large composition for group called "New Dance," first presented in 1934, she not only established herself as the first choreographer of her time, but marked the coming of age of the American dance. Here for the first time the dance took a heroic theme, the relationship of man to man, and treated it heroically in terms of an abstraction as pure as that of music, developing its material at length according to its demands of internal organization, and abandoning story sequence, impersonation, and musical formalism altogether.

Though Humphrey has no space awareness such as Wigman's, she achieved here that objectification of inner relationships that constitutes the basis of theater. This she did in part through spatial emphasis, with sets of blocks to give focal points and contours to the stage area, but it was chiefly through the inner organization of the group of dancers that the work attained that quality that marked it as of the theater rather than the concert hall. Two other works on the same theme followed, "Theatre Piece" and "With My Red Fires," to complete a trilogy which, not only because of its ambitious proportions (it would require nearly three hours to perform in its entirety), but because of the grandeur of its conception and the masterliness of its realization, constitutes the crowning achievement of the American dance thus far.

In these two works, which actually form the earlier portions of the trilogy in spite of the fact that they were composed later, Humphrey has been less absolute, resorting, indeed, at times to grotesquely stylized representationalism and even to a kind of symbolic impersonation. The purely abstract approach is exemplified in "Theatre Piece" almost exclusively in the dominant solo role (in which Humphrey gives probably the most exquisite performance of her career) of a protesting figure in a world of mad caricatures; in "With My Red Fires" the opening group dances maintain the abstract note and gradually materialize into specific characterization and dramatic theme. By these variations of medium, superbly handled in each case, the trilogy as a whole loses nothing of unity or elevation of tone, and gains immeasurably in plasticity of form and freshness of interest.

Certainly Humphrey is not doctrinaire, for she goes easily from this heroic mood to the vein of sheer nonsense, making a hilarious and unrestrained stage version of James Thurber's "Race of Life," replete with characters and dramatic theme (of sorts!), and by no means devoid of comment, as first rate nonsense never is. From this, back again to a work of great nobility of spirit couched in pure abstraction, set to Bach's C Minor Passacaglia for organ. This, she has said, she considers her most mature work; and with reason if only its choreographic aspects are considered, for it is profoundly moving. Yet such music, complete in itself and by no means plastic, proves to be competitive rather than collaborative, for it can scarcely avoid making its separate identity felt and sometimes even taking charge of the choreographic situation.

Humphrey's relation to music, however, is one of great sensitiveness and has led to constant experimentation. Having had her fill of dancing to ready-made music early in her career, she has been keenly interested in developing a kind of music that would really serve her purposes in the dance. She has danced without music, and has used unorthodox instruments such as accordion, drums and gongs, the voice in various manners, drinking glasses set to pitch by varying quantities of water, and even a comb and tissue paper! When she has resorted to the inevitable piano, or the small orchestral ensemble, she has had a clear idea of what she needed from the various composers who have worked with her, and has been eminently successful within the quasi-functional limits that are set by the use of conventional instruments, and by a strictly musical point of view.

Her resort to Bach, however, would seem to indicate that she has found that merely putting modern music to modern dance does not solve the problem, for their respective modernisms are as divergent as the materials that shape them. Eventually, there will have to be a more radical approach to the subject, and for her to undertake it would be thoroughly consistent with her temperament and her record to date.

Her genius for composition seems to go back ultimately to her ability to conceive her emotional ideas not only in terms of movement but directly in terms of form. That interplay between materials and emotional intent which belongs to modernism is apparently a spontaneous process in her mind, with the result that there is never anything labored or mechanical about her choreography. It unfolds by its own logic. This attitude finds itself reflected in her method of training, in which at an early stage she departs from the performance of isolated movements, even in a gymnastic sense, and turns to phrases and sequences. Since it is thus that movements occur in dancing, the sooner the gymnastic sense of movement can be eliminated, the sooner the dance begins to function in its own right.

With that underlying consciousness of the normal balances of life, she uses both men and women in her compositions, and uses them not merely as so many sexless units, but with a clear recognition of their contrasts and relationships. Her long professional association with Charles Weidman has made this possible in practice and has given her a freedom that few other modern dancers have had, to develop along this highly desirable path.

Her own dancing is in every way feminine, though certainly without any touch of coquetry or softness; it is strong, clear-eyed, and lit with the same inner glow that illumines her compositions. The field of subjective abstraction, that is, of movement emanating directly from personal feeling, offers her her richest opportunities; but if this is too high a level to dwell on, she has a wealth of resources in the less absolute territory of characterization. Her Matriarch in "With My Red Fires" is a magnificent piece of stylized tragic acting, and the uninhibited farce of her performance in "Race of Life" is equally a masterpiece, in the vein of low comedy.

Her solo dances, however, are chiefly integral elements in compositions of larger dimensions, and are rarely designed as merely personal vehicles. Indeed, one of the extraordinary features of her compositional approach is that it is concerned not with providing herself and her company with vehicles, but with the creation of independent works of art. Hers is not primarily, then, an art of person, but finds itself most fully in the limitless expansiveness of form. This implies no connotations of structure for structure's sake, however, for her abstractions are rooted in human experience and her forms are organic evolutions instead of invented devices.

There are still a few blank spaces in her method, perhaps; she has gone ahead to such great goals that it is only natural that she should have lacked the time to stop and close all the gaps, though some of them are of major importance. There is still, for example, no technic for the production of movement out of subjective experience, much remains to be done toward the evolving of a truly plastic music, and the subject of space offers riches that have not been tapped. All these things come well within her range, not only of perception but of accomplishment, and no doubt she will come to them in due time. If there is at present any continuity in the native American dance, however, it is with her that it would seem to lie.

Charles Weidman

IN the field of the modern expressional dance, only two other figures are of national reputation, namely, Charles Weidman, who also came out of the wonderfully stimulating atmosphere of Denishawn, and Hanya Holm, who is an American not by birth but by choice.

Weidman's independent career has been closely linked with that of Humphrey, and most of the distinguished accomplishments of either of them have in some way involved the other. They work, however, in different departments of the dance, and it is this, no doubt, that has made it possible for them to sustain a partnership so long and on so free a basis. If he has allowed himself to be overshadowed by her at times, it is not merely because his art departs from the exalted world of absoluteness in which hers dwells, but also because its genial insouciance often approaches that lack of discipline which is so commonly associated with artists.

In its essence, his dance is utterly original and approaches the subject in a manner that is unique. Its basis is a satiric pantomime, reduced to a high degree of impersonality, keenly observant and by no means innocent of malice. Though it necessarily touches upon impersonation, there is no sense whatever of identification, but on the contrary, Weidman himself is always deliberately peering around the corner of the character. If it were only this, it would be excellent high-comedy clowning, but it is considerably more, for it is also dance, and this sets it quite apart from precedent. The mimetic element is treated as movement, less fully abstracted from its normal life dimensions than the stuff of the more absolute dance is, but differing from it only in degree. Its forms are dance forms, determined by motor considerations rather than by story sequence, and frequently the latter plays no part whatever in the procedure.

Weidman's attack upon the problem is distinctly according to the principles of modernism. Since his medium is pantomime rather than pure movement, his method is in a way comparable to that of the painter rather than to that of the musician, for the painter's medium, even in its most modern manifestations, is not ideally one of complete abstractness. Like the painter, Weidman departs from representationalism not only by the surface distortions which reduce his material to pure color, so to speak, but also by the organization of its formal elements according to the laws of its materials, instead of to any superficial demands of its literary or story content.

Thus far, he has achieved complete success in this highly experimental medium only twice, first in a solo called "Kinetic Pantomime" and later in a group composition called "Opus 51." On countless other occasions he has proved himself a gifted mime and a delightfully ingratiating performer, but with this latter work he emerges definitely into the category of a significant composer. It is a long work without program though not without content by any means. Like a kaleidoscope, it presents bits of unrelated action from everywhere—a man taking a shower, a woman sweeping the floor at odd intervals, a pseudo-lyric mazurka, campfire stunts, pompous acrobatics, entrances made with great effort over a pile of blocks instead of through obvious open spaces—and Weidman in the middle of it all, watching, participating, and eventually becoming a kind of ringmaster. Unlike the bits of color in a kaleidoscope, however, it falls into design in no merely fortuitous fashion, for it has a fine clarity of outline and a unity of form. On its surface it is deliberate nonsense, but it is that kind of nonsense that is a fine art and that invariably has overtones quite remote from idle fooling. Curiously enough, this work built on a pantomimic base is perhaps as totally abstract a composition as the modern dance has ever produced.

Apart from his preoccupations with mimetic material, Weidman has composed repeatedly in terms of more absolute movement, but this is not his natural bent. When he abstracts his movement this far, it ceases to have the qualities of illumination, and his handling of its formal requirements leads him into involvement and prolixity. No more is he a dancer with any especial technical leanings or interest in brilliance of execution for its own sake.

What he will do in his own particular vein remains for the future to disclose, but he has developed it already to the point where it is no longer merely a promise but a fulfillment.

Hanya Holm

THE presence of Hanya Holm in the field is filled with potentialities for the American dance. A pupil of Mary Wigman, a member of her first and most famous dance group, and later the principal teacher in her central school, she came to this country in 1931, bringing with her that thing of all things which the American dance most lacks, a method, and furthermore a superb method that goes very near to the source of free creation in the dance.

Though her coming in the first place was simply a transfer of her teaching activities from Dresden to New York, she was quick to find in the vital rhythm of the country a stimulus to the development of her independent career as a dancer and composer, along lines that would never have been possible for her in her own country. With this as a goal she spread her roots in her new environment and eagerly invited its influences. Such an approach was totally different from what America was accustomed to from European artists, for they have all too frequently brought with them an overbearing arrogance and a determination to teach a nation of barbarians how to become civilized. Holm's gentleness and humility marked her as clearly not of this kind; her interest was not to impose her ideas upon America, but quite to the contrary, to allow its vitality and freshness to bring her art to maturity.

As a consequence, it was six full years before she felt that she was ready to subject her work to the critical ordeal of a New York performance. In the meantime, however, she had developed a small group and had danced with them and taught more or less all over the country, for news of both the charm of her work and her great ability as an educator had traveled rapidly from community to community. In these small and rather informal performances, it became clear that her values as a dancer were rather as the focal member of a group than as a soloist, and that her handling of group choreography in general was brilliant and intuitive. But the generally lyric character of these compositions afforded no hint at all of the dramatic power and the theater quality which she was to reveal in her first large work, called "Trend." It was with this that she made her New York debut, after its première at the Bennington Festival, and established herself beyond question as one of the important figures in the American dance world.

"Trend" had all the dynamic quality that is characteristic of the American dance, but it retained, also, the more subjective qualities of the German dance—its sense of space, its fluency, its unbroken relationship of movement to emotion, and at least its attitude to music, if not a full realization of it in practice. All these elements, together with Arch Lauterer's setting, which for the first time supplied the dance with a truly functional stage to work on and in, brought the dance to a new realization of its theater possibilities. The only lapse toward synthesis was in the use of two previously composed works, the "Ionization" and "Octandre" of Edgar Varèse, as part of its musical setting. These were completely right in color and courageous in instrumentation, the former employing highly unorthodox percussion instruments exclusively in tremendous rhythmic and dynamic terms, but they inevitably imposed certain formal limitations upon the choreography. By way of further adventure, the entire musical score was completely recorded and played upon a specially designed reproducing mechanism, thus making possible the use of a variety of instrumental combinations and an artificial control of dynamics that would otherwise have been out of the question.

The works that have followed in the brief period since "Trend" have been of smaller dimensions, more practicable for presentation on tour, and have accordingly not touched the same heights, but they have showed no less authority and imagination. Though their basis of procedure stems from Wigman, they reveal the presence of a composer who is no mere echo of a dominant personality, but who is in every way an individual creating in terms of her own authentic reactions to her environment. For all the lyrical gentleness of her own style, it is in large theatrical forms that Holm apparently has the greatest contribution to make. Her career here as a composer, however, is still young, and on the basis of its brilliant beginnings it should contribute significantly both by its additions to the repertoire and by its influence.

Her acceptance of the rhythms of American life as her own, and America's acceptance of her without question as its own, bring not only a new artist into the field but the seeds of a new maturity. Those principles of Wigman's dance which are without race or country but belong to the universal aspects of the art, have been planted in perhaps the only manner in which their growth is assured. That they will be instantaneously brought to flower is, of course, impossible, but in the fullness of time their universality may very well come to blossom in a new soil with all the hardiness of an indigenous growth.

Ideals of Method

If these individual artists are the outstanding figures in the modern expressional dance, they by no means encompass it, for by its nature it can never be confined to any handful of personalities however great. Since it grows out of the nature of man and his relation to his environment, its field is limitless, and as its true character is being more generally understood, it is seen to be taking independent root ever more widely. In such a country as this, with its many racial strains and its geographical sweep and variety, there must be an inexhaustible range of background for art to shape itself against, provided there are mediums sensitive enough to respond to these distinctions. None could possibly be more so than the dance at this creative level. Perhaps, indeed, in the development of its regional manifestations is to be found a greater importance than in the occasional geniuses who emerge from it, for in this it realizes most fully the scope of its compensatory functions.

Certainly nothing could be more destructive of its fundamental powers than to try to pattern all dance expression upon the personal approaches of a few individual artists. Standardization and the setting up of systems are fatal to an art that draws its sustenance from individual awareness.

But to talk only of awareness and environmental influence and emotion is not to be realistic, for though these elements are enough for the dance on the recreational level, when art enters the picture there enters with it at once the element of method, that is, of how things are done. In the recreational dance, where the dancer is dancing for himself alone, he simply moves in response to an emotional impulse until he is satisfied, using whatever means he has, and conforming without question to the limitations of his natural endowments. In the communicative dance, where he must create in terms that will produce results upon a spectator, the situation is altogether different. He cannot merely please himself, but must state directly and without confusion what is in his mind; he cannot remain within the physical powers he happens to have by nature, but must increase them until they are able to achieve movements larger and more vivid than life. He must have music and costume and setting that will clarify his intention. Since every dancer's temperament and physical equipment differ from every other's, and the forms and types of movement that result from them differ accordingly, there can obviously be no such thing as a standard technic or formula for procedure. Yet the problem that lies at the root of the matter is common to all dancers, for it is the problem of transmuting basic dance into terms of communication, the problem of retaining all the fresh spontaneity of subjective experience while creating an objective thing known as a work of art, definitely formed and capable of repetition.

Let us see what the underlying method that is indicated ideally involves. Its processes are exactly the reverse of those of the ballet, for instead of taking ready-created materials and manipulating them for the fullest display of the dancer's powers and person, it must work outward from the dancer toward the presentation of an emotional concept, creating its materials incidentally on the way.

The dance begins with the body and nothing else. Before it is the body of a dancer, however, it must undergo certain training by which it becomes almost a super-body by reason of its strength, its control, its plasticity, and its ability to respond instantaneously to demands made upon it. This is not specifically dance training, but neither is it sheer gymnastics; it is physical education in the best sense of the term. The development of a perfectly functioning body, whether for the dance or for everyday life, cannot be brought about by the use of dumbbells and mechanical routines, as is being realized more and more in the progressive fields of general education. Psychological factors must be taken into account so that the individual may develop in the line of his own nature instead of being hammered into some predetermined mold, and also so that healthy and efficient practices may become habitual. Superimposed exercises, with no life outside the gymnasium, do not make for a controlled and responsive instrument, whatever the size of the muscles they may produce. The preparation of the dancer's body as an instrument, then, demands a gymnastic training that takes into full consideration the relationship that exists in life between posture and movement on the one hand, and emotion and mental imagery on the other, and that does not attempt to produce dead muscle bulk or to attain physical skills apart from the subjective impulses that belong to them. Nothing could be worse for a dancer, as Isadora Duncan was the first to realize, than to undergo a technical training, no matter how strong it made his body, that led him to arbitrary movements as a matter of habit.

It is only when the body has been transformed into an instrument that is fit to be played upon—responsive, wide of range, and without mechanical weaknesses which demand constant concentration and stopping for repairs—that the technic of the dance can be begun. In this, the affective basis of movement, which has been employed as an agency in the gymnastic period of training, now becomes the dominant issue. Since the dance consists of movement as the emanation of subjective experience, there must be a means developed for the control of the process by which such emanation is made to occur. From simple beginnings of an improvisational nature, there must be evolved a definite ability to deal in one's own emotional evocations with a certain objectivity. It is impossible for the artist to work in immediate emotional experience, for it would carry him away into self-expression and out of art; his medium must of necessity be a remembered, a re-created emotion, which will lead him on but not take possession of him. This is the subtlest and the most important branch of the dancer's craft, for without it he is unable to create the very stuff of his art and must either rely on luck and "inspiration" or resort to habitual routines. Certainly no dancer can be considered an adequate technician, no matter what prodigious physical feats he can perform, until he has mastered this process, for it is the heart of dance technic.

Once the body moves under these impulsions, all the other elements of the dance are brought into being, the rhythms of its dynamic scale, the phrase on which it builds its forms, and ultimately the forms themselves. Automatically he has created space, and from the way he molds it as he proceeds will grow inevitably the basic design of his stage setting. His music flows from sources in his own body, its rhythmic beat from his dynamic pulse and its melodic song from his voice. His costume likewise develops upon the pattern of the body itself, upon the freedom demanded by its movements and their particular quality and flavor. It will naturally devote itself to revealing the body as fully as possible, and not to hiding the communicative instrument of the dance under superfluous trappings however beautiful in themselves.

Few dancers, if any, have mastered all the implications of such a method; it exists, nevertheless, not in some vague realm of fantasy, but as a kind of composite of basic practices of all of them.

There can be little doubt that modern expressional dance is essentially one of the most important contributions to culture that has been made within our time. It has cut through inertias and resistances, both stolid and stubborn, until it has arrived at the bedrock upon which all art must ultimately be seen to rest. On this firm foundation it has built a structure of its own that is broader, simpler and closer to the nature of human experience than anything the arts have hitherto contrived.

Certainly those who have labored for it have done so through inner compulsion, and have had only their success as their reward. Because it is art, and not entertainment, its financial situation has been difficult. Unlike most other artists, the dancer cannot starve in a garret and create art that future generations will hail; his art is immediate and if it is not allowed to function in the moment of its creation it cannot function at all. Because it cares nothing for glamour and coquetry, for spectacle and display, it has little to attract capital investment. What it has done, therefore, it has done through labor and sacrifice and heartbreak. There is a crying need here for subsidy such as is common in the other arts. Without subsidy, indeed, the public would have little access to music or to painting, and it is neither just nor intelligent to expect the dancers, with no financial resources whatever, to pay for the public's access to dance. No art can exist in terms of community value unless the community subsidizes it. What has been accomplished thus far in the dance, therefore, is not only a magnificent artistic contribution but a triumph of the human spirit.

Chapter Nine

MIDDLE GROUND

~~~~~~

I F the dance falls naturally into divisions according to its differences of purpose, it does not erect any forbidding barriers between them. At their points of highest development, recreational, spectacular and expressional dancing are markedly remote from each other, but the same substance composes them all, and there is a definite continuity in their relationships as they shade into each other.

Of the three divisions, the most elemental is the recreational, as we have seen. It is not art, but shades off in two directions toward the two divisions that are art. Thus in the neutral ground that lies between recreation and the spectacular dance, we find folk and ballroom dances so skillfully developed that they are done as exhibitions, and laymen learning tap dance routines. In the neutral ground that lies on the other side of recreation, there is the whole field of the so-called "free" dance for self-expression, that tends toward the expressional dance but stops short of the border. The triangle is completed with another neutral ground that lies between the spectacular and expressional branches, and this time completely within the field of art. It is with that territory that we must now concern ourselves.

The existence of such a territory is essentially healthy, for it allows its neighbors on both sides to expand as fully as they please in each other's direction without cutting themselves adrift from their own institutions and principles. To be sure, its hospitality is occasionally violated, and we find the ballet trying to be altogether expressional with equipment developed through the centuries to be spectacular, and the expressional dance trying to be altogether spectacular with an approach that is designed in no wise to produce brilliance of surface. Nevertheless, there are very few good artists indeed who do not find a measure of freedom in departing from their major concentrations from time to time, and the art as a whole generally profits from their leading it into broader fields.

In the ballet, for example, nobody has dared to expand in the direction of expressionalism so far as Fokine, and his divagations actually gave this great spectacular division of the dance a new lease on life. In the modern expressional dance it is a similar adventurousness, if in smaller degree, that leads Doris Humphrey to such a delightful bypath as that which produced her "Pleasures of Counterpoint," or the gay and technical "To the Dance" which she composed with Weidman. Illustrations abound of these elasticities on both sides, and in none of them is there any denial of dominant tendencies, but only an extension of them.

There is, however, an unhealthy aspect, also, to the existence of this neutral territory, for it harbors a kind of artistic freebooter with allegiance to neither camp who lives by preying on both of them. With him we shall deal presently.

First it is important to point out a group of artists who illustrate the possibility of planting one foot in each field in such a manner that it is sometimes difficult to tell which one bears the greater share of the weight. If their activities keep them altogether in this middle ground, they are there not through opportunism or mischance but through conviction. Assuredly it is only this common territorial range that unites them, for it would be difficult to find three artists less alike than Ted Shawn, Kurt Jooss and Harald Kreutzberg.

Ted Shawn

SHAWN's weight is definitely heavier on the spectacular side, for all that he is frequently grouped with the other camp in the public mind. The tendency to group him thus is due in part, though not entirely, to his long association with Ruth St. Denis. Their individual approaches to the dance, as a matter of fact, have little in common beyond certain rather deceptive theatrical values, and as St. Denis has pointed out in her autobiography, they were constantly standing in the way of each other's fulfillment. Through the many years of their partnership, their essential differences became steadily clearer and eventually led to separation. Of the two, Shawn was perhaps less able to yield because of the indomitable energy and drive of his nature. It was his approach, accordingly, that put its stamp most markedly upon Denishawn, and this approach itself was chiefly what classed him with the radicals. In that it departed wholeheartedly from the established practices of the traditional ballet, it became automatically part of the "new" dance movement.

What Shawn rejected of the ballet, however, was not its technic, its use of objective vocabulary or its emphasis on the person of the dancer, all of which he accepted fully and turned to his own purposes; it was the restrictions of academism that he was congenitally averse to. For his overflowing vitality and his insatiable intellectual curiosity to be pinned down to a strictly outlined course of conduct was clearly impossible. He had ranged through the history of the dance and had been deeply impressed by Havelock Ellis's philosophy of it, and the inclusiveness of the subject no doubt fitted in well with his own expansive temperament. He has said that the system of Denishawn consisted of the fact that it had no system, for the dance was too big to be confined to any one compartment. The technic of the ballet was colored by the free spirit of the "new" dance, with its bare feet and scant draperies, and became one element in the basic method; St. Denis's Oriental dance provided another. To these were added in unending succession the dance of the American Indian, Aztec legends, native folk material, Dalcroze eurythmics, the dance of Spain, the religious attitude toward dancing and ritual, yoga, Duncan-inspired Greek, St. Denis's music visualization, and in later years even a touch of Wigman technic. Now that Denishawn is no more, all these things still make up the nucleus of his individual practice, with others added to them day by day, in what is certainly the most completely eclectic dance method on record.

For all its range and variety, it escapes diffuseness because of Shawn's use of it. He manages somehow to subject all these diverse materials to the dominance of his own individuality so that they emerge purely in terms of his personal style. They serve him much as the comparatively infinitesimal academic vocabulary serves the ballet dancer, as a background against which the artist exhibits himself.

Shawn is a man of action; he is no introvert. His dance therefore has nothing of ecstasy about it. Because of the voracity of his mind, everything it touches must be translated immediately into action so that new fields may be attacked. There is never any indication of ideas being allowed to germinate and grow in their own good time; they are grasped quickly and shaped to the dancer's own purposes. To call this kind of procedure intellectual is perhaps to give an erroneous impression that it is cut-

and-dried; on the contrary, there is an emotional glow in the very act of performance that is closely akin to the satisfactions of self-expression. This is easy to understand when the experience of dance itself has such value for the dancer. Shawn has treated it as something besides an art; it has been also for him in a sense a religion, a medium of education and a way of life.

It is in his insistence on this point of view and the zeal of his preaching and demonstrating of it from one end of the country to the other that his great contribution lies, rather than in any specific works of art he has created. His production of compositions has been prodigious, but they have been, consistently enough, occasions for performance rather than objective creations with lives of their own. The modern movement's approach to form has left him untouched. Indeed, the modern movement as a whole has been unsympathetic to him, and he has rarely missed an opportunity to denounce it with characteristic vigor. It is one of the few things that his adventurous mind has rejected, as, indeed, it could scarcely fail to do, for it is in many ways the negation of his own convictions and practices.

In his advocacy of the dance as an art for men he has done yeoman service all through his career, but especially since his organization in 1933 of a company and school exclusively for men. Here he has developed a magnificent type of young athlete, and his tours across country with a company of them each year have done much to break down the nineteenth century prejudice against male dancers. If in this activity he has not restored anything of the normal balance of the dance in which ideally men and women should be equal participants, it has perhaps been necessary to go to this extreme in order to give emphasis to his purpose.

Similarly he has contributed notably to that same respect for the nude body that Isadora advocated. If this has been a more difficult problem for a man, he has nevertheless triumphed, and has helped to bring about a public reaction that accepts nudity in a dance group with as little question as in a swimming team.

Shawn is at his most effective when he is most completely in the spectacular camp, indulging freely his bent for showmanship, and letting whatever philosophical ideas he pleases animate him, without attempting to project them specifically through the dance.

Kurt Jooss

KURT Jooss divides his weight considerably more evenly between the two fields; indeed, it is rather amusing to find that in America, where the modern expressional dance is best known, there is a tendency to consider his work as a form of ballet, while in England, where the ballet is best known, he is considered as an exponent of the modern dance. Actually, he employs much of the technic of the academic ballet, and many of the principles of the modern expressional dance, but what he concentrates upon is neither of these, but the production of what are best described as dance dramas. Indeed, his work is not to be intelligently approached through any consideration of specific dance methods, for his aim is not independent dance but the creation of a theater form that uses dance as its medium.

In this he differs from the theater ideals of both the ballet and the expressional dance. The former is chiefly a spectacular synthesis of which drama is at best only one element, and frequently is nothing more than a thread upon which to hang dancing. Fokine has developed it farther than this, it is true, and Jooss's approach has certain similarities to his. Both of them, for example, insist that there shall be no alternations of mimed scenes and divertissements, but that all the movement shall be expressive and carry the dramatic development forward. But Fokine works within the framework of the ballet in the capacity of a daring reformer, while Jooss has made a completely fresh start with no reservations or commitments whatever that tie him to the ballet. Where Fokine has inherited the ballet's idealization, Jooss touches his highest level of achievement in his resort to realism and even colloquialism. Fokine, it is said, has never composed a work on a contemporary theme except a single divertissement called "Tennis" for Patricia Bowman. Jooss's repertoire includes "The Green Table," a modern Dance of Death which is a bitter denunciation of the futility of war; its sequel, "The Mirror," which deals with after-war readjustment; "The Big City," which is a cross section of metropolitan life; "Chronica," which tells of a political dictator in a Renaissance setting but with modern implications.

In his response to the world about him, he exhibits his kinship with the modern expressional dancers, but again there is a gulf between them. He translates this response into plot and characterizations and even allegory where necessary; they translate it into immediate motor terms without representational connotations. For them the drama grows out· of the dance, where for him the dance grows out of the drama. Theirs is abstract and consists of direct relationships between dancer and dancer, and between dancer and space; his is specific and consists of relationships between character and character, and between character and situation.

Early in his independent career, Jooss stated his conviction that the new times in which we lived demanded new forms but that the art of the dance was substantially the same as it had always been. Consequently he built his forms from the materials that were at hand. From the ballet, he took that part of the technic that concerns itself with peripheral movement alone, that builds brilliance and control, and discarded that part that was merely designed for personal virtuosity, such as entrechats, multiple pirouettes and the use of points. From the expressional dance, which concerns itself only with movement from emotional sources, he took the principles by which these movements are created. By combining the two sources in their proper relationships, he arrived at a system of movement that was equipped to give him the entire range of movement that any dramatic medium could demand.

In theory this is more convincing than in practice, for the two types of movement do not blend easily. The ballet technic, conceived in the most concentrated vein of artifice, is inclined to cut sharply through scenes that are couched in creative terms of realistic emotion. This is especially true when not only ballet style but familiar figures from the academic vocabulary suddenly appear; though they are not performed with any emphasis whatever on their virtuoso aspects, their very familiarity in the midst of unfamiliar material destroys the dramatic illusion.

For his technical method, Jooss turns chiefly to the principles of Rudolf von Laban, who was his teacher. Though he has naturally colored these with his own ideas and developments, his system makes fundamental use of Laban's theories of space harmony and of creative movement. He has completely given over dancing himself, and devotes himself in the main to choreography. He is a slow and careful workman, and a composer of great talent and individuality. "The Green Table" is unquestionably a masterpiece, and "The Big City," though less heroic, is equally fine in its own way.

His productions have nothing whatever of the ballet's synthesis; they use little or nothing in the way of décor, and concentrate on the choreographic action. All the music is arranged for two pianos. Both these practices make for facility in touring, though their effect upon the compositions themselves is perhaps open to question. Jooss composes with his emphasis entirely upon ensemble instead of upon individual roles, and his company has attained something very near to perfection in meeting his demands in this respect.

In recent years, since he has established his headquarters in England, his work seems to have leaned more and more in the direction of the ballet. Whether this is his natural bent or merely a result of contagion is impossible to determine, but it is gradually putting more weight upon his spectacular base and less upon his expressional.

Harald Kreutzberg

THERE is probably nothing that concerns Harald Kreutzberg less than theory. He is a dancer for no more cosmic reason than that he has an irresistible inclination toward it and a great gift for it. His position in the matter is set forth in a statement he issued at the beginning of one of his American tours.

"I am not a leader nor a creator of any school of dancing," it said. "I dance to express myself. I dance from my heart, blood and imagination. As an actor uses words to tell the story of the drama, as a composer narrates his themes in bars of music, I express my mood, my poesy, my inner feeling with movement, with my body. I do not believe that dancing should tell a story or have a meaning; nor do I feel that a dancer must draw upon his experiences to express fully dances of great joy or great sorrow. I love music very dearly but I do not seek to interpret in my dancing the compositions of the immortals, Bach, Schubert, Mozart, etc. I create my dances and then begins my search for the ideal music, for the music that will best reveal my mood in movement. I think we all should dance, women and men and children. Only through dancing can we throw off the heaviness of body and heart and mind."

Self-expression, however, is far from the complete story, for besides that inner exuberance that moves him to action, there is a superb craftsmanship to hold him within bounds. It is compounded of several things in addition to mere bodily technic—a gift for the theatrical and a phenomenal instinct that tells him how things will look to an audience, a highly developed visual sense and an innate talent for design.

It was Mary Wigman who first recognized his abilities as a dancer when he was enrolled in one of her evening classes for laymen, and it was from her that he gained the groundwork of his art. But such a volatile nature as his could never be satisfied with so subjective and searching a method, and he turned accordingly to a more theatrical approach to supplement it, based on a free adaptation of the ballet. His movement, however, is still basically of the expressional type, dealing in no set vocabulary but creating its material according to the needs of the situation. It is the uses to which he puts it that give it its spectacular quality. There is never so much as a hint of any specific movements out of the ballet's academic vocabulary; indeed, what few clichés he allows himself to fall into once in a while are clearly derived from the Wigman technic.

Kreutzberg is a charming but certainly not a profound artist. With the profound artist it is a vision of intangible realities that drives him to the creation of his art, and he turns to a medium that will convey those concepts that exist only on the unintellectualized level. Kreutzberg is dominated by no such obsessions; he is forced to dance by inner compulsion, it is true, but it is a compulsion simply to dance rather than to deliver himself of any message. As a result he turns naturally to light, decorative and picturesque subjects.

More than this, he is always the showman, in the best sense of the word. Whether he is presenting a purely decorative trifle to music of Mozart, a piece of hilarious nonsense like his "Dances for Children," an excursion into morbid psychology such as his "Three Mad Figures," or compositions in such elevated mood as that of his "Angel of Annunciation," he is definitely exhibiting something to his audience, and saying to them, in effect, "Look at what I am doing now!" It is this that puts the tinge of the theatrical and of the spectacular upon everything he does.

He does not evolve his forms exclusively in terms of movement, but allows them also to be determined by dramatic program at times and by the structure of his music. He has an extraordinary gift, however, for movement simply as movement, and few dancers can deal in it with such freedom, such authority, and such an instinctive feeling for the motor phrase. This, combined with the ebullience of his personality, makes him, though not one of the most significant composers of his time, certainly one of its greatest dancers.

Kreutzberg's visual sense is also very close to being unique. He is so perfectly aware of how he looks, with his square shoulders, his shaven head and his large hands, that he is able to costume himself in a manner to achieve striking pictorial effects. In this, again, he tends in the direction of the spectacular, for he dramatizes the pictorial aspects of his costuming a bit beyond the point where it merely serves to heighten the character of the composition he is performing.

In short, then, Kreutzberg's art grows out of expressional principles, but he is not content to leave it at that; there is in him a kinship with that basic theory of the spectacular dance

that makes the art a channel for the artist instead of the artist
a channel for the art.

Hybridism

IF there are glowing talents like this who use the middle ground
between expressionalism and spectacularism as a kind of stretching space, there are also, unhappily, lesser spirits who try to
stake squatters' claims in it and set up permanent residence
there. It is, however, a barren and dreary land in so far as productivity is concerned, and unless one has a source of supplies
in one fertile region or the other, the maintenance of life is
likely to prove impossible.

The argument that is used to justify the migration into this
middle territory is as follows: The spectacular dance, that is,
the ballet, pays too much attention to surface, to virtuosity
and the exploitation of personality, and not enough to emotion
and expressiveness. The modern expressional dance, on the other
hand, is drab of surface, and neglects virtuosity and personal
glamour in a too great concentration on inner experience. The
best features of each, accordingly, should be combined in order
to achieve a truly worthy dance art.

It must be clear, however, that to try to put together two
forms that are diametrically opposed is to succeed merely in
canceling them both out against each other. The basis of the
expressional dance, for example, is the materializing of inner
experience in terms of freely created movement; the basis of the
ballet is a definite and traditional scheme of movements, subject
to great alteration and adaptation, it is true, but inviolable in
the fixity of its principle. To attempt to put a fixed procedure
or a ready-made vocabulary upon the former is simply to deny
its existence, and to take away the established code from the

latter is to deprive it of its center of reference and the foundation of its effectiveness. If there is some point midway between the two approaches at which movement can be half traditional and half produced by immediate subjective processes, it has not yet been discovered.

Similarly, the expressional dancer concentrates all his forces upon the communication of an experience to the spectator, not trying to win admiration for himself, for his person or his skill; is he to abandon this aim in part or in whole while he exhibits himself? The ballet dancer, on the other hand, is concerned with the presentation of an idealization of himself as the very symbol of personality; shall he destroy this by allowing the realities of his subjective experience to break through?

Throughout the entire range of the two approaches they are seen to contradict each other, even to the mechanics of the bodily technic. The habit, which the ballet dancer acquires only by diligent practice, of making adjustments in his body so that certain specific relationships are always maintained in movement, thoroughly disqualifies him for that constant discovery of new relationships in the body, which is the very basis of the expressional dancer's technic. For the former, the gymnastic technic "is the art," as André Levinson observed; for the latter, the gymnastic technic is only a preparatory stage before the actual creative technic of the dance begins. Nothing could be more absurd, therefore, than the notion frequently expressed that the ballet technic is the groundwork of all dance—that it is, in fact, the only technic. Actually it is the technic of the ballet, and of nothing else.

The only possible manner in which the two types of dance could be put together would be by taking superficial movements from the ballet and superficial movements from specific compositions of various modern dancers and making an arbitrary vocabulary of them. In such a procedure, to be sure, there would be neither rhyme nor reason, and its advocates unwittingly convict themselves of failure to understand either of the elements of their proposed syncretism.

If there are shortcomings in the ballet and the expressional dance as they are currently practiced, as indeed there are, they are not to be corrected by destroying both mediums and substituting a form of sterile hybridism. Indeed, the middle ground provides no permanent dwelling place of any kind, and the nomads who now inhabit it must sooner or later take refuge in one camp or the other.

Chapter Ten

DANCE IN EDUCATION

❧❧❧❧

WHEN Isadora Duncan discovered the principle of the dance to be the translation of subjective experience into overt movement, she made available perhaps the most potent of all educational mediums. Though she eloquently argued its merits as such, it is scarcely surprising that it was not at once accepted by educators, for who would ever think of looking to what was commonly regarded as the most frivolous and inconsequential of the arts for any contribution to the serious business of developing the mind?

A great growth was necessary on both sides before the compatibility of the two fields could be made to appear. Yet Isadora was not advocating anything that had not been anticipated by progressive thinkers in the educational realm for many years. That master romanticist, Rousseau, who was so convinced of the unity of the nature of man, had long ago argued that the body could not be left out of the educator's consideration; Froebel had carried the theory further by his insistence that education could not be brought about through superimposed routines but only through activity prompted by inner impulsion. What Isadora contributed was a medium by which the way was opened to these goals.

It was no longer ago than 1904, however, when she and her sister Elizabeth opened their first school in Berlin, that the police interfered because the children wore only brief tunics in a demonstration of their work. Of the general reaction to their progressive experiment, Elizabeth has written: "The great majority anchored in the standard conceptions of that time, could not follow but remained looking on nervously or sneered. The small minority, mostly artists who saw in Isadora's idea the dawn of a new human freedom, cheered her as she turned her hopes to the child to be the bearer of her message."

What is really remarkable is that in so comparatively short a time as has elapsed since then, so much should have been accomplished toward that rapprochement between dance and education that must inevitably come. Already there is extensive activity in the schools, from the primary grades all the way through the college years. Not all of it is good, by any means; some of it is actually bad, and much of it misses the point, acting on vague intuition rather than a complete understanding of the situation. But it is intrenching itself more strongly all the time, its standards are steadily improving, and when it finally finds itself fully, it may well change the whole course of our cultural approach.

The development that has been taking place in recent years in the science of education itself (or is it more accurately an art?) exhibits a tendency in all directions to abandon the old scholastic opinion that would confine it to intellectual fields alone, and to accept the broader responsibility of developing the whole individual, with a sense of the relationship of his intellect to his hitherto neglected physical and emotional activities. To be sure, there are many rugged unregenerates who cling to the theory that the three R's were good enough for those worthy people, their grandparents, and are consequently good enough for everybody else, and who accordingly scorn what they are pleased to call the frills of modern education. There is also a cult of neo-medievalists who would turn the educational system back to the selective concentrations of monasticism. But those more sensitive minds who see education as a social and a socializing force have recognized that it must be attuned to the needs of a world in which the ability to make ready adjustments is absolutely essential to survival, and that an intellect however great in an unco-ordinated personality is a helpless anomaly. If there is a considerable lag, as there is in every field, between the vision of the leaders and the standard of practice, there can be no question of the liberalization that has taken place in the subject as a whole.

The dance as a basic educator, along the lines of a theory that treats the individual as an integer, is obviously unique, for no other activity calls into play the three departments of the personality with such equality of emphasis and especially such unity of impulse. This latter consideration is what is most frequently neglected, and we find the common systems of education tending to pull the individual apart instead of to put him together. He is trained to exercise his reasoning powers in one department, his muscles in another, and his capacity for feeling not at all, unless the singing of folk songs and the painting of sprigs of pussy willow are supposed to take care of this side of his nature. It remains for the individual thus drilled in sections, as it were, to stumble as best he can upon some method of synthesis, to reassemble what should never have been separated, to achieve in spite of his education that unity of his being that has been so seriously disturbed, if he is ever to find his place in the world.

There are co-ordinations in the method, to be sure, such as the teaching of manual skills, of sports and games; but these are entirely objective and carefully detour around that very center of conscious being, the "inner man." Emotion and the type of compensatory creation that grows out of it are avoided as if they were slightly indecent or at best a violation of good taste. The preparation for life demands an approach exactly the reverse of all this, for every life experience impinges upon the entire man, with no reservation for propriety or good breeding.

By no other means than the dance is it possible to work in terms of the essential stuff of experience, with all its elements balanced in an approximation of the balances of life itself. If intellect perhaps appears to be understressed in it, that is because our habitual standards demand such overstress upon it. In the dance it is by no means inactive, but assumes much the same relations to other elements that it assumes in life. It functions, in other words, in terms not of pure intellection but of applied intellection, as a link between feeling and action.

Art or Exercise?

THUS far the results that come nearest to exemplifying the ideal relationship between dance and education have been accomplished by a few progressive teachers with small children, where the problem is comparatively simple. When algebra and Latin come into the picture, however, and reason and intellect take the field, the dance is usually crowded out. Physical education is relegated to games and the exercises of the gymnasium, and while these are admirable as far as they go, they are one-sided, and do not in the least make up for the omission from the scheme as a whole of the more ecstatic emotional compensations of the dance.

What could be more surprising, then, than to find the creative dance bobbing up of its own volition among the very wall-machines and horizontal bars of this same gymnasium? Forcing its way into the field thus through the back door, it gives rise, indeed, to certain perplexities. Some types of dance are easy enough to reconcile with conventional gymnasium practice: tap dance, for example, or folk dance or even "rhythmic" dance (that is, the performance of simple preordained movements such as skipping, bending, swinging, etc., to the beat and phrase of music). These provide healthy exercise and produce certain skills, disciplines, co-ordinations and a sense of teamwork in exactly the same way that games do, omitting only the element of competition. But this new type of dance introduces another element and a dangerous one, for it touches upon the delicate and fearsome field of emotion. Is it exercise, then, or art? What in the world is one to do with it within the educational framework? If it is exercise, what is it doing with emotion? And if it is art, what is it doing in the gymnasium?

Actually, it is both these things and at the same time neither of them. Its primary concern is definitely exercise, but just as definitely not what is meant by physical exercise. Because it is exercise of a sort, however, it is not art, for its purpose is neither the production of an artifact nor even training directed ultimately toward this end. Nevertheless, it deals with the same relationships within the personality with which art deals.

It is exercise, however, in the acquisition of no single skill, but in the production of experience whole. Its aim is so to broaden and deepen the individual's capacity for experience in fully rounded dimensions that he may learn to live to the fullest extent of his being, not defensively but creatively, intensifying his response to the universe about him but maintaining such a balance of his own forces that instead of being used up by this intensification he is able to translate it automatically into appropriate action. By means of it he finds himself as a feeling and acting creature, using and co-ordinating all his faculties and equipment, giving out what he conceives within him instead of continually taking in what somebody else puts upon him.

The process by which this end is approached must be three-fold; it must deal first with leading the individual to the discovery of the resources within him, second with turning him toward the use of these resources in terms that have value in his environment, and third with increasing his capacity.

The young dancer must inevitably start from where he is and not from where we might wish he were. It is useless to ask him to express what is not in his experience or to perform what his physical instrument is incapable of performing. To put upon him the emotional pattern of some specific musical work or the physical pattern of some specific dance composition is to leave his own repressions exactly where they were and to force him more and more into those faults of movement and those bad bodily practices which have become habitual to him. It is impossible to take him forward along the line dictated by his personal nature until he has first been taken back from all the erroneous and contradictory starts he has made away from this line under the pressure of poor balances within himself and in his environment. In other words, his norm must be established.

So far as his emotions are concerned, this is to be begun in no other way than by easing him away from the haphazard disciplines that are warping him and into the fullest expression of his own desires and feelings. He can find his innate resources only as he is permitted to deny the limitations imposed upon him from without and to abandon the abnormal compensations they have compelled him to develop in himself. This is obviously not to be accomplished by concentration and introspection, but only by the simplest and most natural activity, for it is the denial of outlet to his emotional potentialities that has caused the difficulty in the first place. This is sheer self-expression, in which he is enabled to find the free channel that lies between subjective experience and outward action, and nothing more.

Since movement is the first reaction to all impressions whether from within or without, it is the medium that automatically presents itself for this purpose. Even though perhaps the attention is later to be turned with more accent upon other mediums such as music or painting or drama, this first step cannot be omitted, for dance is the elemental creative medium by the very nature and constitution of man.

It must not be forgotten, however, that the use of the voice enters the picture at this very level, and the basis for that music which is eventually to become the accompaniment of the dance is here laid. Its roots are in the breath, the pulse, and the contractions and relaxations of the voluntary muscles, and it is brought into action by the impetus of the emotional experience. When that experience consists of little more than personal release, it may be perhaps just sound, and as the experience is more centered and focused, it may develop into melody, song, and even speech. It is, nevertheless, the direct product of movement.

All this naturally leads to the consideration of the body itself. Here again there are haphazard disciplines and abnormal compensations that must be destroyed before the perfect balances it demands as an efficient instrument can even be approximated. Though there are mechanical principles that underlie its structure and operation, their particular application varies from individual to individual, for no two bodies are alike. Each is to be developed to its highest functioning powers, then, just as emotional capacities must be developed, according to the particular nature that has shaped them. Except in the case of actual malformation or structural deficiency of some sort, bodily inefficiencies and unbalances are at least as much emotional problems as they are physical. Among the more advanced specialists in the field of changing poor bodies, postural conditions and movement habits to good ones, the emotional element is taken so largely into consideration that its active use forms part of the technic, and mental imagery is called upon to bring into action deep muscles that are not to be reached by voluntary effort.

Ultimately the individual can find himself physically and emotionally only by simultaneous processes. The body is not to be built for any practical life benefit by exercises that are purely physical. Muscles can be increased in size, it is true, by this means, and if they are considered as abstractions to be exhibited for themselves as in the case of the professional strong man, nothing better could be asked. In education, however, the development of muscles is in the interest of normal life activities, and here they function only in conjunction with every other part of man. It is health that is admittedly the physical educator's goal, but health not in the negative sense in which the word is frequently used to denote merely the absence of sickness, but as the synonym of wholeness.

The establishment of such a personal norm, however, is only the first step in the educational process. The young dancer is now ready to begin his exercises in experience. Having found his resources in a measure, he must put them into action, or else he is isolated from his environment. To leave him in a world of his own imagination is to render him helpless in the world of realities. He must learn how to put himself, with all the potentialities that self has been found to possess, into relationship with other people without loss of any of these potentialities. Such a relationship includes both working with others in the pursuit of a common purpose, and working, in a sense, in opposition to others, that is, convincing them of his own concepts and being convinced in turn by theirs.

The socializing influence in this basic approach to education through dance is form; the process by which it is attained is a purely pragmatical one and is known as composition. The dancer who is dancing merely for his own release may enjoy movements that are entirely random, but as soon as he is working with or for others he must begin to order his activity. His pleasure in working with others derives from the fact that thus he is able to participate in a movement experience of greater force and dimensions than any he could create alone. Accordingly it is requisite for all the participants to move either in unison or in certain deviations from unison that specifically supplement each other, and if any individual departs from these fundamental requirements he separates himself automatically from the increased pleasure of concerted action. Thus a certain objective awareness is injected into the situation.

If he is working for others, who occupy the position of spectators, he must again order his activity, this time so that it holds attention and is intelligible. It is now necessary for him to draw upon his inner experience with a heightening of objective awareness, for by this he is guided in the arrangement of his movement so that it will convey his feeling directly and without confusion. Sheer expenditure of personal energy is no longer enough; concepts must replace it. The forces in the life about him that move him to action must be recognized as such and related to the action they incite. Here reason and judgment and definite intellectual skills are brought into play.

The process of composition thus becomes a medium by which innate potentialities adapt themselves to the actualities of a life based on human intercourse. Nothing is lost of full personal expression, of the feeling-acting experience; the will to participate and, even more strongly, the will to communicate, simply put it to work. They cause it to change its shape, they focus and intensify it, but they do not repress or destroy it in any degree. Such a process makes unnecessary the warping disciplines by which in the educational methods of our grandfathers the free impulses of life were forced into conformity with the demands of practical living. Certain outward patterns of behavior which were considered correct and orderly were arbitrarily imposed upon the individual, and his not to reason why but only to do and die. The stream of his own impulses thus dammed was forced to find outlets where it could, and it is easy to understand how they might easily be unhealthy and antisocial. The setting up of such compensations as these is obviated by a process that allows the feeling-acting experience to achieve form by self-discovered, self-administered, purely pragmatical means. These functional means, which replace and destroy the old and rigid disciplines, can never become stereotyped since they must be continually varied by the variety of results they are designed to attain. Instead of being stultifying they are actually creative.

Just as it is possible to build muscles without any relation to life by means of isolated exercises, so it is possible to produce forms of movement by rote. Almost any young pupil of normal intelligence can be taught to invent some kind of action for the various members of his body and arrange them in the A-B-A or the rondo form. This is not to educate him, however, but to impede his progress. It is merely the imposition of disciplines and has nothing whatever to do with his creative forces, in that it does not relate form to function. It does not so much as verge upon the problems of participation and communication which are at the root of the socializing process. It may result in the production of the body of a dance, or if he happens to be a genius, in the soul of one as well, but what is important to him is not merely turning out a product, but the discovery of his creative processes.

In working to achieve form that will function communicatively, the young dancer must necessarily set up a closer relationship with the inner processes of the colleagues to whom he is addressing himself. Their degree of response is his guide to action; he knows when he has succeeded in touching them to sympathetic experience only by his ability to sense their reactions to what he is doing. He finds himself to a large extent in them. Thus he is led to develop an ever keener alertness to the mental attitudes of those about him; and since he is working in a group, he must also acquire an awareness of differences in individual response, and learn bit by bit to adjust himself to these variations. Eventually his sensitiveness to the reactions of those to whom he addresses himself will reach its severest test when he steps out of the intimate and sympathetic atmosphere of the classroom where his purposes and the details of his daily growth are familiar, and shows his compositions to an entirely strange audience. What he creates by all these means may not be truly art, for the chances are that it will have little or nothing of the illumination of life about it, but its process is that of art and for him it is an art experience.

When, in the classroom, he is functioning not as dancer but as spectator, his experience of movement and of the problems of composing will give him an increased responsiveness through the channels of inner mimicry, and he will acquire automatically a facility in interpreting what he sees directly into terms of action and hence into the deepest form of understanding.

The carrying through of the development toward form to the point of actually presenting finished compositions before audiences calls upon a more centered attack upon emotional experience and the application of increased physical and intellectual skills. To maintain a dominating emotional purpose, think it through, and sustain its integrity, while making the countless contributory adjustments demanded by the preparation of a performance, constitutes an experience that can scarcely fail to toughen the fibers of the personality.

Consideration must be given to the evolving of music, to its melodic and rhythmic relationships to the body, to the timbres of the instruments that seem to be indicated by the quality of the movement, and to its actual composition and performance. Costume introduces the necessity for creative activity in designing its form and color to reveal and to heighten the movement. The translation of space patterns into a stage setting opens up still further avenues. With the handicrafts and the mechanical and organizational elements involved, a single emotional impulse will have related itself finally to a whole world of practical activities.

Influence of Professionalism

But what has all this to do with the gymnasium? Or the physical education instructors who have learned their anatomy and their kinesiology and their hygiene, and have been engaged specifically, perhaps, to teach swimming and basketball? Not much, it is clear.

Physical education, however, can never let the dance go completely out of its practices, for progressive thinking makes a link with the emotions an essential to its broader fulfillment. Indeed, though it may not come to the place where it sees the value in carrying the possibilities of the dance through to their own conclusion, involving music, costume, setting, and actual performance, it must inevitably give it an increasing importance in the building of bodies. It is conceivable that the day may eventually arrive when physical education will become not the education of the physique so much as the physical approach to general education.

In the meantime, that is where the dance has found itself placed, and there is no reason to disturb it until it can ultimately be made an independent activity around which education in general centers. There is every reason, however, to advocate its better treatment. There can be no doubt that the majority of physical educators are unqualified to teach it. A few of the more progressive and art-minded have a genuine sense of what it is, what it has to contribute, and what it demands. A somewhat larger number have a certain intuition about it. A great many, however, are teaching it merely because the job they happen to hold requires it, or because it seems to be the progressive thing to do. Most of them, unhappily, have so little recognition of what is involved in it that they do not even know they are not teaching it adequately. It is to them simply another skill to be taught, with its own set of movements and a few rules of form to fit them into. All the routines of procedure one gets by going to summer school and writing them down in a notebook. But it cannot be taught out of a notebook. It is a matter involving the most delicate analysis of personality, an ability to diagnose difficulties by "inner mimicry" and to create in motor terms, and the utmost tact, patience and persuasiveness. It cannot be merely a sideline, thrown in between tap routines and diving lessons; it demands a genuine talent and a dominating one.

Even discounting the notebook mind, however, perhaps the greatest fault lies in the tendency to pattern all procedure on the systems of professional dancers. This is a perfectly natural thing to do, to be sure, for in a subject so comparatively new as the expressional dance, with no tradition whatever within the field of education itself, where is one to turn for guidance except to those few artists who best exemplify its principles? The mistake lies not in the sources that have been turned to, but in the application of what has been found there to the purposes of education. It is a common experience to find classes of youngsters being taught exercises taken directly from the studio of some celebrated concert dancer, or perhaps even several sets of exercises taken from several different studios.

At best no routine of exercises can be put thus upon the body from the outside with any creative results; whether they are called dance or not, and no matter how expressional they may have been when performed by the dancer who originated them, they are simply routine gymnastics, no different from dumbbell exercises. But beyond this, such exercises as these were not designed in the first place to develop the individual for life practice, but only to make one particular dancer capable of performing in a certain manner for specific artistic purposes. They are, in short, professional technics.

In many cases, they are bad to begin with because routinized and lifeless, and do little service even to the artist who employs them for his own ends. If he were more of an educator, he might realize this and release himself from their habit-forming influence. Most probably they have been designed to meet some personal need and have no general application whatever. The artist-dancer's approach to movement is not through general principles but is essentially personal and entirely through his own body. It is therefore marked, and rightly so, by all his peculiarities of temperament and physique, and though it may result in what is for him an eminently healthy manner of movement, it is utterly without merit for other temperaments and other physiques and may even work injury to them. In some instances there may be actual anatomical distortions, for the artist-dancer is not concerned with building bodies but with expressing his convictions in stirring dances.

If the professional dancer's personal practice provides no model for the educator's procedure, neither does his training of his company. He is not concerned with developing the individual members of the group along the lines their natures would suggest; his object is to make them parts of a unified group by means of which to express his ideas, a kind of orchestra for him to play upon. Naturally they must move in the same general style, and also naturally, this style must be based on that of the dancer himself. To treat a group differently, developing each member along his own line, would make for a sorry performance, indeed. To be sure, he will probably select for his company only those dancers who have a certain physical and temperamental aptitude for his personal approach, and there will be no damage whatever done to them as individuals. But when the educator tries to transform his pupils into imitators of some leading artist he happens to admire, he is doing them serious damage, and is certainly doing no service to the artist. He should be interested only in processes by which human beings are developed to their highest individual capabilities, even if they lead him directly counter to the methods of the theater or the concert hall.

Actually the relation between the professional dancer and the educator should be reversed, and it should be the professional dancer who comes to the educator for teaching principles instead of the other way round. The educator, by his ability to establish the norm of posture and movement for each of his pupils, should be able to supply the professional dancer with group members who could take on any number of personal styles without becoming warped by them. If the norm has been firmly enough grounded, the dancer will be able to make what temporary compensations are demanded and return always to his own basic patterns. This is the ideal contribution that a fully developed dance education would make to the professional field. But such a result is not likely to be even within the bounds of possibility until the educator quits going to the professional dancer for routines.

Often the educator so far confuses the two fields that he attempts to give performances with his pupils on a professional basis. Apparently he forgets that the dance with which he is dealing is re-creational and designed not for the edification of spectators but for the growth of the dancers. As we have already seen, they must assuredly have the benefits that are to be obtained in no other way than by performing for spectators, but it is important that both they and the spectators understand that the dances presented are not works of art but exercises in experience.

The dance in art and the dance in education are by no means separate things; indeed, they are essentially one. At the root of both of them is what we might call basic dance, the age-old activity of expressing subjective experience in ordered movement. It is this that education must concern itself with, exclusively, separating it from all those personal adaptations by which professional artists have turned it to their own specific purposes.

Thus far, the greater part of the dance activity in the secondary schools and colleges has been confined to the women's departments, and this is not difficult to understand. The dance crept into the girls' gymnasium in the first place as a ladylike form of exercise more suitable than tumbling and acrobatics. Its very ladylikeness made it unsuitable for the boys and of no earthly benefit to them. Further than this, the nineteenth century opinion of the dance as a medium for coquetry has died hard and the low estimate of the male dancer has clung tenaciously to it. As the dance has developed, however, it is certainly no longer ladylike, and it has begun in the past few years to win ardent masculine support. The stories are legion of football captains who request modern dance classes, and of star athletes who are chagrined to discover that they cannot perform the requisite technics. There is, indeed, a steadily increasing number of colleges introducing it into the curriculum.

This is, of course, a healthy sign, for the dance has nothing effeminate about it. When it last appeared in the educational field in the Western world, that is, in classic Greece, it was exclusively for men and formed the basis of their schooling. In primitive society and in all predominantly masculine cultures, it is a man's art. Perhaps there is some commentary upon our own culture implicit in the fact that among us today such is not the case.

Certainly the time to engage the interest and the confidence of boys is at a point much earlier than these college years. In the preschool and elementary grades, where much good work has been done in the truly creative dance, boys are as amenable as girls. It is at a later stage that they are alienated, possibly by the inertias of ridicule from without, possibly by some essential weakness in the teaching approach, or most likely by a combination of the two. With the eager seeking by progressive forces in education for a medium that will do away with the ancient dualism of mind and body and make possible the education of the individual as an integer, the dance is rapidly coming into its own, and it is only a question of time before the American boy will accept it as enthusiastically as the American girl.

Chapter Eleven

CONTEMPORARY DIRECTIONS

✿✿✿✿✿

THERE is probably no other time in history when the dance has reached such stature, and such awareness of its stature, as it has today. It was perhaps necessary for it virtually to die in the nineteenth century in order that it might be freshly discovered and re-evaluated in the twentieth as the need for it arose. There are frequent expressions of wonder that it should have come to a new flowering in so sophisticated and mechanized an era, but it is just because of the intellectual and sedentary character of the times that it has been brought into being as compensation. More than ever before in a so-called civilized society it is a cultural necessity, both as an activity to be entered into directly and as an art to be participated in vicariously.

Like other necessities, however, it finds itself in a world that does not know how to make use of it. In the long historic trend toward the establishment of the inherent nature of man as the standard of human institutions, another major adjustment is apparently in the making. Certain gains have been made in the direction of social and political democracy, and the next inevitable step is in the direction of economic democracy. The prevailing economic fallacy, which is undeniably in the process of being destroyed, albeit painfully, hangs over the arts just as it hangs over the more tangible phases of living. That paradox which allows great sections of the population to starve in the midst of a wealth of material resources is exactly reflected in the realm of the mind and the imagination, where there is a wealth of cultural resources available only to the few.

It is in this trap that the vital forces of the dance find themselves. A conscious public need and a corps of artists with the power and the will to satisfy it stand facing each other in an economic stalemate that only a subsidy can break.

Without subsidy, indeed, it is difficult to see how the dance can go any farther. Its days of personal experimentation are over; little solo recitals, requiring nothing but a few different-colored tunics and a pianist, have long since served their purpose. They have led little by little to the development of the possibilities of the dance as a great theater form, involving the use of companies of dancers, adequate costuming, stage settings and music by orchestras of special types. But how are these potentialities to be realized? For the individual artists, who have already borne the full burden of the discovery and nurture of the dance to this high state, to assume this enlarged financial responsibility is completely impossible. There is a limit to what personal sacrifice can do, and nobody can sacrifice what he does not possess.

Even artists must eat, and in order to do so, they are driven under the present system to turn away from their true function as creators and become teachers, whether qualified as such or not. And what, indeed, have they to offer pupils in the way of a career? Nothing more than the prospect of eking out a living in turn by teaching others and attempting to devote what time and energy are left over to creating something that can be squeezed and chopped into the parsimonious dimensions of practical production. It is not an inviting prospect.

When the young professional student comes to the place in his training where he is fitted to become a member of a company, he cannot expect to support himself by his activities in this capacity, for he cannot be paid adequately when there is no money to pay him with. He must instead contribute his share of personal sacrifice to the general good, and without the rewards of creative satisfaction that accrue to the major artists. Even though he is willing to work under these conditions, however, he will not be allowed to do so indefinitely, for with the increasing concern of public agencies and of labor organizations with minimum standards of wages, his case cannot and, indeed, should not, go unnoticed. Yet to insist that he be paid a living wage is grotesque when the artist who is technically his employer is himself not earning a living out of his art and must supplement his income from other sources.

Many young dancers find it out of the question to support themselves by outside activities, and are compelled to abandon their careers entirely. Others, understandably enough, lose heart and turn to the more lucrative fields of the Broadway revue or the night club, where if there are fewer artistic satisfactions, there is at least the hope of weekly pay envelopes. Such a situation inevitably lowers the standards of production in the dance itself, by creating a constantly shifting personnel, and adds one more insoluble problem to those of the leading dancers. For the future it creates an even more serious problem, for it is upon these young dancers that continuity and progress depend. When Graham and Humphrey and Holm and Weidman retire, who is to carry on? There is an abundance of talent throughout the field, but how is it to be sustained to the point of maturity?

The ballet seems on the surface to be on a more stable foundation than the so-called modern dance, but is it? Its future, in the present scheme, rests entirely with the box office; when it ceases to pay a profit to its entrepreneurs it will cease to exist. This perilous moment forever threatens, and sets the direction of all experimentation. It is postponed only by two factors; one is that working capital is supplied and possible deficits underwritten by private subsidy, and the other is that the real requirements of the ballet as an art are disregarded and it conforms to circumstance. Not all of this pinching is confined to sacrifice of the art itself, but much of it is taken out of the hide of the dancers. The limitations that are put upon them and their development by the necessities of keeping the company numerically within financial bounds have already been pointed out. The terrific schedule of work without inner refreshment is enough to destroy the artist. Even at that, his salary is pitifully small, and in certain companies young dancers actually pay the management for the privilege of working!

The dictates of the box office (and in general of private subsidy, as well) demand that the dance be entertainment and that it go in for glamour in much the same way that Hollywood does. Whether it manages to be art or not is beside the point. To meet this demand debauches the ballet regrettably, but it does not destroy it, for its interests are primarily spectacular to begin with. The expressional dance, however, cannot even begin to comply, for it has no earthly concern with entertainment. One of the most pitiful manifestations of its financial predicament is its occasional effort deliberately to make itself entertaining for the sake of the box office, and at the same time to keep its self-respect.

Why should the dance be entertaining? No other art has that requirement put upon it. The function of art is not mere time-pleasing, but compensation and enrichment. Why should it be expected to yield a financial profit to investors or even to pay for itself? It occupies much the same position in relation to the public interest that education does. It is a builder of men, a socializing and civilizing force, and an actual increaser of the public wealth. Education is not a profit-making enterprise nor is it expected to pay its way. It is conducted at the public expense because it is a public benefit. Undoubtedly the time is not far off when it will seem as barbaric to leave art to chance and individual whim as it would today to leave education on such a basis. The history of our times bears terrifying witness to the cost of training the intellect and the body and leaving the emotions undeveloped and unco-ordinated.

There have been numerous public-spirited individuals in America who have stepped into the breach where music and painting are concerned and have kept them alive, as far as this can be done by private endeavor. There are symphony orchestras, opera companies, art museums, and public libraries all over the country, supported by private patrons, but there has been nobody thus far who has done as much for the dance. Such support, generous and farseeing though it is, is not ideal, to be sure, for its voluntary aspect inevitably carries with it a sense of personal obligation even where it does not actually include personal dictation and control. Public subsidy, on the other hand, is merely a matter of the conservation of natural resources, and there can be no real cultural democracy until it is put into practice.

The only experiment that has been made in America in the public sponsorship of art, namely, the Federal Arts Projects of the Works Progress Administration, came about simply as an incident in the general routine of unemployment relief, and not in any degree as a direct attack upon the basic problems of the arts. As a result, it was hampered from the start by outside political interference and by the fact that it was compelled, as an unemployment measure, to use good, bad and indifferent artists. But though it was inherently inept and left-handed and it has at

last been mutilated beyond recognition by demagoguery and re-
actionism, it has nevertheless made a signal contribution to the
ultimate solution of these problems. On the one hand, it touched
into cultural life a whole new financial stratum of the population, and revealed the existence of a widespread artistic hunger
that has gone unsatisfied because of the high price of buying árt
experience when it is controlled by haphazard, profit-seeking and
erratic private distribution; on the other hand, it showed that
under contact with this broad and vital public, art itself blos-
somed with new vigor, and artists whose talents had been hid-
den under economic necessity were allowed to come forward to
the general enrichment of the community life.

The dance, as a sub-activity of the Federal Theatre Project,
was treated shabbily enough, in all conscience, even before the
entire Federal Theatre was wiped out by the crassest of political
opportunism. Its old reputation for frivolity and inconsequence
was apparently widespread in governmental circles, and that it
was included at all was perhaps something of a miracle. But
even against odds more serious than any other art had to con-
tend with, it made unmistakably clear the values, to both the
public and the art itself, that would be created by the establishment of an orderly federal dance project, with both educational
and production facilities.

Eventually the solution of the arts problem must come about
in the setting up of a well-administered, politically free Federal
Bureau of Fine Arts, entirely unencumbered by relief considerations. Such a bureau has already been discussed in Congress and
has received the support of many distinguished figures in the
arts, so that it is not so remote as might appear. If we are really
progressing toward democracy, it is inevitable, and the WPA
experiment has proved its immediate desirability too eloquently
to be denied.

Meanwhile, what is to be done to stop the gap? Only widespread private patronage can do it adequately, but what is to take care of the situation until that materializes? The answer, such as it is, seems to lie in the establishment of more and stronger dance "co-operatives," to bring producer and consumer together in this instance as in so many others where more material commodities are to be exchanged. Centers of this sort have been forming for a number of years, not under this name, to be sure, but with this general intent. There are, for example, such organizations as the Chicago Dance Council, the Michigan Dance Council in Detroit, the Philadelphia Dance Association, the common purpose of which is to unite the various creative elements in their respective fields and together to underwrite an audience, so to speak.

In almost every community where there is a college with an active dance department—and their number is very large and extends virtually all over the country—this has been done repeatedly. Performances are given from time to time by the college groups themselves in an amateur way, much like the dramatic performances given by the "little theaters" over the country. Others, however, are by leading professional groups brought from New York or elsewhere. The existence of such centers as these has made possible extensive tours by all the leading modern dance companies and several of the native ballet groups. Such tours, which have been nicknamed the "gymnasium circuit," would be quite out of the question under commercial sponsorship, for there is not enough money involved to make them interesting. As a matter of fact, no profit accrues to anybody from them, but they serve a cultural purpose of incalculable value. Not only do they bring to the various communities a new vision, but they allow the professional companies to perform with a certain amount of continuity and to earn at least a bare living while doing so.

Such a setup as this is significant rather than ideal. It is significant because it is the natural outgrowth of the situation itself and indicates that there is a national demand for the highest type of dance arts. It misses perfection in obvious ways, the principle one being that it does not produce sufficient funds to provide the dancers with the production facilities they so urgently need, or to keep their organizations together between tours. It is frankly a makeshift, therefore, at present, but it already provides a framework for the building of a national dance organization under public sponsorship when the time comes. Its accomplishments in the creation of a national audience constitute an inestimable service, a genuine clearing of the way for the future.

That future, however, must come quickly. The American dance is now at the height of its powers; unless it is given a means for expansion and a richer life, it will necessarily consume itself in frustration.

The influx of artists from Europe adds a serious complication. Though it is an old and familiar type of competition, finding a disproportionate strength in the traditional respect of the American public for the exotic, it has assumed formidable proportions with the contemporary stream of refugees from foreign political persecution. Certainly it would be unthinkable to close the doors to these artists, and the steps that are being taken to place them in their arts here with the least possible interruption to their careers are thoroughly admirable. But somehow nobody appears to have thought of taking similar steps for the American artists to counterbalance this adjustment. Indeed, the sympathy for the alien refugees has at times been consummately lacking in perspective, and with something akin to ruthlessness it has offered security to foreign mediocrity at the expense of native ability.

It is high time that some of this fine concern be shown for the American artists, before they become in fact refugees themselves from European invasion.

It is only out of their creative perceptions that the deep undercurrents of native thinking can be brought to realization in a truly indigenous culture, and if that is worth anything to us as a people it is not a minute too soon for us to begin to foster it actively. We have subsidized farmers, manufacturers, shippers, and mine owners; it is time we gave something more than lipservice to the cultural departments of our national life.

Of all the arts, it is surely the dance, in defiance of inertias, that should be the first to receive attention, for it is first intrinsically in the nature of man. It is the art out of which all others grow, and it touches the issues of life itself as none of them is equipped to do. Its philosophical implications are profound and practical, for it reveals the vision of the wholeness of man and provides a simple means for making that vision real. Surely in a period like the present, with its arguments of escape from the difficulties of individual conviction into comfortable authoritarianisms, no agency can be overvalued which relates man consciously and actively to his environment.

Illustrations

Hopi Niman Ceremony.　　　PAINTING BY FRED KABOTIE

Hopi Eagle Dance.　　　PAINTING BY FRED KABOTIE

Greek hero in mid-eighteenth
century French ballet.

Eros in late nineteenth century
Italian ballet. COURTESY OF THE
KAMIN DANCE BOOKSHOP

Greek style in the early nineteenth century. From "The Code of
Terpsichore" by Carlo Blasis. (London, 1830)

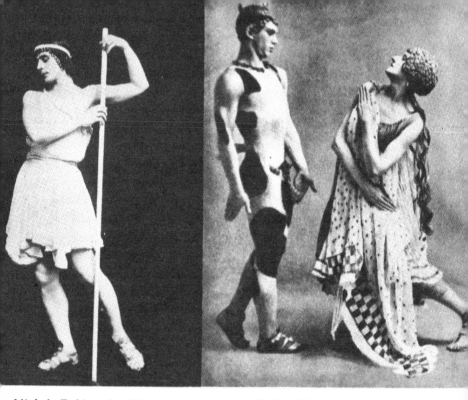

Michel Fokine in "Daphnis
and Chloe," 1912.

Vaslav Nijinsky and a nymph
in "L'Après-midi d'un Faune,"
1912.

Gluck's "Orpheus" as produced by George Balanchine at the
Metropolitan Opera House, 1936.   GEORGE PLATT LYNES

Salome dancing before Herod as pictured by a medieval English artist.

Maud Allan in "The Vision of Salomé," 1908.

Thamar Karsavina in "[?] Tragédie de Salomé," 191[?]

Social dancing—an eighteenth century court ball. Drawn by Pierre Rameau for his book, "Le Maître à Danser." (Paris, 1725)

Lindy Hop at the Savoy Ballroom in New York's Harlem, 1937.

PIX, NEW YORK

A late nineteenth century ballroom position labeled "very objectionable" by Allen Dodworth in his book, "Dancing." (N.Y., 1885)

"*Ballet Comique de la Reine,*" produced by Balthasar de Beaujoyeux at the Court of Henri III, *1581.*

The comedy and ballet of "*La Princesse d'Elide*" by Molière and Lully, *1664.*

"Les Indes Galante," "ballet héroïque" by Jean-Philippe Rameau and Louis Fuzelier, 1735. From the painting by Nicolas Lancret.

Fanny Cerito in the Shadow Dance from "Ondine," 1843.

Michel Fokine's "Petrushka," as revived by Col. W. de Basil's Ballets Russes de Monte Carlo. (Originally produced by the Ballets Russes of Serge Diaghileff, 1911.) Décor and costumes by Alexandre Benois.   RAOUL BARBA, MONTE CARLO

Michel Fokine's "Don Juan," produced by René Blum's Ballets de Monte Carlo, 1936. Décor and costumes by Mariano Andreù.

Bronislava Nijinska's "Les Noces," produced by the Ballets Russes of Serge Diaghileff, 1923. Décor and costumes by Natalia Gontcharova.

Leonide Massine's "Nobilissima Visione" ("St. Francis"), produced by the Ballet Russe de Monte Carlo, 1938. Décor and costumes by Pavel Tchelitchev.

Leonide Massine's "Les Présages," produced by Col. W. de Basil's Ballets Russes de Monte Carlo, 1933. Décor and costumes by André Masson.   IRIS, PARIS

Kurt Jooss's "The Green Table," produced by the Folkwang-bühne, Essen, 1932. Costumes by Hein Heckroth.

Kurt Jooss's "Ballade," London, 1935. Costumes by Hein Heckroth.

R. V. Zakharov's new version of "The Prisoner of the Caucasus," at the Bolshoi Theater, Moscow, 1938. Setting by N. Williams.

Frederick Ashton's "A Wedding Bouquet," produced by the Vic-Wells Ballet, London, 1938. Décor and costumes by Lord Berners.   J. W. DEBENHAM, LONDON

Ninette de Valois's "The Rake's Progress," produced by the Vic-Wells Ballet, London, 1935. Décor and costumes by Rex Whistler.
   J. W. DEBENHAM

Catherine Littlefield's "Barn Dance," produced by the Philadelphia Ballet Company, 1937. Costumes by S. Pinto. IRIS, PARIS

Eugene Loring's "Yankee Clipper," produced by the Ballet Caravan, 1937. Costumes by Charles Rain. GEORGE PLATT LYNES

Helen Tamiris's "How Long Brethren," produced by the Federal Theatre in New York, 1937.

Ruth Page's and Bentley Stone's "Frankie and Johnny," produced by the Federal Theatre in Chicago, 1938.

Uday Shan-kar, Hindu dancer, and his company.

ALFREDO VALENTE, NEW YORK

Kikugoro VI, master dancer and actor of Japan, in a female role.

La *Argentina* (*Antonia Mercé*). D'ORA, PARIS

La Argentina and company in "El Amor Brujo," Opéra-Comique, Paris, 1930.

GEORGES ROUQUET, NEUILLY

Vicente Escudero.
EDWARD WESTON, LOS ANGELES

Argentinita (Encarnación Lopez).

Isadora Duncan.

ARNOLD GENTHE, NEW YORK

Isadora Duncan in her school in Moscow, 1922.

Mary Wigman in "Dances to Polish Folk Songs," 1939. S. ENKELMANN

Mary Wigman and group in Processional from the suite, "Dance Songs," 1936.

CHARLOTTE RUDOLPH, DRESDEN

Ruth St. Denis in "Radha," 1906.

Ruth St. Denis and the Denishawn Company in "The Lamp," at the Lewisohn Stadium, New York, 1930.

SOICHI SUNAMI, NEW YORK

Ted Shawn in "Mouvement Naïf."
FREDERICK KAESER II, MADISON, WIS.

The Shawn Dancers in "Labor Symphony."

Doris Humphrey in "To the Dance," 1937.
ALFRED A. KOHN, NEW YORK

Doris Humphrey and group in "With My Red Fires," produced at Bennington Festival, 1936.
REUBEN GOLDBERG, PHILADELPHIA

Martha Graham in "Ekstasis,"
1933. SOICHI SUNAMI, NEW YORK

Martha Graham and group in
"American Provincials," 1934.
PAUL HANSEN, NEW YORK

Hanya Holm in "In Quiet Space,"
1936.

Hanya Holm and group in "Trend," produced at Bennington
Festival, 1937. Setting by Arch Lauterer.

Charles Weidman and company in "Candide," 1933.
EDWARD MOELLER, NEW YORK

Charles Weidman in "Traditions," 1936.
HELEN HEWETT, CLEVELAND

Harald Kreutzberg.

Ronny Johansson.

Paul Haakon in "Death in the Afternoon," staged by Harry Losee for the revue, "At Home Abroad," 1935.   RICHARD TUCKER, BOSTON

Esther Junger in the Theatre Guild's revue, "Parade," 1935.
VANDAMM, NEW YORK

Sally Rand in her "Bub-
ble Dance."

MAURICE SEYMOUR,
CHICAGO

Dance scene staged by
George Balanchine for
the Rodgers and Hart
musical comedy, "Babes
in Arms," 1937. Duke
McHale and Mitzi Green
in center.

LUCAS AND MONROE,
NEW YORK

Dance scene staged by Felicia Sorel for the Arnold Sundgaard-Marc Connelly play, "Everywhere I Roam," 1938. VANDAMM, N. Y.

Doris Humphrey and Charles Weidman in a dance scene of their staging in Molière's "School for Husbands," 1933. VANDAMM, N. Y.

*Vernon and Irene Castle,
1914.*
COPYRIGHT BY IRA L. HILL,
NEW YORK

*The Hartmans, Paul and
Grace.*
BRUNO OF HOLLYWOOD,
NEW YORK

Veloz and Yolanda.
BRUNO OF HOLLYWOOD,
NEW YORK

Bill Robinson.

Paul Draper.
MAURICE SEYMOUR, CHICAGO

Fred Astaire.
RKO-RADIO PICTURES

Sonja Henie in "Alice in Wonderland," ice ballet staged by Harry Losee for the film, "My Lucky Star."

Radio City Music Hall's Rockettes, directed by Russell Markert and his associate, Gene Snyder.

Index

Abstraction, 16, 33; in ballet, 179, 204 f., 208, 210 ff.; in characterization, 88; in expressional dance, 123 f., 227, 235, 241, 251; in Graham, 255; in Humphrey, 258, 260 ff.; in masks, 140; in miming, 142; in St. Denis, 250; in Weidman, 266; of sex, 214; unsuited to pantomime, 209

Academic ballet, *see* Ballet

Academism, a conservative check, 90 f.; effect of, on native dances, 158; future, 223; in ballet, 101, 106 ff., 121, 182 ff., 186, 188, 191 f., 195, 200, 203, 206, 208, 210 ff., 285 ff.; in form, 56, 59, 71; in language, 114 f.; in religion, 117; in Renaissance, 150, 153; modern, 164 f., 168; modernist independence of, 126, 160, 276; of Noverre, 185; opposed to Russian ballet, 195; opposed to subjectivism and representationalism, 209 ff.; postwar, 199; rejection of, by Nijinsky, 197 f.

Academy of Music and Poesy, 178

Acrobatic dance, 137

Acrobatics, 21, 23, 193, 217, 235; in American modern dance, 241; in ballet, 206, 209 f., 212, 225; in education, 303; in Weidman, 265. *See also* Gymnastics

Act of Piety, 255

Acting, 61, 104; comic, 263 ff.; satiric, 264; tragic, 263. *See also* Characterization, Drama, Theater

Action-theme of modern American dance, 244

Actor, *see* Dancer

Adagio, 137

Aestheticism, 202; cults of, 16; in recreational dance, 146; inherent in classicism, 141; modernist departure from, 243; of Balanchine, 207; of ballet, 137; of Kreutzberg, 284; of St. Denis, 249

Aesthetics, ballet, 173, 208 ff., 217, 219, 221; exotic, appreciation of, 94, 108; in style, 91; modern, 129, 161; of Graham, 252; of movement, 26; relation to motor perception, 46

Alexander (the Great), 112 f.

Alexandria, 113 f.

Allegory, in Jooss, 280

Amateur dancing, 171; professional teaching in, 171

America, aesthetic dancing, 242; amateur activity, 171 f.; American Ballet (New York), 207; Ballet Caravan, 207 f.; Chicago Opera ballet, 207; contemporary ballet in, 207 f.; influences of ballet in, 237; Metropolitan Opera ballet, 207; Philadelphia Ballet, 207; possibilities of ballet in, 222; community relation to dance, 273; contemporary problems, 246; cultural implications, 313; dance in education, 243; emphasis